NEW CHALLENGES IN
THE SOCIAL STUDIES

NEW CHALLENGES IN
THE SOCIAL STUDIES

Implications of Research for Teaching

Edited by Byron G. Massialas
The University of Chicago
and Frederick R. Smith
Indiana University

Wadsworth Publishing Company, Inc.
Belmont, California

New Challenges in the Social Studies: Implications of Research for Teaching, edited by Byron G. Massialas and Frederick R. Smith.

L. C. Cat. Card No.: 65–15098

Printed in the United States of America

PREFACE

BACKGROUND AND OBJECTIVES

The postwar years, though punctuated with periods of national and international crisis, were also characterized by tremendous progress in the acquisition of knowledge. Educators, whose major concerns immediately following World War II had been with providing sufficient facilities to meet increasing enrollments and finding new sources of income, were faced with a new problem—revitalizing the schools so that they might better meet the educational demands of this complex world. The latter part of the 1950s brought with it rapid changes in the education process at all levels: new programs in mathematics and science, advances in the teaching of foreign languages, curricula for the handicapped and the talented, and team teaching. During this period the field of social studies received relatively little concentrated attention. Actually, it was not until the 1960s that social studies began to gain momentum and to attract popular and governmental support.

As a first step toward an educational renaissance in any field, one needs to recapture the cumulative experience of frontier thinkers in the field. For, unless the data gained through research are communicated to those concerned with curriculum development and the instructional process, it is unreasonable to expect changes of any magnitude to take place. Gross and Badger,[1] in the *Encyclopedia of Educational Research,* provided a comprehensive overview of investigations in social studies education, but did not attempt a critical assessment of the quality of the research. Metcalf,[2] on the other hand, provided an excellent analytical review, but he was unable to be comprehensive in the limited space

[1] Richard E. Gross and William V. Badger, "Social Studies," pp. 1296–1313, in Chester W. Harris, ed., *Encyclopedia of Educational Research* (3d ed.). New York: The Macmillan Company, Inc., 1960.

[2] Lawrence E. Metcalf, "Research on Teaching the Social Studies," pp. 929–965, in N. L. Gage, ed., *Handbook of Research in Teaching.* Chicago: Rand McNally and Company, 1963.

available. Thus, in the opinion of the editors, there was a pressing need for a relatively comprehensive critical examination of research in social studies. This book was written to fill that need.

In more specific terms, the present review has three major goals:

1. To provide a summary and a critical appraisal of current research in the social studies.
2. To translate the findings of research into terms which are meaningful to the practitioner.
3. To locate gaps in present inquiry and to suggest areas in which future studies may profitably be conducted.

ORGANIZATION

In order to accomplish these objectives, a team of social studies educators was formed. After making a preliminary survey of recent research to ascertain the general nature of social investigations, the team decided to group the studies under seven major headings. For purposes of consistency and focus, individual members of the team undertook the review of specific topics. Each of the contributors had a good background in a social science, broad experience in teaching of social studies, and previous work in teacher-education programs. The topics were assigned to each writer in accordance with his interest and the extent of his direct involvement in related research. Each member of the team, operating within the general objectives of the project, assumed responsibility for the selection, organization, and analysis of research pertinent to his area of concern; and each has brought his personal judgments, commitments, and interpretations to bear on the relevant studies in his field.

OVERVIEW

Guided by criteria of manageability and availability of studies, the editors have divided research into seven parts. However, many more areas of social studies education are analyzed than those indicated by the title of each chapter. All in all, the review suggests considerable activity in recent years and shows evidence of major breakthroughs in this important field. In reading this material, the classroom teacher will hopefully be motivated to apply certain research findings to his daily tasks and at the same time pursue some of the questions raised in the book from an experimental standpoint.

In the opening chapter Engle suggests that most of those who have written about educational objectives concentrate on the similarities and differences between the social studies and the social sciences. In his essay he attempts to identify the underlying philosophical positions on major issues and thus to enhance our understanding of the implications of accepting one position and rejecting another. Smith, in reviewing the difficult area of curriculum, points out that social studies offerings have changed little during a period of fifty years. However, he sees a definite movement toward the incorporation of social science concepts and tools of analysis into the traditionally history-dominated curriculum. His belief that economics, political science, and sociology should have a definite place in the curriculum is shared by all contributors. In the area of social studies in the elementary schools, Penix indicates that although there is no magic age at which children acquire concepts about society and their role in it, there is some evidence to support the idea that the crucial age in political socialization is the period of pre-elementary and elementary school. Furthermore, he suggests that teachers tend to underestimate the store of knowledge that young school children have of the social world, and that we should begin to question the validity of the theory of the "expanding horizons." Cox and Cousins conclude that the reflective method is the most defensible approach to teaching social studies in that it incorporates psychological and philosophical elements conducive to rational inquiry and the critical examination of social issues, which are so crucial in our time. Furthermore, by employing a model of critical thinking, the teacher can unite the rich theoretical foundations of education with practical considerations in the classroom.

Lunstrum emphasizes the forces operating against freedom of expression in the schools. He advocates the use of objective and analytical models of inquiry in order to deal in an ethically and intellectually defensible way with social inquiry. In this way, much of the emotional mood of certain schools and their supporting communities can be gradually made to disappear. Palmer clearly indicates the dearth of teaching materials and textbooks which include new concepts and developments in the social sciences or notions of valid teaching strategies, but he identifies some studies that show considerable promise. Research in audio-visual instruction needs to include dimensions (e.g., reflective-thinking skills, critical attitudes on the treatment of social problems) other than arbitrary acquisition of information. The last section deals with social studies instruction in other lands, and Massialas suggests that regardless of its prevailing political ideology each country uses social studies to inculcate its own dominant values. Thus, universal history and world politics are generally presented from a narrow, national viewpoint. He suggests that social studies instruction is directly related to nationalism, cultural change, political socialization, and social mobility. This relationship, however, needs to be established more rigorously through world-wide empirical studies. Finally, the essay in the Appendix offers some constructive guidelines to be used by teachers interested in following up the questions raised in this book.

We hope that this book will challenge all teachers to engage in an unending process of discovery.

B. G. Massialas
F. R. Smith

CONTENTS

1

OBJECTIVES OF THE SOCIAL STUDIES

Shirley H. Engle
Indiana University

There is confusion, if not open disagreement, about the nature and hence the purpose of the social studies. On the one hand are those, principally the academicians, who see the term social studies as no more than a general name for a collection of separate, but somewhat related, disciplines —history, sociology, economics, political science, etc. To many at this extreme, the very name social studies is anathema because it does not refer to a particular subject. At the other extreme are those who see social studies as a discipline in its own right, intermingling knowledge from all of the social science disciplines and dealing directly with social ideas and problems as these occur to the average citizen.

Efforts to bridge the gap between these extreme positions, though frequently attempted, reveal, on closer scrutiny, that they have not resolved the basic issue. According to Wesley's now famous definition, "The social studies are the social sciences simplified for pedagogical purposes" (1958, p. 3). Recent general statements of aims of the social studies, notably those of the Ad Hoc Committee on Social Studies of the National Association of Secondary-School Principals (1961, p. 4) and a Committee of the National Council for the Social Studies on the "Role of the Social Studies" (1962, p. 315), begin by accepting the Wesley definition and then proceed to interpret this definition as implying no particular curriculum organization but rather as referring to all the educational activities systematically planned by the school to improve human relations. As Metcalf (1963a, p. 930) has sagely pointed out, detailed listings of social studies aims based upon such statements usually differ little, if at all, from the statements of aims of general education. To such eclecticism in aims, Metcalf (1963b), who would narrow the aim of the social studies to the single one of fostering reflective thought in the "closed areas," has this to say:

The suggestion that the social studies limit its purposes to the fostering of reflective thought in the closed areas will not be popular with those who call themselves eclectics, and who value equally a variety of instructional aims. The trouble with many of our eclectics is that they have not included consistency as one of their philosophical criteria. A careful reading of their stated purposes leaves one with the feeling that they are not really for anything at all, since their lists of impeccable purposes are shot through with contradictory and incompatible destinations. It is fair to say that a person who wants to ride off in all directions is essentially aimless in his equestrian activity (p. 198).

Equally forthright in an opposite direction is Keller (1961, pp. 60–61), who dismisses the claims of the Ad Hoc Committee (and by implication the Council Committee too) as extravagant and harmful. Keller lays what he refers to as the "present unhappy situation" at the feet of the social studies, which he says is not a subject but rather a "federation of subjects often merged in an inexact and confusing way." Keller decries the fact that "too many social studies teachers have emphasized the creation of good citizens rather than the content and discipline of their subject." He would begin the "revolution" by eliminating the term "social studies," which is vague, murky, and too all-inclusive; he would substitute for it the terms "history" and "the social sciences," which are exact and hence "meaningful." Claiming that good citizenship is a by-product of the discipline of the mind which comes from the study of subjects, Keller would have students "study subjects and become acquainted with the facts and ideas" therein as the best preparation for citizenship.

Keller's position is echoed by Berelson (1962, p. 6). Purporting to summarize the thinking of the scholars commissioned by the American Council of Learned Societies and the National Council for the Social Studies to formulate basic objectives for the social studies, Berelson says, "The scholars will accept preparation for responsible citizenship as the goal only if they can dictate the means, which is the presentation of each subject, for its own intellectual sake, in the spirit of the liberal arts." This, it is argued, is the "best preparation for responsible citizenship." With more insight into the necessary complementarity of means and ends than is exhibited by the committees, Berelson, in effect, says: Yes, I agree, if by social studies you mean the separate teaching of the social sciences. Thus, it is clear at the outset that no real agreement exists, except in terms of platitudes, as to the objectives of the social studies.

Two basically different positions with respect to the nature—and hence the objectives—of the social studies are already obvious. To some educators, the social studies are essentially the same as the social sciences. To another group of educators, the content of the social studies is directly related to its goal of developing the attributes of good citizens. Within each major position a variety of alternatives may be found, each predicting a somewhat different end for social studies instruction. Efforts to reconcile these positions have not proved entirely successful. No one has really taken up the challenge to the social scientists thrown down by Robert Lynd in 1948 under the exciting title "Knowledge for What?" Confused and even contradictory aims for social studies instruction persist.

THE SOCIAL STUDIES
AS SIMPLIFIED SOCIAL SCIENCES

Scholars in the social sciences accommodate easily to the notion that the social studies and the social sciences are basically the same, social studies being merely a name which designates a group of broadly related, but at the same time disparate, subjects. Though social scientists as a whole would probably agree with Herring (1958) that "The basic objective of the social scientists . . . is the objective of all men of good will, seeking the good life"; nevertheless, because of their scientific and highly specialized interests, social scientists appear at times to disassociate themselves from the practical problems confronting ordinary citizens. As Herring points out, "The problem of method in the social sciences . . . is best understood in relation to purpose. The more scientific the bent of the investigator, the less he is concerned with overall social problems or broad dilemmas that invite speculative thinking." And again he says, "Social science knowledge can contribute, in some measure, toward the realization of the goals of government or religion or industry, but it cannot function as a rival or a substitute. Should social science be conceived in such terms, it would cease to be science; and, should social scientists contrive for such ends, they would find themselves becoming politicians, theologians, or entrepreneurs." The practical problems which face a citizen are thus placed outside the concern of the social studies inasmuch as they require in their resolution, as Herring says, a, . . . "pluralism of intellectual effort and shared respect for varied methods of inquiry and forms of knowledge." Thus, citizenship education is clearly separate from the more scientific and more limited realm of the several social sciences or, as we are calling them here, the social studies.

The classic statement of the position that the social studies are essentially the same as the social sciences is that of Edgar B. Wesley, cited earlier: "The social studies are the social sciences simplified for pedagogical purposes" (1958, p. 3). While this definition has been quoted approvingly in almost every work on the social studies written in the last quarter century, it clearly falls short of the concept held by those who would make the development of the attributes of good citizens the central purpose of the social studies, a position taken most forthrightly by Metcalf (1963b, p. 198) but seconded—at least by implication—by many others, including Hanna (1962, pp. 190–192), Donald Oliver (unpublished manuscript), Engle (1960, p. 301), and Massialas (1963). Neither does Wesley's definition make it at all clear what, short of citizenship attributes, the outcome of social studies instruction is to be. Is the student to become a minuscule social scientist and the classroom a resonable facsimile of the social science laboratory, as Bruner (1962, p. 14) implies? Is the student to be engaged in some manner and to some degree in the same research in which the scholar is engaged, concerned more, as Herring (1958, p. 2) has pointed out, with fact gathering and the quest for the concrete, the observable, the measurable, and the definable than with overall social problems? Is the acquisition of the insights, skills, and attitudes which constitute the separate methodologies of each of the social sciences—i.e., the method used by the historian, the sociologist, etc.—to be an end of social studies instruction? Is the student to be involved as the discoverer, or perchance rediscoverer, of previously unrecognized relationships, as Bruner insists (1962, p. 20)? Or, as is much more commonly held, is the student to become a consumer merely of the products of research in the several social sciences—i.e., is transmission of knowledge to be the goal? Those who speak approvingly of Wesley's definition do not explicitly exclude the "involvement in discovery" suggested by Bruner (1962, pp. 20–21), Massialas (1963), and others; however, they frequently fall into ways of talking which belie this purpose. Thus, Gross (1960, p. 1296), elaborating on Wesley's definition, says that "the social studies are those studies that provide understandings of man's ways of living, of the basic needs of man, of the activities in which he engages to meet his needs, and of the institutions he has developed." This language clearly implies that the social studies are a body of predigested and organized knowledge ready to be transmitted to the learner. There is no suggestion of the tentative and approximate nature of whatever passes for knowledge in the social sciences at a given time; there is no suggestion of student participation in the process by which larger facts or more general conclusions are sorted out and validated from lesser facts and values; there is no mention of involving students in the act of discovering for themselves the general laws and commonalities of human society, in any of the senses recognized by Bruner (1962).

Many, possibly most, of those who accept Wesley's definition of the social studies interpret it in the narrow sense to mean that it is a storehouse of knowledge, skills, and specific virtues, the presumed product of research in the social sciences, to be transmitted to students. Nor does the following list of commonly accepted aims for the field—proposed by Carr and Wesley in 1950 (p. 1219) and reported by Gross (1960, p. 1298) as having remained fairly fixed—go far in dispelling this suspicion:

1. To respect the rights and opinions of others.
2. To be skillful in securing, sifting, evaluating, organizing, and presenting information.
3. To assume social and civic responsibility.
4. To act in accord with democratic principles and values.
5. To become a judicious consumer.
6. To understand principal economic, social, and political problems.
7. To learn about vocational activities and opportunities.
8. To understand the interdependence of peoples and groups.
9. To become a happy member of a home.
10. To make intelligent adjustments to change.
11. To get along with individuals and groups.
12. To use basic social studies skills.
13. To exercise critical judgment.
14. To understand and promote social progress.

If we may take Herring's (1958) interpretations, cited above, as a fairly accurate description of the way in which social scientists regard the field, items 1, 3, 4, 5, 9, 10, and 11 are clearly beyond the pale of the social sciences and move Carr and Wesley—and, by implication, most of those who hold with the Wesley definition—far into the camp of those who see citizenship education as the central concern of the social studies. This is an interpretation which the authors of the definition could not have foreseen. Neither is it at all clear, even to the social scientist, let alone to those who teach the social studies, just how the content of the social sciences is to be translated into the kinds of behavior listed by Wesley. In fact, as indicated earlier, many social scientists frankly disclaim any intent to teach moral purposes or normative judgment, which are clearly involved in such items as 1 and 4 in the list above. Further, many of the items listed above, especially 13 and 14, are general objectives of all education and therefore could not grow strictly out of the social sciences, as implied by the definition.

Neither does the list, which presumedly is consistent with Wesley's definition, give much solace to those who hold with Bruner (1962) that the central aims of the social studies are involvement in the process of discovery, and attainment of skill in the methodologies of the several social sciences. Item 12 gives a nod in this direction, but it is not at all clear how the preponderant demands of the list for fixed knowledge and behavior patterns could be poured through so scant a funnel. One gets the impression that lip service only is being given to items like 12 and 13 and that there is no clear intent to substitute transmission of knowledge and fixed attitudes for the slow and uncertain process of scientific inquiry.

But we are still not out of the forest into which Wesley's definition leads us. If we agree that knowledge is the goal of the social studies, we still need to define what we mean by knowledge. Is knowledge to be equated with getting the facts? If so, should we, as Larrabee suggests (1945, p. 128), distinguish between facts that refer merely to isolated events, and facts that refer to broad generalizations, theories, or ideas about human affairs? If the distinction is to be made, how can one be said to really know or understand a more general fact or principle unless he is also master of the myriad lesser facts which go to provide the grounds upon which these principles rest, as Massialas (1963, p. 186) has pointed out? Further, as Herring (1958, p. 2) has indicated, the enterprise in which the social scientist is engaged is not merely that of amassing data; it also involves the interpretation of data: speculating, hypothesizing, generalizing, theorizing about relationships between events, and searching out the lesser and relevant facts to substantiate or repudiate the theory. To this process, the so-called social sciences, simplified for pedagogical purposes, have no clear resemblance. As Metcalf (1963a, pp. 953–954) has emphasized, the simplification of the social sciences for pedagogical purposes requires, because of the increasingly great mass of material that must be covered, the progressive boiling down of the content to ever more general propositions which are presented as facts, on the authority of the scholar or textbook writer, without benefit or even a suggestion of the factual grounds, if indeed there be any, for holding the belief. Potter (1954, Part I) has brilliantly demonstrated how grievous can be the errors that result from this procedure. What is more to the point here is that the "simplification of the social studies for pedagogical purposes" concept may compound errors in knowledge without ensuring that students will really attain what is possibly a more lasting objective of the social sciences—a readiness always to inquire, and skill in conducting the inquiry, along lines most clearly laid out by Metcalf (1962), Donald Oliver (unpublished manuscript), Engle (1960), and Massialas (1963).

THE SOCIAL STUDIES AS CITIZENSHIP EDUCATION

In sharp contrast to those who conceive of the social studies as essentially the same as the social sciences are those who see the social studies as directly concerned with developing the attributes of good citizens. Although there is some overlapping, there are three discernible schools of thought within this group.

One would approach the problem of citizenship development through the restructuring and unification of the content of the social sciences, to bring this content more directly to bear on the broad social problems of the society; hence, the content of the social studies is conceived to be unified, synthesized, and applied social science. Another school sees the purpose of the social studies as that of developing the process of decision making (frequently referred to as problem solving or reflective method). To this group the content of the social studies is limited to data that are relevant to the problems confronting citizens [and to the process by which information (and perchance values) is put to use in solving these problems]. Still a third school conceives the social studies to be that content (including myth as well as fact) by which budding young citizens may be indoctrinated with the "right" beliefs and attitudes believed to be necessary for the unity of the nation and the loyalty of her citizens. A few in this school would limit such an approach to the formative years, being willing later, after a proper set has been established, to lay bare the facts of life. But others would conceive the social studies as a means of indoctrination even through the college years. Obviously such a position, which tends to be taken by some patriotic organizations and is not without its adherents among educators, removes the social studies from any very clear relationship to the social sciences.

UNIFIED SOCIAL STUDIES

Foremost among those who equate the social studies with unified and applied social science are Paul Hanna and his associates at Stanford. Hanna (1962, p. 64) sees, as sources of content in the social studies, the on-going activities of the community and the responses of children to experience. He summarizes his concept of the social studies as follows: "The contemporary professional education literature clearly reflects the acceptance of the nation that 'today we teach children something' and that something is the resultant of a synthesis of content from all three sources built around generalizations drawn from the social sciences." Again Hanna (1963, pp. 191–192) refers to the desirability of a "unified, coordinated, wholistic study" of "men living in societies," particularly in the elementary school. He adds, "we believe the child is psychologically helped, when we start his systematic school study of men in groups by having him observe and generalize about total cultural patterns rather than concentrate on the separate social science threads pulled out of the cultural textile (as is done by scholars engaged in sophisticated and detailed analyses)."

From the literature of six selected social sciences, Hanna and his students were able to identify and synthesize 3,005 generalized statements "universally applicable . . . and relevant to all time or to a stated time about man engaging in a basic human activity" and to assign these statements to nine basic areas of human living (protecting and conserving life and resources; producing, exchanging and distributing goods and services; expressing aesthetic and spiritual needs; educating; organizing and governing; etc.), each of which cuts across the several social sciences, and each of which corresponds roughly to an area in which persistent social problems may be found. What Hanna (1963, p. 193) refers to as the "grid of basic human activities"—i.e., the various basic categories into which human activities fall—each with its attendant set of generalizations, is somehow applied, though exactly how is never made clear, to the study, at different grade levels, of expanding communities of men—i.e., the family, the school, the neighborhood, etc.

Among others who conceive the social studies as a unified and applied social science is a Committee of the National Council for the Social Studies. This Committee proposes 14 basic themes, somewhat like Hanna's basic human activities, which are to serve as the framework of the entire social studies program (1957). As with Hanna, the Committee has identified a number of generalizations drawn from the content of the several social sciences which cluster about each theme and tend to support and further amplify it.

Similarly, the State Central Committee on Social Studies of the California State Department of Education (1957), with the aid of scholars in eight of the social sciences disciplines, sought to identify the generalization thought to be most important in each field, and to prepare a synthesized list of high-order generalizations (18 such were identified), which would serve to unify the entire social studies program—in all subjects and at all grade levels.

Engle (1963) suggests nine basic ideas, corresponding roughly to the principal areas of persistent social problems, which should receive recurring emphasis in the social studies. As with the others, he does not make it completely clear how this grid of basic ideas and problems is to be worked into the social studies program at the level of grades, subjects, and topics.

In somewhat the same vein, Johnson (1963) places himself squarely in the camp of those who, while recognizing the necessary dependence of the social studies on the social sciences, feel that the social studies have a larger role—that of synthesizing. Taking sharp exception to the views of Keller (1961) and Berelson (1962), quoted earlier, he calls attention to the obvious necessity for the citizen to live and make decisions (judgments about values) in a "life space" or "area of experience" which goes far beyond and cuts across the discrete boundaries of the classical conception of the social sciences. He disputes the academicians' claim that the separate study of the several social sciences provides sufficient and suitable preparation for the judgmental responsibilities of citizens. He denies that the study of such broad areas as the "family and community" and "social knowledge and social policy," which he suggests as timely subjects respectively for a freshman and senior high school social studies course, is any less a firm intellectual pursuit than the study of one of the classical subjects taken alone. He sees the clear aim of the social studies as "improvement in judgment about values" and objects to Keller's (1961, p. 62) attempt to limit it to a study of separate subjects and an acquiring of facts.

Johnson's forthright position symbolizes the sharp variance in aim between those who would merely simplify the social sciences for pedagogical purposes and those who seek to synthesize these subjects around the life experiences of students. To the former, the aim is some degree of mastery through exposition of each of the separate subjects comprising the social studies. Mastery is interpreted knowledge of, or ability to recall, the important facts and generalizations which presently frame each subject. The claim of some educators in this group that such a process directly influences the quality of decisions made by citizens is based on somewhat questionable and mysterious assumptions. Since the nature of the relationship between knowledge and values has never been clearly demonstrated, can it be assumed that the individual will discover for himself the interrelationships that exist between fact and value, thus achieving a balanced view of the life scene of which he is a part? More important still, it is claimed that the more intense study of a single subject, presumedly any one will do, will give the student a disciplined and discriminating way of thinking, which will automatically transfer to the demands of the broader social scene.

Encouraged by the research in psychology, those who would unify and synthesize the social sciences around life experiences deny the claims of the "separate-subject" group that broad transfer of intellectual training takes place from the study of the separate disciplines to the making of judgments in the context of a broad social problem. There is no evidence, they say, that the narrowly trained economist or historian is any more able to cope with the broad problems of citizenship. They note that among the social scientists themselves sharp variances exist over both matters of interpretation and methodology. Thus, sociologists may claim that historians mislead themselves into erroneous conclusions by narrowing their research interests to artifacts and written documents while ignoring psychological and sociological factors not represented in the written or spoken word; likewise, economists and political scientists, often so narrowly concerned with the economic and political structure of society that they ignore sociological forces, have drawn an overly-simple and unrealistic picture of this structure.

Moreover, the group that seeks a synthesis in the social studies contends that improvement in the quality of beliefs which people hold in the broad areas of life experience is possible, and that such improvement, far from being a result of rigorous intellectual activity in a discipline, is to be reached only through direct experience in examining one's beliefs systematically and "holistically." More important still, this group holds that the methodology through which one seeks synthesis and balance in his beliefs cannot be derived by adding together the separate methodologies of the several social sciences; rather, it has an integrity of its own and operates under rules and procedures that distinguish it from the methodology used in any of the social sciences, requiring intellectual veracity of an exceedingly high order and perfectable only through practice.

The clear, and some would say extravagant, aim of those who wish to unify and synthesize the social sciences is to influence, and perchance improve, the quality of people's beliefs about both matters of fact and matters of value, as these beliefs relate to broad and important areas of life experience. Those who wish to teach the separate subjects, however these may be simplified for pedagogical purposes, would settle for a more remotely useful if not actually lesser aim—i.e., the mastery through exposition of a considerable body of facts and generalizations selected from the social sciences. Though some relationship may be assumed to exist between knowledge so acquired and the ultimate beliefs which people come to hold, the direct and systematic development of beliefs is not an operational objective of the "social sciences simplified for pedagogical purposes" group, but it clearly is one for those who wish to work for synthesis.

INDOCTRINATION

A question remains which plagues both those who wish to synthesize the social studies curriculum and those whose goal is the mastery of individual subjects: What beliefs are to be taught (beliefs concerning values are an especially difficult problem here) and on whose authority? Specifically, the subject-oriented group asks, What facts and what interpretations are to be selected for mastery, and how do we provide for the eventuality that our facts are in error and our interpretations biased or faulty? Concern for this problem has resulted in recent years in a spate of commissions, committees, etc., composed of so-called authorities who are charged with the responsibility for preparing impeccable lists of generalizations held to be true beyond all reasonable doubt and therefore safe for educational purposes. All of which forcefully reminds us that Hanna, Johnson, Metcalf, and others who see the social studies as concerned focally with citizenship education are uncomfortable bedfellows with a group which sees the role of the social studies as indoctrination. Furthermore, in agreement with Johnson, Ballinger (1963), and others, though not clearly with Hanna (1963), this group is centrally concerned with values. But in sharp contrast with Metcalf (1963b), who seems to see perfection of the process of valuing more than values per se as an appropriate end of the social studies, this group looks upon values as being final and absolute, to be accepted unquestioningly from one's elders throughout the years of schooling. Facts, too, are treated as the unquestioned facts, the right facts, the values everyone should know, serving as the rationale for the right values, those that everyone should accept. The objective of the social studies is to teach the student what to value, not how to choose from among competing values.

Many teachers and laymen, either unwittingly or by deliberate choice, subscribe to this objective of social studies teaching. A few would limit such an approach to the formative years, being willing later, after a proper set has been established, to lay bare the facts of life. Extremist groups and patriotic organizations such as the American Legion (1957) seem to conceive the social studies as a closed body of facts and values, even through the college years. Though such a position obviously removes the social studies from any very clear relationship to the objectivity and the open-endedness of the social sciences, some social scientists, by declining in the name of science to deal with values and valuing, abdicate in the realm of values to those who would willingly indoctrinate.

THE DECISION-MAKING PROCESS

At this point, those who believe the social studies should teach the process of decision making launch barbs at the other schools of thought. Metcalf (1963a) and his mentor, Alan Griffin (1942), may be taken as the foremost proponents of this school. For the sake of clarity, it may be well at this point to draw a distinction between Metcalf's position and that of Bruner (1962). Bruner too sees the process of inquiry and participation in discovery of general ideas as of central importance, but he seems to see it in the more restricted context of the separate social sciences, while Metcalf sees the process in the context of broad and current social problems.

Metcalf (1963b, p. 198) chides those who ascribe long lists of impeccable and general purposes to the social studies (which, he says, are usually operationally vague and poetic expressions shot through with contradictory and incompatible destinations). He suggests instead a single purpose: "to help students examine reflectively issues in closed areas of American culture, i.e., in such areas as sex, economics, religion, race, and social class." Engle (1960), Massialas (1963), and Oliver (unpublished manuscript) make common cause with Metcalf, though all of these clearly see the tested beliefs which the student achieves through the process of inquiry as complementary objectives of social studies instruction and none would limit this approach to the study of critical or closed areas of American culture. Like Bruner, they see opportunities for what Massialas (1963, p. 186) calls the "creative encounter" in history or in the social sciences.

Swift (1961) and, in more general and somewhat like vein, Hullfish and Smith (1961) have spelled out the decision-making process operationally: i.e., what is involved in solving problems of *definition;* what is involved in solving problems of *explanation;* what is involved in solving problems of *valuing;* in short, how does one ground the generalizations which he holds or may come to hold in any area in which human beings are in disagreement.

Ballinger (1963) has called attention to the marked tendency of the social studies to neglect problems of value. As Oliver (unpublished manuscript) has pointed out, the problem of what to value or of what choice to make between values in a given situation is at the heart of all social problems. Yet Ballinger found that only one of eleven authors of textbooks in social studies methods had anything substantial to say about teaching values. Only those who see the central concern of the social studies as the teaching of decision making seem to be sensitive to the process of valuing as an end of social studies instruction. And these would sharply distinguish the end they have in view from the indoctrination advocated by some writers. By indoctrination is meant a deliberate stacking of the cards in favor of particular values, deemed "right," and against others, considered "wrong." To the "decision-making" group, the primary end is perfection of the process of inquiry into questions of value, all of which posits a far different concept of knowledge and a different image of the end product—i.e., the citizen—than is evident in any of the other positions. In all the other positions taken, knowledge is looked upon as relatively fixed, something to be known; the end is the all-knowing student, one who commits to memory all the "correct" answers. To those who make perfection of process the end, knowledge is taken as always changing, open continually to new interpretations as the circumstances of life change; the end in view is the student who knows how to achieve reasonably accurate conclusions.

CONCLUSIONS

A variety of sometimes contradictory aims is ascribed to the social studies. The contradictions run so deep that they are impossible to arrange on a single continuum, but we can get some idea of the differences which exist if we consider them on two separate continuums, one of which we shall call the "content" continuum and the other the "process" continuum. On the content continuum, we see the social studies varying at the extremes from the study of separate subjects, with no claim to any direct bearing on the broad problems of citizenship, to the direct study of broad areas and problems taken from the "life experience" of citizens. The latter is an enterprise held to be clearly separate, if not over and above, the study of subjects. The clear aim at the first extreme is knowledge, by which is meant the ability to recall multitudinous facts and principles in each of several of the social sciences. If, indeed, one studies a subject to the point of being able to abstract from experience and to discover a model of human behavior (i.e., a model of economic man, of sociological man, of political man, etc.), such a model is necessarily incomplete, because it is detached from real-life problems, which always appear in complex and patterned configurations requiring whole, and not piecemeal, solutions. At the other extreme of the continuum the clear aim is the possession of valid ideals and values as these relate to broad areas of human experience drawn from a wide range of subjects.

On the content continuum Keller (1961) and Berelson (1962), representing essentially the traditional academic position, are at one end. Hanna (1963) and Johnson (1963) are at the other. Wesley and the members of the Committees are essentially unclassifiable because their writings are so clouded in platitudes.

On a second continuum, the "process" continuum, the extremes vary from those who see the central process in social studies instruction as the mastering of subject matter to those who see it as a problem-solving process. To master subject matter is taken to mean to fix in one's mind, memory, and understanding in meticulous order the facts and principles which form the separate content of each social science discipline. Problem solving emphasizes the function of synthesis and imagination as ideas from a variety of related sources are tested in the context of broad areas of social experience. The goal in the first instance is the ability to recall arbitrary associations from each of the social sciences as well as diligence in the process of committing these facts to memory. The goal in the second is a continual development and refinement of the ability to solve problems and arrive at valid answers to the perplexing circumstances which confront citizens. On the process continuum, academicians are at one extreme, just as they were on the content continuum. Metcalf (1963b), Griffin (1942), and Oliver (unpublished manuscript), and possibly Engle (1963) and Massialas (1963) are at the other extreme, with Bruner (1962) somewhere in between.

Perhaps all of the philosophical positions are to some extent worthy of consideration. The difficulty with general statements of goals, like those of the Committees cited above, is that they encompass indiscriminately all of the goals mentioned, with the result that the reader is likely to take out that to which his bias inclines him, relegating other goals of equal or even greater importance to limbo. Future studies should focus on operationalizing the objectives of social studies instruction by relating goals to curricula, to methods of instruction, and to more specific student behavioral outcomes.

BIBLIOGRAPHY

American Legion. A Resolution Adopted by the National Executive Committee, Register No. 23, November 20–26, 1957.

Ballinger, Stanley E. "The Social Studies and Social Controversy." *The School Review,* LXXI (1963), 97–110.

Berelson, Bernard. "Introduction," in American Council of Learned Societies and the National Council for the Social Studies, *The Social Studies and the Social Sciences.* New York: Harcourt, Brace and World, Inc., 1962.

Bruner, Jerome S. *The Process of Education.* Cambridge, Mass.: Harvard University Press, 1962.

California State Central Committee on Social Studies. *Building Curriculum in Social Studies for Public Schools of California.* Sacramento: California State Department of Education Bulletin No. 26, 1957.

Carr, Edwin R., and Edgar B. Wesley. "Social Studies," in Walter S. Monroe, ed., *Encyclopedia of Educational Research,* rev. ed. New York: Macmillan Co., 1950, pp. 1213–1238.

Engle, Shirley H. "Decision Making: The Heart of Social Studies Instruction." *Social Education,* XXIV (1960), 301–304, 306.

————. "Thoughts in Regard to Revision." *Social Education,* XXVII (1963), 182.

Griffin, Alan. "The Subject Matter Preparation of Teachers of History." Unpublished Doctor's dissertation, Ohio State University, 1942.

Gross, Richard B., and W. V. Badger. "Social Studies," in Charles W. Harris, ed., *Encyclopedia of Educational Research*. New York: The Macmillan Company, 1960.

Hanna, Paul R. "Revising the Social Studies: What is Needed." *Social Education,* XXVII (1963), 190–196.

————, and John R. Lee. "Content in the Social Studies," in John U. Michaelis, ed., *Social Studies in Elementary Schools,* 32nd Yearbook, National Council for the Social Studies. Washington, D.C., 1962.

Herring, Pendleton. "Toward an Understanding of Man," in Roy A. Price, ed., *New Viewpoints in the Social Sciences,* 28th Yearbook, National Council for the Social Studies. Washington, D.C., 1958.

Hullfish, H. Gordon, and Philip G. Smith. *Reflective Thinking: The Method of Education.* New York: Dodd, Mead and Company, 1961.

Johnson, Earl S. "The Social Studies versus the Social Sciences." *The School Review,* LXXI (1963), 4.

Keller, Charles R. "Needed: Revolution in the Social Studies." *Saturday Review,* September 16, 1961, p. 60.

Larrabee, Harold A. *Reliable Knowledge.* Boston: Houghton Mifflin, 1945.

Lynd, Robert. *Knowledge for What?* Princeton, N.J.: Princeton University Press, 1948.

Massialas, Byron G. "Revising the Social Studies: An Inquiry-Centered Approach." *Social Education,* XXVII (1963), 185–189.

Metcalf, Lawrence E. "Research on Teaching the Social Studies," in N. L. Gage, ed., *Handbook of Research on Teaching.* Chicago: Rand McNally, 1963a.

————. "Some Guidelines for Changing Social Education." *Social Education,* XXVII (1963b), 197–201.

————. "The Reflective Teacher." *Phi Delta Kappan,* XLIV (1962), 7–11.

National Association of Secondary-School Principals. "Social Studies in the Comprehensive Secondary School." *Bulletin of the National Association of Secondary School Principals,* XLV (1961), 1–17.

National Council for the Social Studies, Committee on the Role of the Social Studies. "The Role of the Social Studies." *Social Education,* XX (1962), 315–318, 327.

National Education Association, National Council for the Social Studies. *A Guide to Content in the Social Studies,* Report of the Committee on Concepts and Values. Washington, D.C., 1957.

Potter, David M. *People of Plenty.* Chicago: University of Chicago Press, 1954.

Swift, Leonard F. "Explanation," in B. Othanel Smith and Robert H. Ennis, eds., *Language and Concepts in Education.* Chicago: Rand McNally, 1961.

Wesley, Edgar B., and Stanley P. Wronski. *Teaching Social Studies in High Schools.* Boston: D. C. Heath, 1958.

2

THE
CURRICULUM

Frederick R. Smith
Indiana University

The problem of determining the nature and content of the social studies curriculum is still one of tremendous proportions, despite renewed efforts in this direction in recent years. The task of preparing responsible citizens for a dynamic democratic society forces social studies educators to penetrate an unsolvable labyrinth of traditions, points of view, claims and counter claims, attitudes, and beliefs. The only reasonable course of action for educators who wish to achieve a successful resolution of the problem is to conduct a systematic, objective, and rational examination of issues and alternatives. The following review of research concerned with the social studies curriculum in grades K–12 undertakes to do this.

For purposes of analysis, studies concerned with the social studies curriculum were organized under three general classifications: reports and surveys of existing curriculum patterns; systematic investigations of the selection and organization of content; and research in delimited areas of the curriculum—i.e., a specific grade level, a course, or a given discipline. The following considerations were foremost in selecting the studies examined within this basic framework: (1) They should have attempted to examine some aspect of the curriculum or curriculum-related problems in a logical, systematic, and consistent manner, and must have been published in the last five years. (2) The primary concern of the study must have been pertinent to the selection, organization, and sequence of content in the social studies curriculum rather than to supervisory and administrative organization or processes. (3) Studies might deal with objectives and methods of instruction if they have implications for curriculum development.

A number of studies published during the period under review did not satisfy these considerations and were excluded. Other investigations not primarily designed to do so provided data relevant to the question of curriculum planning, and it was therefore deemed essential to include such data where appropriate, even though the entire study is not reported in this review.

CURRENT CURRICULUM PATTERNS

Intelligent and realistic judgments in curriculum planning must consider the nature of existing patterns and their relation to justifiable objectives for the social studies. However, the results of curriculum surveys, which describe these general patterns, must be subjected to rigorous analysis, using carefully determined criteria based on a sound philosophical and psychological approach to curriculum development. Too often, in a sincere effort to do good, overly zealous individuals are willing to accept "trends," "new patterns," and "recent developments" as being desirable prima facie without the benefit of thorough examination. The results of such action are a continual patching process in which existing courses are modified, emphases are changed, and new areas of concentration are added, but—in almost every case—nothing is deleted. Real progress will never result from slipshod approaches to educational planning.

Because an assessment of social studies curricula must start with those now in existence, the studies reported are viewed as an important first step in establishing a logical point of departure for this review.

ELEMENTARY LEVEL

Adams (1962) conducted a survey of all state departments of education, the District of Columbia, the Canal Zone, and representative cities of differing populations in each state, for the purpose of determining the nature of curricular offerings, and basic materials utilized in social studies programs in grades 1 through 9. Topics most frequently reported at the various grade levels were:

Grade   I: Our Families, Homes, and Schools. Work and Play. Pets. Farm. Holidays. Safety.

Grade   II: Helpers in the Community. Units on the Post Office, Firemen, Dairy, Bakery, Grocery Store, etc.

Grade III: The Town or Local Community—its relation to other general types of communities (rural, large city, etc.). Food, Clothing, Shelter, Communication, and Transportation. Also frequently mentioned are Indians and other ethnic groups, pioneers, etc.

Grade   IV: World Folk, Contrasting Communities in the United States, Local State. These three topics are taught with almost equal frequency. Two, and sometimes all three, topics are taught in the same school system at this same grade level. Exploration and Pioneer Days are also taught in the fourth grade.

Grade   V: Our Country: Its History and Geography. Our Neighbors in the Western Hemisphere. (Canada is taught more frequently at this grade level than at any other.)

Grade   VI: History and Geography of Latin America, or History and Geography of the Eastern Hemisphere.

Grade VII: History and Geography of the Eastern Hemisphere or, less frequently, United States History.

Grade VIII: United States History, Geography, and Civics. The Home State.

Grade   IX: United States Civics and Citizenship. World Cultures.

This sequence of topics is similar to that discussed by Furman in *Social Studies in Elementary Schools* (1962). Both represent the "expanding-environment" philosophy of curriculum organization, in which the curriculum broadens as the pupil gains additional experiences and greater maturity.

Particularly significant trends noted by Adams include: more emphasis on world cultures (especially the non-Western world of Asia and Africa); more current events—even in grades two and three; concern with Americanism versus Communism; and increased emphasis on "social economics," especially at the junior high school level. Human relationships, the problems approach, and a movement toward the fused or unified type of curriculum received significant emphasis at the elementary level in the past ten years. One cannot help being encouraged by the optimism of Adams' observation that social studies teachers are alert to the necessity of constantly improving the curriculum.

After an examination of reports on the contents of elementary textbooks and state educational bulletins, as well as recommendations of social studies educators, Alilunas (1961) concluded that the geographic-areas approach continues to be the most widely based plan for organizing social studies instruction in the middle grades. This is in keeping with the developments previously cited and seems to represent a generally accepted principle of curriculum development in the school years through grade seven.

SECONDARY LEVEL

Several studies concerned with social studies programs at the secondary school level provide a comprehensive picture of the curriculum at state, regional, and national levels. Jones (1963) was concerned about the progress of the social studies during the five years since the launching of *Sputnik I*. As a result of a study of 130 school systems in cities of 100,000 or more in the U.S., he concluded that in the large cities the social studies are in a stronger position than they were eight years ago. Thirty-nine city school systems reported that they had increased their high school social studies graduation requirements during the past five years, and 14 indicated that they were in the process of increasing these requirements. Only two of the systems reported a decrease in social studies requirements for graduation. The preponderance of increases in requirements came in world-history courses, with 64 school systems reporting that world history was now a required course, as compared with the 28 school systems reporting the same requirement in 1953. United States history was required by all of the school systems reporting.

The "required problems" course declined somewhat, and there apparently is a trend toward moving civics or government out of the ninth grade and into grades eleven or twelve. Economics as a required course showed a considerable increase and is now ahead of geography and local and state history as a requirement in the cities reporting. Jones also discovered that the median number of courses required in social studies instruction in grades nine through twelve had increased from four to five since his 1953 survey. The most substantial increase in social studies requirements geographically was in the South, with the Far West and Middle West following, in that order.

Jones' data also indicated an increase in interest in the area of world affairs. He concluded that this increase at a time when there is great interest in science and mathematics in the public schools was due to an increased awareness of the tasks of the social studies on the part of school administrators. This conclusion seems to carry with it the implication that the central responsibility for the social studies curriculum lies for the most part with the administrator. If this is a valid inference, it is essential that the situation be changed. Those teachers who are prepared in the social sciences and who know and understand the purposes of social studies education must make the important decisions in their curricular area. The school administrator who is frequently not prepared in the social studies must provide an atmosphere which will encourage his teachers to assume this responsibility.

Curriculum trends in the social studies were also reported by Moreland (1962), following a study of 500 schools selected as a representative cross section of secondary schools in the United States. In an examination of the required social studies courses in grades seven, eight, and nine, he found that geography is the most frequently required subject of students in grade seven, American history is the social studies course most commonly required in grade eight, and civics is the predominant social studies course in grade nine. Depending upon the school system, the junior high school program offers these courses either independently or in combination with other subjects, such as American history, state history, or social studies.

The pattern of required courses is apparently more firmly established in the senior high school than in the junior high school according to Moreland. World history is the predominant social studies requirement at the tenth grade level, with American history being almost exclusively the required social studies course in grade eleven. A full year's course of "problems" is most frequently found at the twelfth-grade level.

An alternative approach at grade twelve is the offering of a one-semester course in American government, accompanied by a semester offering on problems of democracy. He also reported that the study of economics, sociology, and psychology as separate courses, usually one semester in length, is increasingly apparent at the twelfth-grade level.

A second area of inquiry reported in this study is concerned with elective courses available in the social studies. There were very few elective courses reported in either grades seven or eight. Some freedom of choice did exist in grade nine, with civics and geography being the elective courses most frequently noted. The most common elective in grade ten was world history, or world history in combination with other courses. The second most common elective in the sophomore year was geography. Economics was the most frequently offered elective at the junior level, being offered by some 24 schools in the study. The greatest variety of electives were available in grade twelve: courses in economics, psychology, sociology, and world history.

Several general observations are evident from Moreland's study:

1. The pattern of required courses today reflects the influence of the Committee on the Social Studies of 1916 and indicates the need for a re-examination of the sequence of social studies instruction in the 1960s.

2. There is no basis for the belief that increasing use of the term "social studies" has meant a decline in history, geography, and other more traditionally organized subject-matter courses.

3. The general pattern of curriculum revision in the social studies is characterized by an emphasis on changing the subject matter within existing courses rather than with the reorganization of basic course titles. There is a trend toward including more work on international understanding and cultures, particularly as they relate to current events.

4. Elective offerings in the social studies, especially in the nonhistorical social studies, are increasing.

Perhaps one of the most interesting results of Moreland's study is the indication that geography, formerly considered an integral part of the junior high school program, is receiving additional emphasis at the senior high school level as an elective. This finding is supported by a study conducted by Gandy (1960) in the public high schools of

California. He discovered that—considering an apparent shortage of well-prepared geography teachers—there were a surprisingly large number of schools offering geography courses. One-third of the schools surveyed were offering special courses in geography—usually world geography.

This apparent resurgence of geography as a separate course in the secondary schools is undoubtedly related to the emergence of the United States in a world-leadership role. Whether this emphasis will culminate in the re-establishment of physical geography as a common offering is questionable in view of the previously discussed emphasis upon world cultures. In any case, these developments carry with them serious implications for teacher education.

A comprehensive examination of social studies curriculum offerings of high schools accredited by the North Central Association of Colleges and Secondary Schools was made by Masia (1963). Using a random-sample technique, he surveyed 400 public and private secondary schools in an eighteen-state area in November 1962. He found that the basic social studies offerings in grades nine through twelve are much the same as they were in the mid-twenties: civics in grade nine, world history in grade ten, American history in grade eleven, and various combinations of government, economics, and social problems in grade twelve. The requirement that all pupils take four years of social studies in grades nine through twelve was most uncommon, with three of every four schools surveyed requiring from two to three years of instruction in social studies courses.

Required courses appear in the following pattern: an initial requirement of American history in grade eleven for all students, with most schools adding a second-year requirement of government or a combination of government and social problems or economics at the twelfth-grade level. Although most required social studies offerings appear in the last two years of the high school curriculum, there seemed, according to Masia, to be ". . . a pronounced trend toward adding a sophomore-year world-history requirement to form a continuous three-year sequence" (p. 209).

The number of elective offerings is generally proportional to the size of the school, with the smaller high schools offering only enough elective courses to satisfy the required number of semesters of social studies instruction. Thus, in these schools, it is not a question whether the pupil will elect an additional social studies course, but rather which of the electives in economics, problems of democracy, or world history he will select to fulfill his graduation requirement.

Sixty-four percent of the schools had not dropped a social studies course in the two years preceding the study. All schools reported a total of only 41 course deletions, while some 155 courses had been added (primarily as electives) in 125 different schools reporting. Most course additions were in geography, international relations, and economics. Masia suggests that world events and other pressures on the social studies curriculum accounted for a renewed interest in these areas.

The investigation was also concerned with the nature of units included in the most commonly taught social studies courses. In assessing the findings of this portion of the study, Masia concludes that a considerable amount of "new" content is included in traditional course offerings, especially as it relates to international relations, foreign affairs, supranational economic matters, and areas of the world other than Western Europe.

Haggerson and Weber (1963) also conducted a study of course offerings, patterns of requirements and electives, and emphases in social studies programs in grades seven through twelve. Following an analysis of historical trends in the social studies curriculum, the report agrees with other studies in its conclusion that the basic program required nationally for all pupils has changed little from those proposed by the Committee on the Social Studies in 1916.

Secondary schools in Arizona were asked to respond to two questionnaires, the first of which was on curricular offerings, while the second was designed to yield data concerning the preparation, methods, materials, and evaluative procedures of Arizona social studies teachers. One hundred seventeen schools and 589 teachers participated in the study. The results showed that less than half the participating schools had a written statement of goals and objectives for the social studies and less than two-thirds of the same schools had written courses of study. Only approximately one-third of the schools reported any plan for articulation between the various grade levels. There was a direct relationship between the size of the school and the existence of these provisions.

A few schools reported dropping courses in the last five years— always in fields other than history and geography. Additional courses are planned in the newer social sciences and on understanding of other cultures and governments.

The study vividly points out that the social studies programs of Arizona are still primarily oriented to the more traditionally organized subject-pattern courses. The patterns of course offerings differed somewhat in sequence but not necessarily in nature from those reported by Moreland and Jones on a nation-wide basis.

The authors concluded that there is need for a broader program of offerings in social studies at the high school level. They went on to point out that: "A substantial percentage of schools indicated a need for more emphasis upon the areas of anthropology, sociology, and economics. Yet, courses which have been dropped from the social studies program in the last five years have included topics from these three areas. It would appear that more attention needs to be given to these areas, especially as elective courses" (p. 24).

Since the preparation of teachers must be considered an important factor in developing the curriculum, it is noteworthy that the Arizona teachers studied have the greatest number of hours of preparation in American history, followed by those in world history and political science. The average teacher had two or fewer three-hour courses in sociology, economics, and geography, and even less in anthropology. While the average total preparation of all social studies teachers participating in the study exceeded minimum North Central Association and Arizona requirements, teachers in the larger schools had a greater average semester-hour preparation in the social sciences than did those in the smaller schools. If the assumption can be made, however, that the subject-matter preparation of the individual influences even to a limited degree the selection of content in teaching, it is not difficult to see why history continues to maintain its key position in the social studies curriculum. Any increased emphasis in the curriculum on anthropology, geography, economics, or sociology will depend in part upon the extent to which these disciplines are included in the preparation of the social studies teacher. Thus, one important avenue for effecting curricular change lies in changing the pattern of formal preparation which is required of the classroom teacher.

Evidence that curriculum revision is in progress is offered by Crowe and Dimond (1963) as a result of a study of 800 school systems enrolling 30,000 or more pupils. From more than 500 replies received, a majority of the schools stated that curriculum work of some type was either under way or in the planning stage. Although the investigators made no attempt to evaluate the studies, some trends can be discerned from the report. A number of schools report revision of units on "ism," usually Communism, and an increased emphasis on non-Western cultures and geography. It appears that the world-history course in a number of schools is being expanded to include much more of the world than was formerly the case. Apparently, the geography courses introduced and/or revised include considerably greater emphasis on a cultural approach. Other studies reported additional elective courses and various types of experimentation in team teaching, student seminars, and in-service training and workshops for teachers.

IMPLICATIONS OF RESEARCH ON CURRICULUM PATTERNS

While the studies reviewed make it apparent that major course offerings in social studies have changed little in the past 45 years, there are indications that existing courses are receiving new emphasis. One also gets the impression that some effort is being expended toward making a breakthrough into such areas as non-Western studies and current problems of society. There is further indication that the curriculum is being broadened to include more elective courses—particularly at the senior high school level.

It is essential that individuals concerned with the improvement of the curriculum keep abreast of recent regional and national developments. Although the perspective gained through the examination of research of this nature is important, caution must be exercised in adapting new programs or modifications of programs without rigorously evaluating these research data in terms of carefully determined philosophical and psychological criteria. Many of the developments reported in the general studies are in all probability the result of a systematic analysis of the problem, based on valid assumptions regarding the needs of the individual and of society. Unfortunately, it is impossible to determine when this is the case, and the user of this research must subject these data to his own carefully determined criteria for the selection and organization of content in the social studies program.

These studies serve to illuminate the formal academic preparation of the teacher as a significant obstacle to curriculum change. State certification requirements and college and university curricula for social studies teachers frequently restrict the teacher to a relatively narrow scope of academic preparation in the social sciences. The demand that the teacher "major" in a given discipline, usually history, tends to reinforce and perpetuate the influence of the university upon the high school curriculum. Further, the preponderance of public-school social studies vacancies are found in the required course of American history, a situation which encourages the prospective teacher, faced with the necessity of selling his wares in the academic market place, to prepare himself in this area of relatively high demand.

This is not to deny the importance of a thorough preparation in history, but it does help to explain why there are not more teachers with academic majors in the other social sciences. Until more teachers possessing a broad understanding of the social sciences are available, it is doubtful whether significant changes in the traditional curriculum will be originated in the classroom.

SELECTION AND ORGANIZATION
OF CONTENT

Even the most superficial examination of recent professional literature leaves little doubt that, on the theoretical level at least, the social studies are being subjected to rigorous analysis. As Engle has so expertly illustrated in an earlier chapter of this publication, any suggestion that unanimity exists among investigators concerned with basic questions of social studies objectives would be extremely inaccurate. Likewise, an analysis of research concerned with the selection and organization of content reveals divergent points of view, although those studies which deal with the problem in depth suggest that a great deal of common ground exists among the various positions represented.

While there is considerable debate between those who envision the social studies merely as simplified social sciences and those who advocate the development of a separate discipline—one whose structure may be derived from other disciplines—there is considerable agreement that part of the content for the social studies curriculum is to be drawn from the social sciences. Earl S. Johnson (1963) speaks for many who are concerned with finding a more reasonable solution to the problem when he states, "Let it be noted, however, that because I am against a return to the classic disciplines, now to be named high school subjects and taught as such, I do not endorse a good deal of what now goes on under the aegis of the social studies" (p. 389).

One group of studies reviewed is primarily concerned with determining which concepts and generalizations are basic to the study of the various social sciences. A second group, although tending to emerge with similar initial ideas, pushes the inquiry further in an attempt to form concepts and generalizations of an interdisciplinary character. The difference between the two, then—at the risk of oversimplification—is one of degree. This may best be explained in terms of the "synthesis" which the latter group seeks. Generally, studies within the first group are concerned with specific courses at the secondary-school level, while research in the second group is broader in scope, frequently viewing the social studies as a continuous program in grades K–12.

THE CONCEPT OF STRUCTURE

Bruner (1961) has provided a most convincing justification for the determination of a base from which each group may move. In examining the problem of how to construct curricula that can be taught effectively by an average teacher while retaining basic or underlying principles of a given field of inquiry, Bruner develops the concept of "structure." He states that the task is essentially one of representing the structure of the subject in terms which the child can comprehend, and that it is possible, psychologically speaking, to teach any subject effectively to any child at any stage of development. The immediate task then becomes one of determining what comprises the basic structure of the social sciences. Once this is determined it is the responsibility of the educator to design a continuous curriculum through which the pupil may come to comprehend this basic structure. This problem is not easily solved, however, for there is no easy solution or ready agreement as to the nature of structure. Indeed, there remains much speculation as to the meaning of the term.

Wronski (1959) develops a rationale not unlike that of Bruner, and consequently assists somewhat in providing clues regarding the problem mentioned above. He states that organizing content and method in a manner conducive to the development of basic tools of the social scientist is a key element in what he envisions as a major breakthrough in social studies. Whereas a "conventional" attempt to improve the social studies curriculum would be to add new topics to the curriculum, Wronski suggests an approach which would consist of "going to the very nucleus that generates these new topics, new interpretations, new research, and new knowledge—the basic composition of this entity called the social scientist" (p. 215).

Apparently, structure will vary from discipline to discipline; and although there obviously will be similarities among the structures of the various social sciences, each will be unique. Thus, to determine the structure of a discipline, one must look to basic assumptions, the procedures, skills, and strategies by which hypotheses are formulated, examined, and subsequently validated. "Structure" involves not only basic principles but also the process by which these principles are derived. Although it is already possible to find social scientists moving in this direction, it remains a rich domain for future research.[1]

Once past this point of agreement that it is first necessary to define the structure of the disciplines, however, research concerned with the

[1] See Bernard Berelson and Gary A. Steiner, *Human Behavior: An Inventory of Scientific Findings* (New York: Harcourt, Brace, and World, 1964), 712 pp.

formulation of a basis for the social studies curriculum seems to proceed in one of a number of directions, depending primarily upon the manner in which the investigator perceives the educative process. In the selection of content, Metcalf (1963) relies heavily on the application of a concept of structure. He emphasizes that the logical result of this approach will in all probability be the removal of history from its dominant position in the curriculum, and an increased emphasis upon other social sciences. Consistent with this emphasis, the arbitrary dissemination of knowledge is de-emphasized as a major purpose of public education. Knowledge finds its major worth in relation to the systematic examination of values. Metcalf warns that since knowledge of the social sciences does not in itself dictate a particular set of values to be taught, teaching which focuses on structure will undoubtedly be a threat to those who have been satisfied in the past to teach their own values. He stresses that knowledge of the structure of the social sciences has a key role to play in the formation of values, and that there is no conflict between teaching the basic content of a field and the process of examination of values. Johnson (1963), in discussing the role of social knowledge and the development of students into "cultured persons," asserts that ". . . improvement in judgment about values" is the chief aim of social knowledge (p. 392).

Massialas (1963) attempts to analyze the curricular structure and methodological procedures which are essential to a social studies program designed to develop a systematic method of inquiry. He suggests that a sound social studies curriculum should be based on (1) Principles and generalizations *which explain human interactions,* and (2) Models of search, verifiability, and invention which the learner employs in his quest to find dependable knowledge.

It is apparent that Massialas visualizes structure as being composed of both method and content, which are inseparable and dependent upon one another. Thus, the learner must be engaged in a process of inquiry in which he is confronted with "ideas about man." He suggests that such data, presented in an appropriate psychological context, will stimulate the individual's desire to seek further data in order to follow the problem through to its *logical conclusion.* Furthermore, he points out that under the existing curriculum value contradictions and incompatibilities in society are either ignored or glossed over. He would include not only the study of social conflicts but also a consideration of alternative courses of action essential to their understanding or to their resolution. A similar proposal was developed by Hunt and Metcalf (1955).

When one examines this thesis carefully, it becomes evident that Massialas, like Metcalf, envisions a curriculum which draws from the structure of each of the social sciences. The process of inquiry in which the learner is engaged must be consistent not only with the methods and strategies utilized by social scientists but also with basic principles of learning theory. The major criterion for the selection of content, however, is its relevance to human and natural problems.

The National Association of Secondary-School Principals (NASSP) Committee on Curriculum Planning and Development (1961) did not really come to grips with basic issues in its statement on social studies in the comprehensive secondary school, although its report did underscore several "desirable trends" which are in accord with the previously examined ideas of social studies educators.

Of the twenty-two included in the report (pp. 9–10), the following trends seem especially noteworthy:

> The core of the social studies lies in critical inquiry into man's political, economic, and social experience.

> The social studies program must help students understand the "special methods" of inquiry utilized by historians and social scientists.

> Curriculum revision in the social studies is characterized by "systematic efforts" to develop articulation in the scope and sequence of the program from the elementary school through the university.

> The social studies teacher must be up-to-date in his knowledge of research in the behavioral and social sciences.

This report can, in essence, be assumed to support the ideas previously discussed, but these major considerations in curricular development are lost within the report itself. Its contents tend to remain at a level which suggests an all-inclusive descriptive approach rather than a systematic analysis of criteria for the organization and selection of content in the social studies.

This is a major concern of Hunt (1962) when he states that the social studies curriculum is constantly reviewed and revised but that in doing this curriculum workers rarely consider basic assumptions upon which the course offerings in the social studies curriculum are founded. He points out that it has been nearly half a century since the program as a whole has been systematically reviewed.

DEVELOPMENT OF CONCEPTS AND GENERALIZATIONS

Platt (1963), discussing the adoption of a concept-developmental approach to social studies, points to a basic problem—the definition of terms. The term "concept" seems especially difficult to define, and he suggests that many people merely substitute other words or labels, such as idea, abstraction, principle, generalization, value, theme. Platt defines a concept as ". . . something about an idea expressed in the words of our language." He suggests that a concept should be stated as simply and directly as possible, avoiding compound sentences, which he sees as generalizations. An illustration of his point is the following "concept": "man must adjust to his geographical environment in order to survive" (p. 41).

Quillen and Hanna (1961) present a much more concise definition: "A concept is a general idea, usually expressed by a word, which represents a class or group of things or actions having certain characteristics in common" (p. 187). They provide examples of concepts, one of which is democracy. As one can readily note, there is a great deal of difference between Platt's definition of a concept and that suggested by Quillen and Hanna.

The lack of a "common language" in social studies education was also recognized by Massialas (1962) in a detailed analysis of research in the social studies. He underscored Platt's discovery that the absence of agreement as to the definition of words such as "concepts," "ideas," "generalizations," "conclusions," and "hypotheses" hampers the use of this research.

Despite problems of definition, a number of investigators have attempted to wrestle with the task of establishing basic concepts and generalizations which would lead to the development of a defensible curriculum for grades K–12. Engle (1963), in a thoughtful examination of the problem, proposed that the emphasis be placed upon "general ideas or concepts" and "social problems." His course of study would focus upon a recurring emphasis on these "basic ideas or concepts": *culture, man in a culture interacting with the forces of nature, social groups, economic organization, political organization, freedom, interdependence, science and the scientific approach to knowing, and the suprarational, including religion, aesthetics, and philosophy.*

Each basic concept should provide a focal point for the selection and examination of relevant data which the learner may utilize in developing appropriate understandings. While some subjects within the social studies curriculum will relate more directly to certain of the basic concepts than others, the key factor in organizing an adequate curriculum is the careful structuring of subject content in such a way that it "can be continuously and usefully related to certain basic ideas essential to thinking clearly about human affairs and to the social problems attendant on these ideas" (p. 196).

A recent proposal (Hanna, 1963) suggests that the elementary and secondary school program should be developed largely along anthropological lines. The basic structure would be "man living in an ever-expanding society." Beginning with the family, the school, and the neighborhood, the curriculum would eventually encompass the world as a community. In order to use this type of structure to the greatest advantage, the sequence of community studied should take priority over grade-level placement, although the latter must be considered. A major strength of this proposal lies in its identification of certain basic activities as common elements in all societies.

Cammarota (1963) points out that in an elementary curriculum based upon the expanding-environment concept, principles of government and politics are incidental rather than central. In an analysis of the work of Easton and Hess (1962) regarding social studies and politics and government in the elementary school, she suggests that "The main ideas of the disciplines should form the framework for the total social studies curriculum in K–12 curriculum" (p. 207). She also proposes that a curriculum organized on a spiral concept should present these main ideas again and again, providing they are introduced in subsequent grades in more intricate and more complicated form. The author, however, is confronted with the "structure problem" mentioned earlier. Consequently, she does not provide concrete examples of these "main ideas" except that they are "underlying principles" and "concepts and content from the political science area."

Paul R. Hanna and John R. Lee (1962) report a series of doctoral dissertations which attempt to arrive at generalizations[2] upon which teachers, administrators, and curriculum workers may draw in curriculum planning. A generalization was defined as "A universally applicable statement at the highest level of abstraction relevant to all time or stated times about man, past and/or present, engaging in a basic human activity" (p. 73). Dissertations by Geer and Hofstrand discussed below were conducted as a part of this study. For a more complete discussion of other dissertations in the project the reader should consult the 32nd Yearbook of the National Council for the Social Studies. Generalizations were developed for the following broad topics: Organizing and Governing; Providing Recreation; Protecting and Conserving Human and Natural Resources; Expressing Religious Impulses; Expressing and Satisfying Aesthetic Impulses; Transporting People and Goods; Producing, Exchanging, Distributing, and Consuming Foods, Clothing, Shelter, and Other Consumer Goods and Services; Communicating Ideas and Feelings; Providing Education; Creating Tools, Technics, and Social Arrangements. Specialists in each of the social sciences aided in applying established criteria for the identification of generalizations from literature considered appropriate to the particular topic of inquiry.

Geer (1959) utilized the basic definition of generalization of the Stanford Studies in arriving at his own definition: "A universally applicable statement at the highest level of abstraction relevant to all time or stated times about man in his relation to society engaging in the basic human activity of conservation and protection of human and

---

[2] For examples of generalizations, see page 39.

natural resources" (p. 2879). In attempting to derive generalizations relating to human activity, six specialists from the various fields analyzed basic books from each of the social sciences. Two hundred and twenty-five generalizations were derived in this manner. Geer views his work as providing an orderly group of generalizations which illustrate the extent of concern which social science writers have for the human activity of conserving and protecting human and natural resources. He suggests that they serve as sources of curriculum material for elementary social studies as well as a convenient means of cross-disciplinary analysis. A sample generalization from his study is, "Since mineral resources are exhaustible . . . only through wise and careful use can the supply be maintained for use" (p. 2879).

Hofstrand (1959) utilized essentially the same definition of a generalization as did Geer. He developed several points by which a generalization might be identified. (1) Opinions, literal facts, concepts, definitions, are not generalizations. (2) The stated generalization should not be limited by reference to specific geographic or cultural boundaries. (3) The generalization must deal with man in a societal orientation, not as an isolated individual. (4) The generalization or the context in which it appears should show that the author believes that there are no exceptions.

In an analysis of the literature from the various social sciences, he attempted to draw up and classify generalizations according to the following categories: (1) creating tools, (2) technics, (3) social arrangements. Samples of generalizations are as follows: "Invention . . . materially modifies the conditions of social living." "A discovery or invention, once it is made, is without result and sterile unless it is adopted" (p. 3223). (In many respects there seems to be little difference between the "concept" of Platt and the "generalizations" suggested by Hofstrand and Geer.)

The Indiana State Committee for the Revision of the Social Studies Curriculum (1963) took a somewhat different approach in attempting to find a basic structure for the social studies program in that state. The study postulated five questions which were to serve as guides for the selection of content. The questions are as follows: (1) Who is man? (2) What arrangements has man made to meet his needs and desires? (3) What factors beyond the immediate control of man have influenced his behavior? (4) What effect does learning have upon the directions man takes and the changes which he has made in his culture? and (5) What are the persistent problems man has faced in his effort to meet his needs and aspirations? Sub-questions under each of the major headings were designed to assist the committee in its effort to organize a plan for the social studies curriculum in grades K–12. This committee suggested that the curriculum should ensure that pupils at every grade level should study materials which will help them to understand and make relevant judgments about those basic questions. Each pupil should be encouraged to evaluate the effectiveness of man's efforts to meet his needs and to solve his problems. One of the tasks remaining for the committee in treating each of the individual questions is the formulation for each grade level of the supporting structure, basic concepts, generalizations, and/or principles, and suggested content for a systematic pattern of curriculum development.

Perhaps the most comprehensive state plan for the social studies curriculum for grades K–14 has been accomplished as a result of the work of the California State Central Committee on Social Studies (1959). The intent of the report, developed cooperatively by both professional and lay workers, was to provide an overall framework for the structure of the social studies curriculum on a state-wide basis from which courses of study in local situations might be derived. Significant portions of the report include a statement of twenty-one characteristics of a social studies program and a systematic analysis of factors essential to the implementation of a social studies curriculum.

The strength of the report lies in its development of specific generalizations for the selection of content and instructional procedures. As a result of an analysis of each of eight social sciences (geography, history, political science, economics, anthropology, psychology, sociology, and philosophy) the committee developed specific generalizations basic to the education of every young citizen. It was recommended that these generalizations be utilized as guides in the development of a basic social studies curriculum.

Following an analysis of the nature of the learner at the various stages of growth and development, general recommendations for the scope of the curriculum from K–14, with major themes and anticipated outcomes, were proposed. The following two generalizations are drawn, for example, from the study: (1) "In organizing government, it is essential to endow rulers with power, and make provisions for making them responsible for its use" (p. 14). (2) "The well-being of the state is dependent upon educating its citizens for life" (p. 17).

In addition, eighteen synthesis statements for social studies are developed on the basis of main and recurring ideas. While these statements are in many cases fairly complex and thus very unwieldy, their value in building a curriculum which emphasizes an interdisciplinary approach is obvious. For instance, note the wide range of choice for the selection and organization of content at almost any grade level given in the following statement. "People of all races, religions, and cultures have contributed to the cultural heritage. Modern society owes a debt to cultural inventors of other places and times" (p. 38).

From these eighteen synthesis statements it should be possible to develop definitions of more sophisticated concepts, such as culture, interdependence, society. Although the process of generalizing provides greater flexibility in curriculum development, it likewise carries with it certain demands. Primary among these demands is that we prepare teachers and curriculum workers possessing the knowledge and understanding of both content and intellectual strategies essential to the development of a curriculum which will enable the learner to inquire into, and understand the nature of man more effectively.

A RE-EXAMINATION OF SPECIFIC PRACTICES AND COURSES

Much of the attention of social studies investigations is devoted to the question of the type of structure upon which a continuous, articulate program of instruction may be based. Research limited to specific areas of inquiry is also being pursued in an attempt to determine how existing social studies courses may be improved.

A number of traditional assumptions relating to the selection and arrangement of content have served to restrict certain topics, units, and even entire courses to specific grade levels. For purposes of illustration, let us examine one such example. One proposal of the Indiana revision committee (1963) places the study of American history in grades eight and nine. Various groups have raised serious, even heated, opposition to this proposal. At this writing the problem has not been resolved, but it does raise a number of interesting questions. Upon what basis does one assume that the teaching of American history is more appropriate to grade eleven than to grades eight or nine? Does the assignment of this course to the intermediate grades imply that the content of the course is less important or will be taught less well than in the junior year of high school? Does this imply that American history is being de-emphasized? Possible questions are endless, but those raised above provide ample illustration of the necessity of examining in a systematic manner proposals for change of modification of traditional practices. There is considerable evidence that inquiry in social studies education is meeting this challenge—particularly in current research concerned with the study of concepts in the elementary schools, and a re-examination of the content in specific courses in the secondary schools.

THE ELEMENTARY SCHOOLS

Spodek (1963) initiated a trial curriculum in the social studies at the kindergarten level based upon the hypothesis that kindergarten children could begin to understand significant concepts in the social sciences. History and geography provided the content of this project, for which concepts of "New York as a Harbor" were developed. These were further broken down into specific understandings judged to be at the level of attainment of these children. Instruction over the unit followed a spiral pattern which was integrated within the regular kindergarten work. Evidence was collected on the process by which the children learned these basic concepts and additional information was obtained through the administration of pre- and post-tests. The results of the tests and the recorded observations provided the basic data for evaluating the learning of the kindergarten children.

As a result of the study, it was found that kindergarten children are capable of developing significant social science concepts. Although there was no single avenue upon which the children relied for gathering information, kindergarten children were able to deal successfully with ideas over long periods of time. The physical tools as well as the intellectual tools of the social sciences were used successfully by the children, who were able to transfer their understandings to new situations. Spodek concluded that children in kindergarten can begin to develop social science concepts as stated by social scientists, and that social studies programs in the kindergarten can become more closely related to programs in the rest of the child's school career.

Rusnak (1961) was concerned that many skills and concepts in the social studies were not being introduced until the later grades in the elementary schools, primarily because children do not read well at earlier levels. Apparently this practice stems from the assumption that children are not mature enough to understand notions of space and time and related ideas until the later elementary grades. In a three-year study of social studies instruction at the primary level, Miss Rusnak explored the problem of adapting some important skills and concepts to first grade instruction. Skills chosen for presentation were research methods, reporting, committee work, and organizing information. Concepts introduced were concerned with historical sequence, cause and effect, geographical space, adaptation to environment, and comparison of simple and complex societies. All work was done within the framework of the existing first-grade curriculum.

Problems which appeared in the program derived from the inability of first graders to read material on social studies projects, the complexity of teaching both skills and concepts, and the short attention span of young children. Thus, it was necessary for the teacher to direct and guide the first-grade pupils in a systematic manner. When instructional practices took into account these limitations, the development and use of advanced concepts and relationships in the social studies was possible, and the pupils indicated an increased interest in and knowledge of the social studies. This is a promising development in view of the results of other studies which indicate pupil disinterest in social studies at a very early stage in the educational process. It also serves as supporting evidence to Bruner's contention that basic concepts are adaptable to instruction at any grade level.

The teaching of generalizations in the sixth grade was studied in an experiment by Beaubier (1962). A control group was taught in what the investigator considered a typical approach for achieving mastery of certain factual information. The experimental group was exposed to a variety of instructional materials and techniques designed to develop an understanding of three reasonably complex generalizations. The conclusion that pupils in the sixth grade can understand generalizations and ideas which are more complex than those commonly taught at this grade level is in agreement with the results of other studies reviewed. All of these studies suggest that the present elementary school curriculum has a tendency to reserve the study of subjects of a complex nature until later in a pupil's experience, a practice which is being seriously challenged by those concerned with the improvement of the social studies curriculum.

Greenbladt (1962) suggests that this situation may, in part, account for the lack of interest which pupils have for the subject. In a study of subject preferences of elementary school children, approximately 300 children in the middle grades were asked to list, in order of preference, their favorite school subjects. He found that the position of preference of the social studies is unclear when compared with other subjects in the curriculum. Apparently the subject does not impress the pupils. Can one conclude from these data that the present social studies curriculum is of so little consequence that it lacks any impact on the child even as early as the elementary years? This is alarming, especially when one considers the degree to which the present program in the elementary schools concentrates upon experiences and environmental elements which are familiar to the pupils. Can the problem be attributed primarily to inadequate instructional practices?

Apparently not, according to Jarolimek (1962), who, following an analysis of curriculum content in social studies in the elementary school, suggests that there have been fewer basic changes in content than in methods of teaching. He contends that inadequate attention has been devoted to research designed to provide a solution to this problem. The program is too often described in big and general terms, such as "Building Good Citizens," "Teaching Democracy," or "Developing Responsible Behavior." The classroom teacher meets with considerable difficulty in planning a program described in such vague terms. Jarolimek proposes that the content of the social studies should be drawn from the parent disciplines of the social sciences, focusing on major ideas from geography, history, economics, sociology, political science, and anthropology. While he discusses a number of other related problems facing the social studies educator, his conclusion is a simple one—either we resolve some of the problems of subject-matter content within the profession or others will solve them for us.

THE SECONDARY SCHOOLS

Research pertaining to the social studies curriculum in the secondary school is characterized largely by the examination and revision of existing courses and proposals for the addition of new courses or even entire areas of concentration. These inquiries conducted by both professional educators and representatives of the various academic disciplines indicate an increased awareness on the part of social scientists of the necessity of contributing their knowledge to the task of curriculum improvement. Many of the studies reviewed have relevance to specific courses rather than to the social studies curriculum as an entity. This may be attributed in part to the scholar's dedication to a specific discipline. The American-studies and world-cultures courses do indicate a trend in some quarters to adopt an interdisciplinary approach. The first group of studies reviewed is concerned with world history and cultural areas. The following ones are concerned with American history and American studies, and those which are classified as projects.

WORLD HISTORY. Siemers (1960) surveyed 100 world-history teachers, representing various geographic areas in California, for the purpose of determining whether tenth grade students were exposed to a variety of methods and materials, and the extent to which history teachers were trained in history and the social sciences. A major assumption underlying the study was that inadequacy of teacher preparation is reflected in the negative attitude which high school students hold toward the subject. Nearly three-quarters of the teachers sampled indicated that they attempted to teach all of the world's history, giving equal coverage to each topic or area. The rest indicated that they concentrated on Europe, ancient and medieval civilization, or ancient and modern

history. Further data indicated an overwhelming reliance on a chronological organization of the course, with at least one-third of the teachers
using this approach exclusively. A topical organization was reported by
30 percent of the teachers, with 8 percent of them indicating this as their
predominant approach to teaching. These data caused Siemers to
conclude that, "If world history is to hold broadening influences for
tenth graders, areas involving social, geographical, and economic import
must assume equal importance with those in the political realm" (p.
154).

The preparation of the teachers of world history indicated that of
those who held bachelor's degrees, 37 percent had majors in history or
social studies, while of those who possessed the master's degree, 17
percent had concentrated in history or social science at the graduate
level. Thus, 54 percent of the California world-history teachers in the
survey had course concentrations in either history or social science
(although data do not indicate that this preparation was concentrated in
world history per se). The major concern of the investigator, however,
was the 46 percent of the teachers who reported no history or social
science concentration in their college preparation. As the teacher is
undoubtedly the most significant factor in determining the effectiveness
of any curriculum, this research vividly underscores the necessity of
planning curriculum offerings with a great deal of consideration not
only for course content, but also for the selection of capable personnel
possessing the academic background, skills, and interest essential to the
successful implementation of the program.

Social studies educators are slowly coming to the realization that
the world-history course can no longer be envisioned as a complete story
of mankind and that the content must be modified. The suggestion has
been made that less emphasis be given to early history and more to
specific themes and movements.

Bruntz (1960) suggests that the teaching of world history be
organized around central themes that are common to all areas of the
world. His basic assumption is that the student will have a better
comprehension of world history if he studies these themes and the data
which are relevant to them than he will through a mere repetition of
chronology. The nine themes proposed are (1) the rise and decline of

civilization; (2) world governments and the development of democracy; (3) the contributions of science, inventions, and technology to civilization; (4) how man has made a living—trade, commerce, and industry; (5) the fine arts and education as they affect civilization; (6) revolutionary movements; (7) religions of the world; (8) war and peace; (9) the influence of geography.

Bruntz concludes that while there will be a great many problems in developing a thematic approach to world history, they can be no worse than they are now—there should even be an improvement.

CULTURAL AREAS AND ANTHROPOLOGY. Another promising solution to the problem lies in the cultural-area approach. Stavrianos (1962) suggests the use of a flash-back technique in which the past is directly related to the present in order to make world history meaningful and relevant to pupils living in the twentieth century. A textbook which develops this approach, *Global History of Man,* by Stavrianos *et al.,* was published in 1962.

Other suggestions for the improvement of the world-history course also endorse an anthropological approach. Miller (1962) reports the basic content of a world-cultures course as including: The development of understandings of basic cultural patterns and the ways in which man lives; the study of cultural aspirations, problems, values, and differences; and the study of the variety of ways in which these problems have been approached. Specific courses in anthropology have been reported in some school districts (Dunlap, 1961) (Reese, 1963). The American Anthropological Association (1963) has organized a project for the purpose of determining ways of introducing anthropological concepts and approaches into the high school classroom. Some teaching materials for use in the secondary schools are now available or are in the process of preparation. While it is not possible to determine the extent of influence which anthropology will have upon the whole social studies curriculum, there appears to be little doubt that it has already brought about significant changes in world-history teaching. If this development continues—and there is every reason to believe that it will—it is imperative that teacher-education programs include more emphasis upon this subject.

AMERICAN HISTORY AND AMERICAN STUDIES. Research in the area of American history is equally as encouraging as that in world history. Halsey (1963) reports that a committee has been organized in western Massachusetts for the purpose of developing materials for a "new" eleventh grade United States history course. This committee, composed of university and secondary school teachers, has organized a series of units which deal with important aspects of American history. The new course proposes to enable the student to see facts in a meaningful context rather than as pieces of isolated information. The units, which make maximum use of original sources, provide an avenue through which students are asked to formulate and confirm historical generalizations inductively rather than deductively. It is assumed that the student, having gone through this process, will be more skillful in using his own generalizations and those of others. Some of the interesting assumptions which underlie the work of the committee are: The United States history course, if organized in a systematic fashion in a radical new manner, will require the rethinking of the social studies courses which immediately precede and follow it; it is no longer desirable for a student to attempt to learn all of American history or to gain an overall "summary" knowledge; the teacher must select content more carefully—he must cease accepting (and consequently, encouraging the students to accept) unexamined generalizations. The committee envisions the role of the teacher in this curriculum not as that of a dispenser of a predetermined body of knowledge, but as that of an individual dedicated to the development of the student's capacity to learn and to inquire.

A number of investigations propose the development of secondary school programs designed along the lines of American studies. Baker (1963) suggests that a curricular model similar to that of American studies will help pupils understand the forces, events, and circumstances from which our society has evolved. In this sense, the "model," as described by Baker, serves a function similar to that of Bruner's concept of "structure." The interdisciplinary approach employed in American studies must, according to Baker, result in the construction of a model which is "eclectic," "functional," and subject to continuous evaluation. Although there is at the present time no model which is fully acceptable to scholars, continued study of the problem should eventually result in the development of one upon which there will be general consensus. Baker suggests the following four-year program for the social studies in the secondary schools. Designed primarily like American studies, it includes some content not generally found in this program.

> First year—Area Study, a study of culture, geography, politics, and problems in major areas of the world.
>
> Second year—American Values and Ideals, an analysis of basic values, prominent Americans, and the examination of the societies from which many of these values have been derived.
>
> Third year—American History, study in depth of major periods and forces which have shaped our nation.
>
> Fourth year—American Issues—An examination of major issues facing American society, including Communism and the responsibilities of the individual in a democratic society.

Another proposal for a three-year program in American studies (Cordier, 1962) relies more upon history than does that of Baker. It purports to facilitate the integration of content while providing a systematic program in which each year of study provides background for content studied in the following year. It includes, in grade eight, United States History to 1876; in grade nine, state and local history for one-third of the year, and national, state, and local government for the remaining two-thirds of the year; and in grade ten, United States history since 1876.

A major consideration in the development of an American-studies program or a program patterned after American studies in the secondary schools is that it be based upon an interdisciplinary approach in which "synthesis" plays the key role (Hague, 1963). Such a program must not only be broad, it must also stress the interrelatedness of knowledge drawn from the various disciplines as it applies to the topic or problem under examination. The program suggested by Baker appears to meet these criteria extremely well and reflects the influence of the concepts of structure and synthesis previously discussed. The second proposal (Cordier) tends to place more emphasis on course sequence, although it derives much of its strength from the interrelatedness of content and the social studies program. This program does not appear to have the scope or flexibility of the Baker proposal.

This type of program with its broad, interdisciplinary, and flexible approach offers a concept of curriculum development which promises to tear down the barriers built up by subject-matter departmentalization. The public school social studies teacher, by virtue of having a broad, although not always deep, social science background, is less apt to be bound by the confines of departmentalization than is the university professor (Fishwick, 1963). Thus he tends to be a more mobile individual who is ". . . willing to experiment with new concepts, courses, and approaches" (p. 421). American-studies programs may, therefore, find many advocates in the ranks of secondary school teachers, with the result that—in the judgment of Fishwick—the future of this movement may rest more with the high schools than with the universities.

ECONOMICS PROJECTS. One of the most significant efforts to revise a portion of the social studies curriculum has been made by the Committee for Economic Development (1961). The primary obstacles to a satisfactory program of economics in the secondary schools, according to the committee's report, are (1) a shortage of teachers prepared to teach economics, (2) lack of properly defined goals for economic education, (3) unavailability of quality teaching materials, (4) lack of adequate evaluation instruments, and (5) lack of coordinated efforts on the part of those interested in economic education to improve the situation. Significant recommendations made by the Committee are the following: (1) Where possible, the course in social studies usually given in the twelfth grade should be directed toward developing economic literacy; and, if possible, high schools should offer an elective course in economics. (2) Economics should be taught at all grade levels through the enrichment of existing social studies courses.

The committee has made specific recommendations regarding the nature of the content and the approach to instruction. The minimal understandings needed for effective citizenship in the modern American economy center around three questions.

1. What shall be produced and how?
2. How much in total can be produced, and how fast shall we grow?
3. Who shall get the goods and services that are produced?

Each of the questions are examined at some length in an effort to describe a number of institutions, facts, and approaches that are essential to the questions raised. While it is not the purpose of the report to develop a course of study in detail, the material discussed does provide a source of ideas which is invaluable in the improvement of this phase of the social studies curriculum.

GEOGRAPHY PROJECTS. A joint effort to improve high school geography has been undertaken by the Association of American Geographers and the National Council for Geographic Education (White, 1961). The plan began with the definition of basic ideas and skills in geography which could be taught at the high school level. Through the cooperation of teachers and professional geographers, a one-year demonstration course in high school geography has been instituted. A primary goal for this course is that it shall be suited to the secondary school social studies curriculum at the ninth- or tenth-grade level.

OTHER PROJECTS. Further research indicating an increase in emphasis on the above areas and in the degree of cooperation between individuals representing the various disciplines and social studies educators may be found in the following publications: *High School Social Studies Perspectives* (1962), *The Social Studies and the Social Sciences* (1962), and the 31st Yearbook of the National Council for the Social Studies (1961). These publications indicate a significant effort on the part of experts in the various social sciences to provide basic understandings and new interpretations in their disciplines. Evident in these writings is the increased emphasis on area studies and cultures other than those of the West. Unfortunately, the first two do not deal extensively with problems of structure or methods of inquiry in the various social sciences, nor do they adequately consider the psychological and societal dimensions of the social sciences.

In addition to cooperative projects in anthropology, geography, and economics, a number of other groups have been organized, both with and without the support of foundations (Michaelis, 1963). As with the areas previously mentioned, there is a tendency for this research to focus on specific disciplines which are or may be included in the social studies curriculum, although several focus upon the curriculum as a whole. A number of reports should soon be forthcoming. In general, these efforts support the conclusion that social studies educators representing all levels of education, the various social science disciplines, and professional education, are engaged in cooperative efforts to bring about significant changes in the social studies curriculum. In view of these developments, perhaps the warning issued earlier by Jarolimek is unnecessary.

SUMMARY AND IMPLICATIONS

Recent research concerned with the social studies provides a comprehensive body of knowledge about the problem involved in selecting and organizing content. Essentially, the studies reviewed fall into three categories: surveys, experiments, and theoretical inquiries. Data obtained through surveys on a national and regional basis provide essential information for the development of a frame of reference by which existing practices can be determined, and assessed in relation to new theories and interpretations.

The limited number of experimental studies reviewed were generally sound, although in several instances the rationale for the design and criteria of evaluation were not complete. In conducting research of this nature, it is imperative that the investigator construct his research design within acceptable philosophical and psychological limits. Basic assumptions and propositions must be warranted, and strategies and techniques must be carefully selected. If these factors are not rigidly considered, data which are derived from the study will be of little value.

The majority of studies reviewed were of a theoretical nature or were derived from a theoretical examination of the problem. While the quality of the research is difficult to evaluate, it is apparent that the investigators operated within the confines of specific frames of reference which relied upon various assumptions regarding the purposes and objectives of social studies education. Too frequently, these assumptions were not discussed; and, consequently, it was impossible to determine the extent to which they had been subjected to rigorous examination. Most of these studies appeared to have a central point of agreement—i.e., that the proper basis for the selection of social studies content is the "structure" of the social sciences. A number of investigators stop at this point, obviously accepting the assumption that, once this structure is determined, the next logical step is to present it to the pupil in terms which are compatible with his intellectual and emotional development. A second group of investigators contend that certain problems, concepts, and generalizations which are basic to an understanding of society should form the core of the social studies curriculum. These ideas, problems, or themes, cannot be adequately explored within the confines of the structure of a given discipline; rather they demand a synthesis of relevant knowledge, principles, and processes drawn from appropriate social sciences.

A second facet of the problem, considered in a lesser number of the studies, is the process by which the pupil develops skills of inquiry which will enable him to acquire, examine, and verify data. Research which does not consider the relationship of the learning process to the selection and organization of relevant content will be of limited value in structuring a social studies curriculum which will be effective in educating American youth capable of making intelligent decisions in a complex society.

A number of other trends and developments are evident in the major findings of the studies reviewed:

Curriculum offerings in the social studies have changed relatively little in the past fifty years. Modifications in the programs at both the elementary and secondary school levels are characterized by new emphases within existing programs, and the addition of elective courses—in the secondary schools particularly courses related to the "newer" social sciences. There are numerous reports of a re-emphasis upon geography at all levels of the educational ladder. Concepts from anthropology and sociology are assuming increasing importance—particularly in the high school years. Nevertheless, data relating to the entire curriculum on a nationwide basis suggest that relatively little progress has been made in establishing a systematic, articulate program from kindergarten through grade twelve.

Despite the fact that the lack of a "common language" in many instances obstructs systematic analysis and effective communication, a number of investigators have set forth basic concepts and generalizations which promise to provide the foundation from which a more effective program may evolve. There is still a basic disagreement as to what constitutes the major purpose of social studies instruction. Until this problem is resolved, the nature of the curriculum will continue to depend upon the basic assumptions, warranted or otherwise, which are made by those in the schools.

There is evidence that the philosophical gap is being narrowed— particularly by those who advocate a cultural approach to the study of mankind. Proponents of such programs suggest that it will be necessary to bridge artificial departmental barriers in order to examine those basic concepts which are common to man's persistent problems. The concept of knowledge for knowledge's sake is giving way to one of selecting ideas because of their value in assisting pupils in gaining an understanding of society, and the significant forces, events, and circumstances from which society has evolved.

Experimentation suggests that a conceptual approach to instruction in the social studies is possible at the primary levels of instruction, and that key concepts may be successfully taught when presented at a level appropriate to the intellectual development of the pupil. A number of investigators indicate that the assumption that pupils in the early grades are not able to understand basic social science concepts is not justified.

Studies concerned with the secondary schools focus both on individual courses and upon area studies. In a re-evaluation of the American-history and world-history courses, there appears to be a trend to move from the chronological approach toward a thematic or unit study based upon the development of key concepts or problems. There is considerable agreement that those who select content for these courses must consider the student in the role of discoverer of knowledge relevant to the study of these topics or problems. More emphasis is being placed upon the development of skills of critical inquiry in an effort to develop the student's ability to carry out this task.

There is a growing emphasis upon world-cultures and American-studies courses, which stress the interrelatedness of content from the social sciences and other disciplines. Anthropology, cultural geography, and sociology thus play a prominent role in the development of area-studies courses. It is evident that these developments will necessitate major changes in the preparation of teachers who have at the present time considerably more depth of preparation in history than in other social sciences. The adoption on a wide scale of many of these proposals will also require numerous teaching materials not now available.

Several major projects have been designed specifically for the purpose of contributing to this ferment in the social studies. National studies in economics, geography, anthropology, and sociology, involving both representatives of the individual subjects and professional educators in cooperative ventures, promise to add much knowledge to that gained from other investigators. These projects will have considerable influence on the nature of content, the development of new materials, and the future preparation of social studies teachers. It is encouraging to note the tremendous strides taken in social studies research in recent years. Nevertheless, this research is of little value if it is not communicated to the profession as a whole. The lag between theory and practice in examining and subsequently restructuring existing curricular offerings at all levels is deplorable. There is an imperative need for social studies educators representing all aspects of the educational spectrum to come to some agreement as to the function and design of the social studies curriculum. First steps in this direction have been taken. Will those on the local level, in whose hands rests the task of curriculum revision and implementation, be willing to subject themselves and their teaching procedures to evaluation in terms of evidence obtained through research? Can traditional practices and their underlying assumptions be re-examined? To what extent are we willing to view the problem critically? The typical classroom teacher must recognize, however, that many of the weaknesses evident in present curriculum organization are clearly beyond his ability to correct. The determination of the structure of a given discipline, for instance, must in the final analysis be made by the specialist in that subject. Clearly, even within the individual disciplines, the nature of structure is debatable.

It is possible, however, to pinpoint a number of specific implications for the social studies teacher. Little will be accomplished if the desire to change is not present. The teacher must assume the responsibility for curriculum improvement. Too often we are complacent, content to carry on the day-to-day tasks of instruction, never questioning or examining basic purposes or practices. The assumption that teachers instruct and someone else, usually the administrator, determines curriculum, though invalid, is all too frequently accepted. The social studies teacher should welcome, and actively pursue, the responsibility to improve the curriculum. In order to do this, of course, he will have to cooperate with other social studies teachers. Social studies departments must be concerned with the problem, for the systematic improvement of any program must be a concern of all the teachers in that program. Departmental and staff meetings, which are so often concerned with the mundane, must become hotbeds of intellectual dialogue in which professionals are able, even though they sometimes disagree, to hammer out new and exciting approaches to teaching.

The traditional isolation of the elementary, junior, and senior high school teachers from one another must give way to an organizational scheme in which teachers at all levels of the educational ladder strive for a continuous program from kindergarten to graduation from high school. Operating within this organizational framework, each classroom teacher has the responsibility to become better informed in social science. He must rigorously examine the nature of these disciplines. He must re-examine his existing course organization, his units of instruction, his daily lessons, in terms of a realistic appraisal of the knowledge and skills his students must have if they are to cope intelligently with the complexities of contemporary society.

The teacher must improve his own understanding of the strategies and procedures by which old knowledge is evaluated and new knowledge is gained. He must actively engage in these activities himself, and he must plan his classroom instruction in such a way that the learner will be actively engaged in the process. This will undoubtedly result in the sacrificing of some of our "sacred cows." And it will certainly demand more of the teachers' time. It may mean changes in the sequence of course content which has been followed for years, and it may even mean that "old" content will be updated or replaced.

Models of inquiry will be developed and subsequently refined in the classroom. New methods of evaluation will be devised, and entire courses may be reorganized. It may be necessary to supplement existing faculty with social studies teachers prepared in specific disciplines, such as anthropology, sociology, and "area" studies. New patterns of staff utilization such as team teaching may be employed in developing new courses or in improving present course offerings.

Further consideration should be given to an assessment of the opportunities for experiences in the democratic processes which the school curriculum offers to the learner. The co-curricular program may be strengthened by the addition of specific activities designed to enable the pupil to assume roles of leadership, to secure practice in decision making, or to examine social or economic phenomena, etc. These activities logically provide a laboratory in which skills learned in the classroom may be applied and reinforced and should therefore be carefully planned and evaluated by competent social studies teachers. They must not be viewed merely as extra duties which add to the burden of already busy teachers. Perhaps some system may be devised to provide such opportunities during the regular school day.

Finally, the social studies curriculum in our school systems must be evaluated in terms of evidence gained through research. Research must be conducted in order to determine the extent to which the existing curriculum is achieving the objectives for which it was intended. Likewise, the effectiveness of innovations must be continually examined. The teacher, of course, occupies the central position in this evaluative process.

These are exciting times in the social studies. The atmosphere is right for progress, but there is much work to be done before progress can be realized. The degree to which each teacher makes a contribution to that progress will depend upon many variables, but each must make his contribution no matter how small. As professionals, we can do no less.

BIBLIOGRAPHY

Adams, Fay. *Curriculum Content and Basic Materials in the Social Studies.* Los Angeles: University of Southern California, 1962.

Alilunas, Leo J. "An Analysis of Social Studies Content in the Middle Grades." *Social Studies,* LII (November 1961), 210–218.

American Anthropological Association. *The Anthropology Curriculum Study Project Report.* Chicago: The Project, 1963.

American Council of Learned Societies and the National Council for the Social Studies. *The Social Studies and the Social Sciences.* New York: Harcourt, Brace and World, Inc., 1962.

Baker, Donald G. "American Studies, Social Studies, and the Process of Education." *Social Education,* XXVII (December 1963), 427–430, 455.

Beaubier, Edward W. "Capacity of Sixth Grade Children to Understand Social Science Generalizations." Unpublished Doctor's dissertation, University of Southern California, 1962.

Bruner, Jerome S. *The Process of Education.* Cambridge: Harvard University Press, 1961.

Bruntz, George G. "A Thematic Approach to World History." *Social Education,* XXIV (February 1960), 67–68.

California State Department of Education. *Report of the State Central Committee on Social Studies* (revised). Sacramento, July 1959.

Cammarota, Gloria. "Children, Politics, and Elementary Social Studies." *Social Education,* XXVII (April 1963), 205–207.

Cartwright, William H., and Richard L. Watson, Jr., eds. *Interpreting and Teaching American History.* Thirty-first Yearbook of the National Council for the Social Studies. Washington, D.C.: National Council for the Social Studies, 1961.

Committee for Economic Development. *Economic Education in the Schools.* New York: National Task Force on Economic Education, 1961.

Cordier, Ralph W. "A Three Year Package on American Studies." *Social Education,* XXVI (April 1962), 185–188.

Crowe, Ruby H., and Stanley E. Dimond. *Survey of Current Curriculum Studies in Social Studies 1962–63.* Washington, D.C.: National Council for the Social Studies, 1963.

Dunlap, Robert. "Teaching Anthropology in High School," *Education Digest,* XXVI (April 1961), 52–53.

Easton, David, and Robert D. Hess. "The Child's Political World." *Midwest Journal of Political Science,* VI (August 1962), 229–246.

Engle, Shirley H. "Thoughts in Regard to Revision." *Social Education,* XXVII (April 1963), 182–184, 196.

Fishwick, Marshall W. "Where Does 'American Studies' Begin?" *Social Education,* XXVII (December 1963), 419–422.

Furman, Dorothy W. "Content, Trends, and Topics in the Social Studies," in *Social Studies in Elementary Schools,* Thirty-second Yearbook of the National Council for the Social Studies. Washington, D.C.: National Council for the Social Studies, 1962, pp. 89–106.

Gandy, William Eugene. "The Status of Geography in the Public Senior High Schools of California." Unpublished Doctor's dissertation, Stanford University, 1960. Abstracted in *Dissertation Abstracts,* XX (May 1960), 4347.

Geer, Owen Chapman. "Social Science Generalizations for Use in the Social Studies Curriculum: Protecting and Conserving Human and Natural Resources." Unpublished Doctor's dissertation, Stanford University, 1959. Abstracted in *Dissertation Abstracts,* XIX (May 1959), 2877–2879.

Greenbladt, E. L. "An Analysis of School Subject Preferences of Elementary School Children of the Middle Grades." *Journal of Educational Research,* LV (August 1962), 554–555.

Haggerson, Nelson L., and Del Weber. *Social Studies in Arizona Secondary Schools.* University of Arizona Research and Services Bulletin No. 13. Tempe: Arizona State University, 1963, 43 pp.

Hague, John A. "American Studies and the Problems of Synthesis." *Social Education,* XXVII (December 1963), 423–426, 439.

Halsey, Van R., Jr. "American History: A New High School Course." *Social Education,* XXVII (May 1963), 249–252, 271.

Hanna, Paul R., and John R. Lee. "Content in the Social Studies," in *Social Studies in Elementary Schools,* Thirty-second Yearbook of the National Council for the Social Studies. Washington, D.C.: National Council for the Social Studies, 1962, pp. 62–89.

Hofstrand, John Milton. "Social Science Generalizations for Use in the Social Studies Curriculum: Creating Tools, Technics, and Social Arrangements." Unpublished Doctor's dissertation, Stanford University, 1959. Abstracted in *Dissertation Abstracts,* XX (February 1960), 3222–3223.

Hunt, Erling M., and others. *High School Social Studies Perspectives.* Boston: Houghton Mifflin Company, 1962.

Hunt, Maurice P., and Lawrence E. Metcalf. *Teaching High School Social Studies.* New York: Harper & Row, Publishers, 1955.

Indiana Department of Public Instruction. *Interim Report of the State Committee for the Revision of the Social Studies Curriculum.* Indianapolis: Department of Public Instruction, Spring 1963.

Jarolimek, John. "Curriculum Content and the Child in the Elementary School." *Social Education,* XXVI (February 1962), 58–62, 117–120.

Johnson, Earl S. "The Social Studies versus the Social Sciences," *School Review,* LXXI (1963), 389–403.

Jones, Emlyn. "Social Studies Requirements in an Age of Science and Mathematics." *Social Education,* XXVII (January 1963), 17–18.

Masia, Bertram. "Profile of the Current Secondary Social Studies Curriculum in North Central Association Schools." *North Central Association Quarterly,* XXVII (Fall 1963), 205–213.

Massialas, Byron G. *Research Prospects in the Social Studies.* Bloomington: Indiana University School of Education Bulletin, XXXVIII, no. 1 (January 1962).

————. "Revising the Social Studies: An Inquiry-Centered Approach." *Social Education,* XXVII (April 1963), 185–189.

Metcalf, Lawrence E. "Some Guidelines for Changing Social Studies Education." *Social Education,* XXVII (April 1963), 197–201.

Michaelis, John U. "Social Studies," in *Using Current Curriculum Developments.* Washington, D.C.: National Education Association, 1963.

Miller, Stanley N. "The World Cultures Course," *Social Education,* XXVI (February 1962), 69–70.

Moreland, Willis D. "Curriculum Trends in the Social Studies." *Social Education*, XXVI (February 1962), 73–76, 102.

NASSP Committee on Curriculum Planning and Development. "Social Studies in the Comprehensive Secondary School." *The Bulletin of the National Association of Secondary-School Principals*, XLV (September 1961), 1–17.

Platt, Myles M. "Concepts and the Curriculum." *Social Education*, XXVII (January 1963), 21–22, 41.

Quillen, Isaac J., and Lavone A. Hanna. *Education for Social Competence*, rev. ed. Chicago: Scott, Foresman and Co., 1961.

Reese, Herbert J. "Introducing Cultural Anthropology into the Curriculum." *The Indiana Social Studies Quarterly*, XVI (1963), 31–34.

Rusnak, Mary. "Introducing Social Studies in the First Grade." *Social Education*, XXV (October 1961), 291–292.

Siemers, Alan A. "World History: Practices and Problems." *Social Education*, XXIV (April 1960), 153–157.

Spodek, Bernard. "Developing Social Science Concepts in the Kindergarten." *Social Education*, XXVII (May 1963), 253–256.

Stavrianos, Leften S. *A Global History of Man*. Chicago: Allyn and Bacon, Inc., 1962.

White, Gilbert F. "A Joint Effort to Improve High School Geography." *The Journal of Geography*, LX (November 1961), 357–360.

Wronski, Stanley P. "A Proposed Breakthrough for the Social Studies." *Social Education*, XXIII (May 1959), 215–219.

3

TEACHING SOCIAL STUDIES IN ELEMENTARY SCHOOLS

Findlay C. Penix
University of Michigan

A review of the literature of elementary school social studies reveals that the writing devoted to the interrelated areas of curriculum and method can be placed in two broad categories: (1) opinions, personal experiences, and descriptions of practices; and (2) experimental studies designed to provide data about specific problems in this area.

Although descriptions of experiences and practices may be useful, evidence resulting from research studies in curriculum and method seems to provide a sounder basis for improvement in the social studies. Therefore, this chapter focuses on experimental studies reported during the five-year period that contributed additional knowledge to the field or indicated promising areas for future investigations.

The following criteria were used for selection of the studies reviewed here: (1) The investigation must deal with or have implications for methods in teaching elementary school social studies. (2) The results of the investigation must refine, contrast with, or add new dimensions to earlier studies. (3) The findings of the investigation must suggest or imply ways for improving instruction in elementary school social studies and provide a base for further investigation.

DEVELOPMENT OF TIME SENSE
AND CHRONOLOGY

To develop in the student a sense of time and chronology has long been an instructional goal of the school. Although many questions about the development of children's concepts of time and space remain unanswered, it is clear that these concepts are particularly important in the social studies because social events become more meaningful when they can be placed chronologically and geographically and are causally or functionally interrelated. It is possible to single out a number of factors relevant to these concepts which the elementary social studies program should stress: the dimensions of time and a related vocabulary of definite and indefinite expressions of time, familiarization with time concepts encountered in reading and listening, the relationship of dates to personal experience for use as points of orientation, and the placing of related events in chronological order.

Many research studies have been concerned with the point of maturation at which children learn the conventional divisions of time and a vocabulary associated with time. Investigators agree that mastery of the different divisions of time and the relationship of one to the other is achieved as the result of a very complex process that appears to be closely related to maturation. They also agree that children have little or no sense of chronology before they are in the sixth grade and that instruction in such concepts should be delayed until children have matured sufficiently to profit from it. These conclusions are based, for the most part, however, on studies made twenty or more years ago. Today, these conclusions are questioned by some investigators, who believe that many children are capable of greater depth of learning and greater understanding of concepts at an earlier age than has been asserted in the past. These assumptions are based on the belief that there will be wide variations in children's understanding of time and chronology at any age level due to individual differences in maturity, to children's participation in varying classroom learning experiences related to time and chronology, and, especially, to their direct and vicarious experiences in today's rapidly changing world.

Two studies provide data about the differences found in children's understanding of time concepts. Lovell and Slater (1960) were interested in assessing the child's understanding of various aspects of the concept of time—simultaneity, equality of synchronous intervals, and order of events. The experiments used to study these aspects of time were very similar to those devised by Piaget [1] and are described fully in the Lovell and Slater study. The subjects were one hundred pupils from schools in England. Fifty of the children were considered to be average or above in attainment and were divided into groups of ten from each age group, five through nine years inclusive. The remaining fifty children were drawn from special schools for the educationally subnormal. Seven tests related to the experiments were administered individually to the subjects. Among the findings of the study were the following: (1) There was a steady increase in "perception of simultaneity with age," although children at all ages recognized it more easily in relation to the beginning than the ending of action. (2) The ability of the child to "coordinate instants and intervals in his mind so as to have a concept of time" can be improved under certain conditions. (3) With increasing age, there was a clear increase of the understanding of the order of events. Overall, the children of this age group were able to "appreciate order of events." The investigators stated that many of Piaget's findings were substantiated in the study, but that "children's notions of time are not available to them in all situations at once and to the same degree" (p. 190). Further data indicated that the educationally subnormal student of sixteen or seventeen years of age had an overall understanding of time about equal to that of an average nine-year-old child.

Chase (1961) reported the results of a test on time relationships. His study, completed in 1960, was based upon an earlier study by Callahan.[2] Subjects for the study were 192 fifth-grade children and 200 sixth-grade children. The test consisted of twenty-four questions requiring the placement of five items in each question in chronological order.

[1] J. Piaget, *La développement de la notion de temps chez l'enfant* (Paris: Presses Universitaires de France, 1946).

[2] Mary G. Callahan, "The Construction and Evaluation of a Test in Time Relationships for Grades V, VI, VII, and VIII." (Master's thesis, Boston University School of Education, 1952.)

Four categories of questions were used: (1) past events or artifacts which are related to each other or to a given present event or artifact; (2) past events or artifacts which are unrelated to each other but are related to a given present event or artifact; (3) related past events or artifacts without a present event or artifact being given; and (4) unrelated past events or artifacts without a present event or artifact being given. For example, this question appeared under the last category:

Here is another set of newspaper headlines of events that have happened in history. Put 1 in front of the event that happened first, number 2 in front of the event that happened next, and so on through number 5.

    ——LAFAYETTE COMES TO AID OF WASHINGTON
    ——EISENHOWER CHOSEN LEADER OF NATO FORCES
    ——BELL INVENTS THE TELEPHONE
    ——FULTON'S FOLLY REACHES ALBANY
    ——ATOMIC TESTS AT BIKINI SUCCESSFUL (p. 337)

The correct ordering of all items obtained a score of five for the question; the incorrect ordering of two items resulted in a score of four, since there can never be just one item out of place in a sequence. Therefore, the children's quality of understanding of time relationships was determined by the percent of scores of five and four out of the total possibilities in the twenty-four questions.

The percent of success in ordering chronological events for the total grade group was 34.7 percent for grade five and 37.5 percent for grade six. The upper 27 percent of the children in grade five scored 56.7 percent and in grade six, 61.8. The lower 27 percent of the class scored 16.9 percent in grade five and 19.1 percent in grade six. The scores for the total grade group in the four categories ranged from 44 to 53 percent for grades five and six, respectively, in the category of related past events to present event, to 31 and 30 percent for the category of unrelated past events without present event.

The results of this investigation showed the range of individual differences apparent in these aspects of time relationships among these fifth- and sixth-grade students. The investigator suggested that, although a large percentage of children at these grade levels may not yet be ready for intensive instruction in time relationships, it is not necessary to defer instruction for all children. Giving attention to the individual child would mean developing time relationships with some children in the middle grades and moving ahead in this development with other children as rapidly as readiness and ability permit. This would seem to be a more valid approach than the practice of allocating the teaching of certain aspects of time relationships to specific grades.

McAulay (1961) conducted a study to determine second graders' understanding of time as it relates to self, the immediate environment, and historical events. Information was sought concerning children's understanding of the relationship of the past to the present, of periods of time, of the continuity of time, and of past social reality, as well as their ability to project themselves from the immediate present into past time.

The subjects for the study were 165 second-grade children selected from suburban middle-class families in a large industrial city, from lower-class families whose livelihood centered about the railroad industry, and from families in a professional college community. The children responded orally and individually to problems related to three dimensions of time relationships: (1) time concepts associated with self: for example, Do you think your mother or grandmother (or grandfather) has lived longer? Draw a line showing how old you are, how old your mother (brother, sister, or grandmother) is; (2) time concepts associated with the immediate environment: for example, Is a week or a month (a month or a year, a second or a minute) longer? Will Christmas or Easter be here first? Is summer or Christmas vacation longer? (3) time concepts associated with historical events: for example, Did Washington or Lincoln live first?

McAulay found that these children had "difficulty associating past with the present in the immediate environment," but they did "seem to have an understanding of past as related to present if time is removed from self and immediate environment" (p. 313). Other findings indicated that second-grade children can understand periods of time, particularly if the periods of time are concerned with events rather than with persons and places; that they have some understanding of past social reality if it is not related directly to their personal environment or to an area of immediate concern to them; and that they have little understanding of the continuity of time, especially when related to the present or associated closely with self. The investigator concluded that the seven-year-old child seems to lack understanding of time when related to his immediate family and community, but he does seem capable of comprehending known events of the past related to the present, of associating persons from history with one another, and of retaining some information about each person and event. Thus the typical second-grade curriculum, which emphasizes family and community studies, "underestimates" the child's ability to understand other aspects of time relationships.

A well-designed study related to geographic time zones was conducted by Davis (1959, 1963), who tried to determine whether children in the intermediate grades can profit from instruction in concepts of time and space related to geographic time zones. Location, distance, direction, orientation, and chronology were some of the concepts deemed necessary to an understanding of time and space. The subjects for the study were 163 students from six different public elementary schools. The fourth-, fifth-, and sixth-grade levels provided two classes each. One class at each grade level was designated as the experimental group, and the other class served as the control group. Prior to the beginning of the study, there were no significant differences among the groups in intelligence, social studies achievement, and understanding of time zones.[3]

The experimental group was taught a unit containing specific material designed to convey an understanding of geographic time zones. Instruction was given for fourteen days over a three-week period during the regular thirty-minute social studies class period. The investigator taught the unit in order to control for variation in subject matter, teaching methods, and instructional materials. The control classes received no instruction in geographical time zones except that included in the regular program of studies.

[3] As determined from scores on the *Lorge-Thorndike Intelligence Test*, Level 3, Form B, Non-Verbal; and the *Sequential Tests of Educational Progress: Social Studies*, Form 4A.

The experimenter constructed a test of forty-six items related to clock time, the International Date Line, standard time zones in the United States and the world, and direction and period of rotation of the earth. Reliability of the test was computed and accepted as valid by the investigator and by two "competent authorities" in the social studies. The criterion test was administered as a pretest, an immediate post-test upon completion of the unit, and a test of delayed recall one month after completion of the unit. All data were treated statistically.

Davis found that the experimental classes profited considerably from instruction about geographic time zones. In all tests, sixth-grade students demonstrated significantly better understanding than fifth- and fourth-grade students; fifth-grade students had significantly higher comprehension than fourth graders. Fourth-grade children gained significantly more understanding of geographic time zones as a result of instruction than did sixth-grade children (possibly, according to Davis, because the upper limits of the criterion test were too low). Finally, it was found that all classes in the experimental groups gained continuously in understanding from the beginning of unit instruction through the test of delayed recall.

Davis concluded that the results of the study provided evidence that children can profit from instruction about geographical time zones at an earlier age than is generally believed and that "firm and substantial beginnings" in the development of geographical time and space concepts can be made as early as grade four. Although in no way minimizing the importance of maturation in developing the ability of pupils to think in terms of concepts, he noted that if the findings of the study are indicative of possible findings in other areas of concept development, the "deferment-of-instruction theory" of curriculum, based on maturation, needs "radical revision."

The teaching of chronology in the sixth grade was investigated by Arnsdorf (1959, 1961). The purpose of the study was to investigate instructional materials and methods which might increase understanding of words and phrases relating to time and historical chronology. The experiment was conducted over a seven-week period with 536 sixth-grade children from self-contained classrooms, divided into experimental and control groups split between boys and girls. The groups were tested for IQ, reading ability, and success in social studies, and found to be closely comparable.[4] Both groups studied the same social studies unit from the same textbooks. The instructional program for the experimental groups stressed activities related to chronology—for example, the identification of and instruction in the terms in the textbooks relating to time, the use of time-lines and charts to add concreteness to time-terms, and the writing of biographical and autobiographical sketches to stimulate interest in past and present events.

The investigator devised an original test battery consisting of six subtests: Vocabulary of Chronology, Ordering Four Events without Dates, Ordering Two Events without Dates, Relative Time, Ordering Four Events with Dates, and Time Absurdities. The items of the test were selected from basal textbooks, supplementary social studies books, and reference books used by students in the intermediate grades. Reliability coefficients and intercorrelations were computed for the tests.

The results of the study showed that the planned instructional program for the experimental groups helped children at the sixth-grade level (a) comprehend definite and indefinite time-terms; (b) recognize the relative length of time between periods and note similarity of time-distances with reference to given events; (c) develop skill in ordering events with dates; and (d) develop competence in recognizing time absurdities. This instructional program had little or no effect upon other study skills as measured by an appropriate test.

Arnsdorf concluded that "children can profit from systematic instruction of the kind undertaken to increase considerably their understanding of and ability to use time relationships common in the social studies" (p. 312). He noted that the instructional program for the experimental group had few provisions for handling individual differences and that it was a single program confined to the time-

---

[4] *The Lorge-Thorndike Intelligence Test,* Non-Verbal Battery, Level III, was administered initially to determine intelligence. Mean IQ for Experimental Group—101.01; Mean IQ for Control Group—99.23. *The Gates Reading Survey* (Comprehension Section) was used to control reading ability as a factor in later analysis of data. *The Work-Study Skills: Iowa Every-Pupil Tests of Basic Skills,* Test B, was administered initially and finally to determine achievement.

terms found in the textbooks used. He asked whether better results might not have been obtained with different or better instructional programs.

The findings of this carefully planned experimental study contrast with those earlier studies which indicated that maturity in understanding time concepts is the result of a slow process of development. The design of the study provides an excellent base for similar experimental studies using other instructional aids and methods of approach. Along this line, Arnsdorf suggested the value of long-time, longitudinal studies beginning in grade one as a means of accumulating data which would provide more evidence about the development of children's time concepts and the way in which instructional methods and devices are related to this development.

One other study concerned with time concepts should be noted. Gill (1962) studied the differences between students and the difficulties they have in interpreting indefinite expressions of time commonly found in textbooks and used in class discussions. Four groups of students participated in the study. Sixty-eight college juniors and seniors, 56 high school juniors and seniors, 68 eighth graders, and 62 fifth graders. All of the college students were prospective social studies teachers; all other students were enrolled in American history classes. Each subject was asked to respond to eighteen indefinite expressions of time often used in American history by placing a definite date before each of the terms. Included in the list of expressions were such terms as: "In colonial days," "At the beginning of modern times," "In the near future," "In ancient times," and "Until recently."

Based upon an analysis of the range and median of the dates given for the items at each grade level, Gill found (a) loose interpretation of indefinite expressions of time at all grade levels; (b) superior grasp of the meaning of indefinite expressions of time at the higher grade levels, particularly college; (c) no clear progression in understanding from the fifth to the eleventh and twelfth grade on many indefinite expressions of time; (d) difficulty in understanding words like "century" and "decade"; and (e) lack of precise meaning for terms like "ancient times," "modern times," and "Middle Ages," with lack of precision particularly noticeable at the lower grade levels. He concluded that indefinite expressions of time convey widely different meanings to students and that specific instruction is needed in helping them "fix meaningful boundaries" to these indefinite terms as well as help in understanding more definite time terms. He suggested that "possibly the best approach would be to substitute where feasible definite dates for vague expressions of time so that a pupil sees events in a mathematical sequence" (p. 456).

From the studies reviewed in this section it is possible to draw a number of conclusions about children's understanding of various aspects of time relationships. Increasing evidence suggests that (1) although there is a steady growth with age in the ability to understand time concepts, this understanding varies considerably with the individual child and occurs with some children at a much earlier age than has heretofore been believed; and (2) planned instruction relating to time concepts reduces difficulties and increases understanding. Strongly implied here are revision of the curriculum to provide for flexibility rather than the fixed introduction of time concepts at stated grade levels, experimentation with methods which utilize both in-school and out-of-school time experiences of children, and more intensive investigation of the levels of understanding of time concepts and the ways in which such understanding develops.

ATTITUDES TOWARD GOVERNMENT AND POLITICS

Typically, an informal approach has been used in teaching and reinforcing attitudes toward law and government (citizenship) in the elementary grades. This approach has emphasized national holidays and heroes, patriotic events, the pledge of allegiance to the flag, and attention to election processes during an election year. Generally, specific instruction in this area has been delayed until the junior and senior high school years. It appears, however, that attitudes and ideas concerning law, government, and the political world may have their beginnings at a much earlier age.

Estvan (1962) reported a study of the teaching of government in Wisconsin elementary schools. Major attention was centered on goals, learning experiences, materials of instruction, evaluation, and organization. Data for the study were collected from a twelve-page questionnaire returned by 369 of the 432 teachers selected for the study through use of a stratified-sampling approach. The data were carefully tested for statistical reliability of differences.

The two most important goals reported by the teachers were the development of desirable attitudes toward "democratic governing processes" and an "understanding about government." Methods used to realize these goals were largely verbal—reading, writing, discussion— along with audio-visual experiences and pupil participation through teacher-pupil planning. Books and audio-visual resources were the most useful tools for carrying out experiences. In evaluating pupil progress, teachers stressed knowledge and understanding rather than attitudes, critical thinking, work-study skills, and group processes; in over half the cases assessment of growth was made through observation and group discussion. The study revealed no clear-cut patterns of organized instruction, planned sequence, or continuity of experiences. Instruction was incidental about as often as it was a part of a current-events period; it was introduced even less frequently in special programs or extra-class activities. More attention was paid to government as children moved up through the grades. Experiences in the primary grades dealt with individual responsibilities, symbols of government, and services. In the intermediate grades, more emphasis was placed on organization, representation, democracy, and history. Teachers at all grade levels reported the usefulness of materials covering many facets of government.

Estvan reported teaching problems related to changes in grade levels from "children's lack of maturity to cope with political concepts to their lack of interest in government, from problems of methodology to curriculum considerations, and from lack of opportunities for pupils to participate in government to the abstract and complex nature of political science data" (p. 295). In an earlier study (1959) he concluded that boys and girls enter school with little conception of government, and that, although the grasp of governmental processes increases by the sixth grade, ideas and attitudes about government are slow to appear and mature. Among the suggestions made for continued efforts to improve civic education at the elementary school level were (a) the development of an abundance of readily available teaching resources on different ability levels, and (b) the identification of various stages in children's growth of concepts, attitudes, and skills related to government.

Easton and Hess (1960, 1962) attempted to discover the nature of children's political orientation—the concepts, attitudes, and values held about the political world. The study involved 12,000 elementary school children from grade one through grade eight. Research is continuing, but present data provide some new insights in this area. Data collected over a five-year period appear to support these major findings: (a) The child's "political world begins to take shape" and undergoes rapid change even before his entrance into the elementary school. Furthermore, many basic political attitudes and values have become firmly established by the time the child has completed the elementary grades. (b) The child's basic political orientation to regime and community undergoes little change during the four years of high school. In fact, there is little evidence that fundamental attitudes and values toward regime and political community are any different at the end of high school than they were at the beginning. (c) The years between the ages of three and thirteen are the "truly formative years" for political orientation.

Easton and Hess concluded that the child's motives and actions indicate a highly positive political orientation during his early school years and that he is as ready to learn about citizenship then as he will ever be.

Cammarota (1963) used the Easton and Hess findings to draw a number of conclusions relating to content and organization of the elementary social studies program. She stated that if new content is to be selected, there is need to redefine the learnings considered appropriate for children of various ages; for example, areas such as government and politics have been largely ignored, even though children are learning about them from a very early age. She suggested that concepts and content from political science be placed on a curricular spiral; thus study about government would begin in the first grade and continue each year through the elementary school. Subject matter would be different at each grade level, but underlying principles would remain the same. This type of organization would build upon and extend the knowledge children acquire outside of school and would help to put "unrelated facts and ideas into a framework where relationships are apparent."

These studies stop short of prescribing methods other than to suggest the development of appropriate instructional resources. If findings from investigations such as those conducted by Easton and Hess are to be incorporated into the elementary social studies curriculum, then appropriate methods must be found which will help children clarify and refine understandings. Techniques which would utilize children's experiences from their immediate environment along with a strong emphasis on related current affairs of national and international significance would appear to be one approach.

KNOWLEDGE AND THINKING

A number of studies relating to the general area of knowledge and thinking were reported during the review period. Investigations by Kaltsounis (1961), Rabozzi (1961), and Arnsdorf (1963) were concerned with various aspects of children's knowledge of social studies material. However, only three studies are reviewed here: one study because the findings are in contrast to some current writing, and two studies because they provide some evidence for approaches to the development of thinking ability.

Mugge (1962, 1963) undertook a study to determine what information young children can be expected to have in the area of social studies prior to the introduction of topics for class study. A total of 180 beginning second-grade children (90 boys and 90 girls) from urban, suburban, and rural residential areas participated in the experiment. All the children were from the middle-class groups. Data were obtained from four instruments: an information test based on seven generally used second-grade social studies textbooks; a test of information beyond the immediate environment, derived in part from recent courses of study for primary-grade social studies; a definition questionnaire which served to clarify responses on the information test and to procure comparative evidence of responses to two types of questions; and an experience questionnaire concerning experiences children might have had in relation to travel and mass media of communication.

The investigator found that the second-grade children responded correctly to approximately one-third of the questions on the information test and the test of information beyond the immediate environment. More than one-half of the questions on the definition questionnaire were answered correctly. Responses to the experience questionnaire indicated that, in general, the relationship between the variety of the child's experiences and his score on the social studies information test was a significant one. There were no significant differences in the information possessed by urban, suburban, and rural children, but boys responded correctly to more items than did girls. However, the results of the study indicated that there were many misconceptions and gaps in the information possessed by these children. A lack of precision in answers to questions, difficulty in remembering two factors at one time, and difficulty with time and place concepts were evident also.

Mugge concluded that although second-grade children do have social studies information on many topics, the overall findings of the study indicated that "many of these young children lacked readiness for comprehensive studies of faraway places and advanced content in community studies" (p. 438). Suggestions were made that teachers assess the information, concerning possible topics for study, that each child in the group has mastered before choosing definite topics and that children be given help in organizing present and newly acquired information into meaningful patterns.

An experiment in teaching critical thinking in the intermediate grades was conducted by Maw (1959). The purpose of the study was to determine whether critical-thinking ability of children in the fourth, fifth, and sixth grades could be improved by using prepared exercises to teach selected skills of critical thinking. Twenty-one experimental and twenty-one control classes from upper-middle and middle-class suburban communities were used in the eight-week study. Critical thinking skills tested were selecting relevant facts, judging reliability of data, making generalizations and inferences, recognizing situations in which evidence is insufficient for a conclusion, determining cause and effect, and evaluating arguments. Twenty-four prepared lessons—three per week—were used with the experimental group. Data were obtained from the *Davis Eells Games* and a test of critical thinking prepared by the investigator. In addition, teachers in the experimental classes used checklists for evaluation of individual lessons and made reports of the general effectiveness of the lessons.

Maw found that the mean gain of the experimental classes exceeded the mean gain of the control classes on both tests. The difference in mean gain was highly significant on the test of critical thinking, but was not significant for the *Davis-Eells* test. Differences in mean gains among grades and ability groups and between boys and girls were found to be insignificant. There was a strong indication that the lessons were effective in improving the thinking skills required by the test of critical thinking. Teachers of the experimental classes reported that students showed improvement in the "general disposition" to consider evidence before reaching conclusions to problems.

The productiveness of children's thinking was investigated by Crabtree (1961) in an unusually fine study. The purpose of the experiment was to determine whether different approaches to structure—"organization imposed upon the learning situation"—would effect changes in children's predisposition to thinking and to measure the effects of different approaches to structure on children's classroom-participation patterns. The six-week study was conducted with 24 second-grade children in a single classroom. The subjects were tested to obtain measures of their predisposition to thinking on the *Torrance Product Improvement Task,* paired, and randomly assigned to one of two groups. Both groups received, in alternate sequence, two experimental programs (Program A and Program B) that used different teaching methods. Each program utilized a harbor and an airport study as content.

Program A was of emergent structure, with children's interests furnishing cues for the sequence and pacing of discussions. Subject-matter resources and teaching aids were withheld until the pupils showed that they were able to profit from them. The teacher's role was that of supporting children's ideas, helping in the development of purposes, encouraging identification and definition of interests and problems within content areas, and adding depth to discussions. The establishment of a classroom climate that supported independence and initiative in thinking was the teacher's responsibility. Program B was predetermined in structure by a selected discussion-topics teacher. The teacher-structured discussions were directive and commanding, held children to systematic, logical lines of deductive reasoning, and were evaluated for conceptual accuracy against norms of an adult world.

Study in both programs began with a discussion period, followed by a play period in a dramatic play center. No limitations were placed upon play; differences which occurred were a function of the type of structuring which had taken place in the discussion period. Teachers became nonparticipating observers. The play environment in Program A was unarranged and consisted of ambiguous materials; in Program B it was prearranged with high-realism materials organized to invite certain patterns of response. Data were collected from scales developed for the measurement of children's thinking and involvement in play. Independent teams of observers obtained both quantitative and descriptive data by point-time sampling and anecdotal recording techniques.

Crabtree found that divergent thinking was expressed by children's responses which created new patterns of play, used original ideas, organized materials for new uses, or extended new organization and order to play. Such thinking was characterized by originality, spontaneity, and flexibility of responses and comprised a mean of 47.46 percent of observed thinking responses in Program A; in Program B, the mean was 17.81 percent with the areas of differences highly significant. Convergent thinking (characterized by the degree to which it was conceptually accurate, logically deductive, and led to the correct but restricted conclusions a well-defined situation was intended to invoke) totaled a mean of 53.53 percent in Program B as compared with 21.29 percent in Program A. Again, the differences were highly significant. Program A, which withheld teacher-structuring and encouraged exploration of ideas initiated by the children, established predispositions to thinking which were maintained in the play periods following discussion. Program B encouraged significantly fewer of these divergent responses. Decrements in divergent thinking were experienced by all but one child in Program B, with the greatest discrepancy scores noted for those children in Program A who had displayed greater divergence. Girls, more often than boys, seemed to respond with convergent thinking patterns to the highly structured cues of Program B. There was no difference in high-involvement levels in either program during the initial eight to ten minutes of each play period.

In discussing the study, Crabtree raised a number of questions related to curriculum and method which need further study. Among these were the following: The children in this study utilized different thinking styles. Are there learning tasks where one or the other of these thinking styles is more appropriate? Are sustained, vigorous periods of convergent thinking necessary in learning tasks which require validating and systematizing of knowledge? What would be the effects of long-term teaching programs expressly designed to elicit divergent and creative responses in children?

Much has been written about the desirability of upgrading the content of elementary social studies curriculum because of the increased knowledge possessed by today's children. However, there is danger in assuming that all children possess this knowledge and have the skills necessary for successful experiences with content placed at predetermined levels. Prior to revising the curriculum, it is important that more effective ways of assessing levels of knowledge and skill be devised to provide a base for decisions concerning curriculum. More experimentation is needed to determine methods that will help children develop skills in thinking. Both the Crabtree and Maw studies point to possible directions for further investigation in this area.

MAP-READING SKILLS

Specialists in geography have stated that skill in understanding and using maps and globes is necessary for developing a geographical point of view—a better understanding of the relation of man to his environment. The ability to read and interpret maps is essential in understanding social, economic, and political interdependence, spatial relationships, and the effect of the physical environment upon the economic and social development of the peoples of the world. Instruction in the use and understanding of maps and globes is one of the important tasks of the elementary teacher.

The increased emphasis being placed on maps and globes in the elementary school curriculum is evident from an examination of curriculum guides of school systems, articles in professional journals, and discussions found in social studies "methods" textbooks. This emphasis is apparent also from the extensive incorporation of map material at all grade levels in the newer graded series of social studies textbooks for elementary grades. Sequential programs of map and globe skills development, which place skills at specific grade levels from the early primary years through the later elementary grades have been proposed; other proposals present a continuous, sequential pattern from the simple to the more complex skill. Today the trend, at least in theory, is to introduce map and globe skills in the primary grades instead of adhering to the traditional pattern of delay until the middle grades—usually in grade four. However, more experimental studies are needed to determine how and when children develop an understanding of map and globe skills in order to provide a sounder basis for approaches in curriculum and method.

Rushdoony (1963) undertook a study to ascertain whether third-grade children could learn, with advanced instruction, map-reading skills recommended for children in grades four and five. The experiment was designed also to determine the relationships between achievement in map reading and achievement in reading and arithmetic. The sample for the study was composed of 129 third graders randomly assigned to experimental and control groups. Advanced instruction in fourth- and fifth-grade map-reading skills was received by the experimental group for fifteen weeks; the control groups received instruction as "outlined in the social studies teaching guide for grade three" from their school system. Prior to the training period, standardized tests [5] of intelligence, map reading, reading, and arithmetic were

---

[5] *California Test of Mental Maturity,* 1957 Edition, Primary Level, S-Form *Iowa Tests of Basic Skills,* W-1 (Work-Study Skills: Map Reading), Items 1–47, Forms 1 and 2. *Stanford Achievement Test,* Elementary Battery (Reading and Arithmetic Tests), Forms M and J.

administered; at the conclusion of the fifteen-week period tests of map reading, reading, and arithmetic were administered again.

The investigator found that children in the third grade can learn many of the map-reading skills traditionally taught at the fourth- and fifth-grade level. At the end of the training period the experimental group made greater gains on nearly all items on the map-reading test than did the control group. Both groups had greater difficulty on test items related to "determining distance from scale, tracing travel routes, determining distances in relation to time, and comparing facts on distribution maps" (p. 73). Analysis of the data revealed that high, positive, linear relationships exist between map-reading achievement and intelligence, map-reading achievement and arithmetic, and map-reading achievement and reading. Rushdoony concluded that instruction in map reading of the type used in the study "contributed to achievement in arithmetic as well as to growth in map-reading skills" (p. 74). There was no evidence, however, that advanced instruction in map reading improved general reading achievement. He stated that the "most fundamental implication" resulting from the study was that third-grade children can profit from instruction in map-reading skills from the primary level to those recommended for the fifth-grade level and that downward placement of map skills throughout the curriculum appears to be warranted.

ECONOMIC EDUCATION

The importance of increasing the student's awareness and understanding of the nature and character of the American economic system is being increasingly realized.[6] Studies have hypothesized that economic concepts can be introduced to and understood by children in the elementary grades; the major concern has been the identification of appropriate concepts and teaching techniques. Two studies illustrate research in this area. The first study, although reported late in 1958, will

---

[6] For example, see *Economic Education in the Schools*. A Report of the National Task Force on Economic Education. (New York: Committee for Economic Development, 1961.)

be reviewed at length because of its close relationship to the second study.

The major purposes of a study conducted by Darrin (1958) were to determine (a) what can be provided in economic education within the framework of elementary social studies curriculum; (b) how well children can learn economic concepts and generalizations; and (c) identification of effective teaching techniques. The subjects in the experiment were 1,332 children in the kindergarten through grade six in 47 classes from two laboratory schools of the District of Columbia Teachers College. A total of 28 topics and 10 subtopics for study were selected from a basic list of 88 topics, "Key Understandings in Economics," compiled by the Council for Advancement of Secondary Education. A jury of over 1,000 leaders from business, agriculture, and labor had derived the 88 topics from an original list of 10,000 economic understandings. The selection of the 28 topics used in the study was made on the basis of probable present and future utility to the elementary school child and the degree to which the topic might be taught to children of varying learning capacities. The topics and subtopics were then translated into illustrations believed to be understandable to children at each grade level and were incorporated into teaching guides.

Teachers used the suggested illustrations for stimulating discussion and planning activities around the topics and subtopics. Two forms were developed: a standard worksheet for each economic topic at each grade level, and an evaluation form on which the teacher recorded whether the suggested illustration (or one of his own) was found to be "highly effective," "effective," or "not effective" in stimulating discussion about the topic.

An expected general finding was that the higher the grade level, the more effective the topic was for stimulation of discussion. Specific findings were (a) that 57 percent of the topics and subtopics were reported "highly effective" in grades two through six, 3.5 percent "not effective," and the remaining thirty-nine and one-half percent "effective"; and (b) that 39 percent were "highly effective" and 9 percent "not effective" at the first-grade level, and 28 percent "highly effective" and 19 percent "not effective" in kindergarten. The remainder in each case were reported "effective." Topics reported as being taught most successfully at all grade levels were travel and communication, labor as a factor of production, science and research as elements of a dynamic technology, economic growth and progress of the American economy, regional and occupational division of labor, the Industrial Revolution, economic geography, automation, effect of natural resources on economy, kinds and functions of money, saving and investing (thrift), private property, ethical values, management, taxation, government spending, and wise use of goods and time. Topics that were most difficult to teach were determining processes of production in a free economy, individual and social implications of unemployment, law of supply and demand, changing situations in agriculture, and competition as a foundation of capitalism.

Among the learning experiences reported useful in building economic understanding were visits to places such as grocery stores, drug stores, construction sites, and freight yards; use of current news events and audio-visual materials—charts, bar graphs, scrapbooks, newspaper clippings, and bulletin boards; introduction of economic topics in classes in arithmetic, science, and reading; and making and using collections such as coins to illustrate kinds and functions of money.

Darrin concluded that more economics can and should be taught at the elementary school level and that it can be taught successfully in areas other than the social studies. He stressed the need for development of more adequate "training aids" and the need for further study to identify other topics for investigation.

The Elkhart Project, a twelve-year experimental program begun in 1958, was described by Senesh (1960). The purpose of the experiment is to develop a "new dimension in the social studies curriculum, an *organic curriculum*." The study is based on the hypothesis that with proper motivation children at all grade levels "can become excited about the abstract ideas underlying their experiences, and that these ideas can be presented in such a way as to reflect the basic structure of the body of economic knowledge." The first- and second-grade teachers in Elkhart public schools have identified concepts representing basic economic relationships and activities and have incorporated these into their conventional social studies units; thus children will be exposed to the most important economic relationships and activities in the first grade, and as the study moves forward, will encounter these same relationships and activities from grade to grade, adding depth to their understanding of them by relating them to more mature experiences.

Units on "My Home" and "What My Father Does" have been developed for the first grade and "My Neighborhood" and "My School" for the second grade. The units include statements of the concepts, accompanied by a statement of curriculum interpretation and student-learning activities. The activities integrate the economic concepts with other social studies and with skills of reading, writing, arithmetic, and the arts. Suggested activities include such experiences as discussions, trips, securing information from varied sources, writing stories, drawing pictures, constructing models, and dramatizing situations. Some examples of economic concepts which appear in the unit on "My Home" are: A division of labor takes place within the family which increases the efficiency of the family; within the home all members of the family are consumers, but only some are producers; the needs of a neighborhood are fulfilled by means of economic, social, cultural, and political institutions producing goods and services; and the neighborhood and the rest of the economy are interdependent.

Multiple-choice tests, combined with cartoons, will be used to evaluate the project at the beginning and end of each academic year. Thus far the Elkhart experiment appears to be a highly successful one. Senesh stated that the study is showing that first-grade children enjoy discovery of the unknown when properly motivated by teachers, and that observers are impressed as first and second graders talk spontaneously about their fathers as producers of goods and services or of the economic aspects of neighborhoods.

SUMMARY

Experimental studies related to development of time sense and chronology, attitudes toward government and politics, knowledge and thinking, map-reading skills, and economic education were reviewed in this chapter. Although these investigations were concerned with different areas of elementary school social studies, employed different research designs, and involved children of different age groups, the findings are strikingly similar in nature and implication. Evidence from these studies indicates that: (1) There is no "magic age" at which children acquire understanding of certain social studies concepts. Although understanding increases with age, individuals vary both in the ability to understand and in the degree of their understanding of these concepts. Moreover, in some areas (the Easton and Hess studies) the elementary school years appear to be the formative years in fixing concepts. (2) Instructional methods and teaching devices planned in relation to the teaching of specific social studies skills and concepts can increase the level of children's understanding of these skills and concepts. (3) Elementary school children appear to have more knowledge related to social studies, even though unorganized, than is often believed. This knowledge can be translated into concepts that are within children's comprehension and understanding provided that levels of knowledge are determined and help is given in organizing this knowledge.

The findings of these studies question the basic assumption too often made in curriculum planning—that certain learnings must be reserved for certain grade levels. The single most important implication of recent research is that flexibility is needed in constructing curricula and choosing methods—in discovering and utilizing teaching techniques which will effectively and continuously build upon the child's present knowledge and understanding of the social studies regardless of grade level.

More research is needed in identifying the stages of children's growth in understanding concepts, and acquiring attitudes and skills in the social studies. Longitudinal studies beginning with early primary children and studies involving large populations would provide useful data in this connection. More emphasis is needed on developing appropriate instructional materials. The work being done by the Harvard-Newton (Massachusetts) Social Studies Project under the sponsorship of the Harvard University Committee on Programmed Instruction, as well as the studies relating to elementary school social studies being carried out under the Cooperative Research Program,

Project Social Studies, should provide new data in the next several years. The studies reviewed here provide a point of departure. It will be interesting to note the progress made in elementary school social studies during the coming five-year period.

BIBLIOGRAPHY

Arnsdorf, Val E. "An Investigation of the Teaching of Chronology in the Sixth Grade." *Journal of Experimental Education,* XXIX (1961), 307–313; and "An Investigation of Teaching Chronology in the Sixth Grade." Unpublished Doctor's dissertation, University of Minnesota, 1959.

——————. "A Study of Intermediate Grade Children's Understanding of Basal Social Studies Materials." *California Journal of Educational Research,* XIV (1963), 67–73.

Cammarota, Gloria. "Children, Politics, and Elementary Social Studies." *Social Education,* XXVII (1963), 205–207, 211.

Chase, W. Linwood. "American History in the Middle Grades," in *Interpreting and Teaching American History.* William H. Cartwright and Richard L. Watson, Jr., eds., Thirty-First Yearbook, National Council for the Social Studies. Washington, D.C.: National Education Association, 1961, pp. 329–343.

Crabtree, Charlotte A. "Effects of Structuring on Productiveness of Children's Thinking: A Study of Second Grade Dramatic Play Patterns Centered in Harbor and Airport Activities under Two Types of Teacher Structuring." Unpublished Doctor's dissertation, Stanford University, 1961.

Darrin, Garney L. "Economics in the Elementary School Curriculum: A Study of the District of Columbia Laboratory Schools." Unpublished Doctor's dissertation, University of Maryland, 1958.

Davis, O. L., Jr. "Children Can Learn Complex Concepts." *Educational Leadership,* XVII (1959), 170–175.

——————. "Learning about Time Zones in Grades Four, Five, and Six." *The Journal of Experimental Education,* XXXI (1963), 407–412.

Easton, David, and Robert Hess. "The Child's Political World." *Midwest Journal of Political Science,* VI (1962), 227–246.

Estvan, Frank J., and Elizabeth W. Estvan. *The Child's World: His Social Perception.* New York: G. P. Putnam's Sons, 1959, pp. 191–205.

——————. "Teaching Government in Elementary Schools." *The Elementary School Journal,* LXII (1962), 291–297.

Gill, Clark C. "Interpretations of Indefinite Expressions of Time." *Social Education,* XXVI (1962), 454–456.

Hess, Robert, and David Easton. "The Child's Image of the President." *Public Opinion Quarterly,* XXIV (1960), 632–644.

——————. "Role of the Elementary School in Political Socialization." *The School Review,* LXX (1962), 257–265.

Kaltsounis, Theodore. "A Study Concerning Third Graders' Knowledge of Social Studies Content Prior to Instruction." Unpublished Doctor's dissertation, University of Illinois, 1961.

Lovell, R., and A. Slater. "The Growth of the Concept of Time: A Comparative Study." *Journal of Child Psychology and Psychiatry and Allied Disciplines,* I (1960), 179–190.

Maw, Ethel W. "An Experiment in Teaching Critical Thinking in the Intermediate Grades." Unpublished Doctor's dissertation, University of Pennsylvania, 1959.

McAulay, J. D. "What Understandings Do Second Grade Children Have of Time Relationships?" *Journal of Educational Research,* LIV (1961), 312–314.

Mugge, Dorothy J. "Social Studies Information of Beginning Second Grade Children." Unpublished Doctor's dissertation, Columbia University, 1962.

——————. "Precocity of Today's Young Children: Real or Wishful?" *Social Education,* XXVII (1963), 436–439.

Rabozzi, M. D. "Extent of Certain Geographic Skills of Latitude and Longitude of Selected Fifth and Sixth Grade Children." Unpublished Doctor's dissertation, Pennsylvania State University, 1961.

Rushdoony, Haig A. "Achievement in Map-Reading: An Experimental Study," *The Elementary School Journal,* LXIV (1963), 70–75.

Senesh, Lawrence. "The Organic Curriculum: A New Experiment in Economic Education," Reprint Series No. 22, Purdue University School of Industrial Management Institute for Quantitative Research in Economics and Management. Reprinted from *The Councilor*, XXI (1960), 43-56.

4

TEACHING
SOCIAL STUDIES
IN SECONDARY
SCHOOLS AND
COLLEGES

C. Benjamin Cox
and
Jack E. Cousins
University of Illinois and
Ball State University

Considering, as Donald Oliver suggests, that the complexity of this field at least equals that of the atom, the research into social studies methodology is neither very rich nor very expansive. Furthermore, not since the days of the famed Eight-Year Study (1942), The Miami Experiment in Democratic, Action-Centered Education (1948), The Detroit Citizenship Education Study (1953), and possibly Bayles' (1956) experiments at the University of Kansas—as questionable as those latter studies may be—has a concerted and integrated inquiry been launched into social studies methodology. Perhaps the methodology theorists have concluded that the problems of what student activities, what classroom management, what lesson organization, and what instructional pattern to employ have already been resolved. Several experimenters, in fact, express this viewpoint explicitly or implicitly in the studies reviewed here.

Principally for the reason that methodological experimentation is obviously crossing a new threshold, we have emphasized the logical and psychological examinations of Smith, Oliver, Rokeach, and Kemp as potentially the most promising in this area. They are saying, we believe, that there are other aspects of teaching, such as the various uses of language and the effect of attitude on learning, which we simply have not explored relative to the social studies, or any other area for that matter.

Most of these studies are done by doctoral candidates, who attempt to be unique in their experimentation in as many ways as possible. As a result, they do not contribute adequately to the building of a systematic body of data which could be used to test a more sophisticated theory of methodology. Metcalf noted this same problem in his recent review (1963). However, we have placed considerable emphasis on four studies that purport to deal with both parts of this problem. *The Indiana Experiments in Inquiry* (1963) represent an integrated attack on the development of reflective thinking as method in the social studies and, at the same time, deal in some ways with methodological theory supporting such reflective inquiry.

Once we had limited our review to those studies concerned with actual social studies classrooms, we were forced to make further judgments about the importance of the research on the one hand, and about its quality on the other. We decided that those studies that dealt with the nature of the teaching-learning situation itself were the most important; and we contend that their quality is evident in the descriptions below. None of these criteria alone would necessarily indicate an emphasis on reflective thinking, but, taken together, they made this focus unavoidable.

PATTERNS OF STUDENT BEHAVIOR IN REFLECTIVELY ORIENTED CLASSES

Several researches have been designed in such a way as to shed light on what actually happens in the social studies classroom. Some of these have accepted or contrived models of classroom management and then attempted to replicate the models within an experimental design. Four researchers at Indiana University, as a part of their design, described and analyzed the methodological procedures followed by a class dealing reflectively with problems. In general, the four studies, recently published as *The Indiana Experiments in Inquiry—The Social Studies* (Massialas, ed., 1963), attacked and confirmed the overall hypotheses that growth in reflective thinking is produced most efficiently in classrooms where reflective thinking is valued, emphasized, and practiced and that the goal of acquiring facts is not sacrificed in classrooms which are oriented toward reflective thinking.

Massialas (1961) and Cox (1961) utilized comparable research designs, which allowed them to divide four classes of tenth-grade world history and four classes of eleventh-grade U.S. history into experimental and control groups equated on the basis of IQ, sex, socioeconomic status, reflective-thinking ability, and knowledge of world history or American history.

These investigators analyzed the results of their investigation both statistically and judgmentally. Pre- and post-test scores were used for the statistical analysis. The judgmental analysis involved the use of daily anecdotal calendars, kept by each of the investigators for each of his classes, and the logical analysis of transcribed tape recordings made early in the experiment and near the end in each of the experimental sections.

Both investigators based their teaching methods in the experimental groups on the general method presented by Hunt and Metcalf (1955) in their text *The Teaching of High School Social Studies*. Method A, the experimental teaching method in each case, involved the use of springboards, or groups of related and thought-provoking facts in standard textbooks, which could lead to conceptualization of some problems of importance. These conceptualizations took the form of hypotheses or insights whose logical implications the class was to explore. A typical hypothesis might state, for example, that *contact with different cultures results in changed values and desires*. These hypotheses were then clarified, elaborated, and tested. In the testing process the textbook and other available evidence were brought to bear on the problems in order to validate, disprove, or modify the hypotheses. The reaching of conclusions or generalizations was the final step of this method.

Method B, as proposed for each of these studies, was a logical adaptation of a traditional attitude toward learning and the social studies. The prime concern of Method B was to impart to the student a body of factual knowledge relevant to the social science involved.

These two investigators independently constructed models of

critical thinking which they used in their analysis of tapes and calendars. Massialas constructed a ten-point model which made reference to specific skills he wished to develop in his students as they learned to deal with materials critically. The model included the following operations:

1. Hypothesizing
2. Defining and clarifying
3. Enlarging the students' perspective
4. Identifying and probing assumptions
5. Drawing logical implications
6. Producing relevant information
7. Generalizing, and distinguishing among different kinds of generalizations
8. Recognizing material fallacies in propositions
9. Relating propositions to one another in terms of their consistency and the extent of their explanatory power
10. Developing a sensitivity to facts and proof

Cox, on the other hand, devised a six-phase operational model of critical thinking: (1) orientation, (2) hypothesis, (3) definition, (4) exploration, (5) evidencing, (6) generalization.

The third of these studies at Indiana University, conducted by Cousins (1962), involved the use of only one eighth-grade social studies class. Although it was concerned primarily with studying the development of the particular skills of reflection, an integrated pattern of these skills, or a reflective model, was implied.

As a part of his study, Cousins reconstructed his model of reflective thinking from an analysis of two bodies of data. One of these was a daily log kept by the teacher in which changes in thinking skills were noted. The other consisted of evaluations of eight classroom discussions, tape-recorded and transcribed during the semester. The typescripts of these recordings were evaluated by a panel of three judges, the original theoretical model of reflective thinking providing the criteria by which the evaluators categorized each student's response in the discussions.

Cousins' reconstructed model contained four major parts: (1)

Generalizing, (2) Deducing, (3) Problem Solving, and (4) Sensitivity to Values.

The fourth of these Indiana studies was that of Elsmere (1961) who experimented with an eleventh-grade class in U.S. history at Elmherst High School, Fort Wayne, Indiana. Elsmere confined his investigation to the testing of the learning and retention of historical facts in U.S. history and the learning and retention of certain steps in problem solving. He hypothesized that a problem-solving approach in teaching U.S. history produces significantly greater pupil achievement in knowledge of historical fact and in problem-solving ability than does a traditional approach. He determined to test these gains by means of (1) teacher-made instruments purporting to measure the acquisition and retention of historical facts and (2) instruments purporting to measure the retention of and the ability to use the problem-solving steps.

Elsmere defined the problem-solving approach as involving four steps: (1) stating the problem, (2) hypothesizing, or selecting, courses of action, (3) discussing the problem, and (4) drawing conclusions.

The traditional approach was described in the study as having the following aspects: the text is read, the facts are discussed through question-and-answer sessions, and then the pupils are tested to see how much of the factual information has been learned.

In designing the study, Elsmere used matched pairs and a single independent variable, the different teaching methods. He also used two conditions: an experimental group A and control group B. Pairs were matched on the basis of intelligence, previous history grades, achievement on a factual history test, and achievement on a subjective problem-solving test.

Intelligence scores consisted of the mean score computed from two forms of the Otis Quick-Scoring Mental Ability Test. Since there is no standardized test measuring the specific content covered during this twelve-week experimental period or specifically measuring the problem-solving steps devised for this study, Elsmere constructed both instruments for this research.

In the subjective test purporting to measure four problem-solving steps, three problems related to the content of the textbook were developed. The problems dealt with the rights of citizens in a democratic society. Each problem presented two conflicting statements. Within these tests students were directed to follow the four problem-solving steps.

The Indiana studies appear to indicate that classroom behavior of students engaged in reflective thinking falls into a certain pattern. The pattern is represented by these researchers as a model to be replicated in social studies classrooms where reflective thinking is desired. The pattern does clearly present distinct phases in which discriminable critical-thinking skills exist. However, the claims (1) that critical thinking can be pursued in the classroom only paradigmatically, (2) that this particular pattern is clear and sophisticated enough to be considered a universal paradigm, or (3) that enough is known about thinking, knowledge, group interaction, and many other relevant factors to construct such a model can at this point only be called hypotheses. Nevertheless, the pattern has many implications, which should influence teachers in the way they proceed in various classroom situations.

First, in the Indiana pattern, students are oriented to a frame of reference through which they acquire "background" information, establish the validity of this information, and form operational definitions. This phase may involve one or more of a variety of activities, such as watching a film, reading the text, reading books, listening to tapes or recordings, or writing responses to questions. A single historical episode, a series of events, or a case may often be the vehicle used to establish this basis for conceptualization. The essential feature of the opening phase is that the students are involved in a situation in which they acquire a frame of reference or orientation to a material or intellectual problem.

In the second phase, students begin to recognize problems, suggest tentative hypotheses as explanations for puzzling situations, or establish the meaning of propositions contained in the materials they are using. This aspect is characterized by free discussion which follows an inductive pattern. It is stimulated by the teacher, who asks leading questions, provides additional information, and encourages widespread participation, so that all possible ideas are generated. Hypothesizing is always heuristic and often intuitional—that is, there is always a certain amount of "guessing" and discovery involved in forming a hypothesis.

Third, the problems or hypotheses which have been suggested are explored in depth, so that assumptions and logical implications are made clear. Again, the students engage in free and largely deductive discussion, in which they challenge each other's logic and use of factual information. Definitions are subjected to further refinement.

The fourth part of the pattern is made up of the acts of concluding and generalizing. The students come to agree as to which of the hypotheses or which solution to a problem is most acceptable. The statement of the problem or the hypothesis is often altered as they arrive at a consensus.

The important implication for the teacher in these studies is that reflective thinking within the classroom setting can be effectively established through the use of a pattern or a model with distinguishable phases. The teacher can introduce reflection into his classroom, or improve his present attempts at it, simply by recognizing and employing these phases.

As stated above, the precise nature of the pattern and its parts has not been described or examined sufficiently to make more than a warrantable assertion that this is *a* way to engage reflection in the social studies classroom. However, when the teacher begins to use the model to guide the investigations and discussions of his students, he will gain an appreciation and understanding of the utility of dividing it into the various phases.

Obviously, if the teacher is uncertain of the overall strategy of reflection as prescribed by a reflective paradigm, he may also feel insecure in his use of the several critical-thinking skills that make up the model. The following section should help to orient him further to this approach to teaching the social studies.

INTELLECTUAL SKILLS EMPLOYED IN REFLECTIVE THINKING

Several recent researches have attempted to deal with individual critical-thinking skills or with a cluster of them. Even the studies that primarily investigated model constructs recognized that the critical-thinking skills are the essential components of the patterns of behavior exhibited by the students. For example, Elsmere, Massialas, Cox, and Cousins tend to agree on the skills evidenced in their experiments.

In a doctoral study at New York University, Rothstein (1960) identified the following critical-thinking skills:

1. Comparing sources of data
2. Interpreting data, drawing inferences, and finding assumptions
3. Identifying strong and weak arguments
4. Evaluating thinking as to its relative criticalness or dogmatism
5. Developing sensitivity to language and meaning
6. Drawing conclusions from evidence

In this 35-week study two groups of eleventh-grade students in American history were matched on the basis of test scores in mental abilities, English reading, and critical-thinking skills. Rothstein found that his experimental group, in which the skills were emphasized, gained in critical thinking and acquired the same amount of information as the control group in which subject matter acquisition was emphasized. However, he found no significant correlation between the information test and critical-thinking ability. Although there was a positive correlation among IQ, reading, and critical thinking, he did not consider these synonymous abilities. He observed further that the experimental group exhibited a broadened perspective and "free play" of the mind, showed more enthusiasm, and recognized a relationship between their school work and daily life.

Rothstein concluded that growth in critical-thinking ability can derive from instruction focused on "increased ability to apply the techniques." These "techniques," of course, are the critical-thinking skills he emphasized in the study. Though these skills cannot be adequately described within the limits of this review, the implication is that the student gains in his ability to think critically as he is directed and encouraged, for example, "to compare sources of data" in appropriately critical ways.

While it may appear tautological to draw such a conclusion, the concomitant increase in subject matter, perspective, and enthusiasm—a finding common to most studies in this area—makes the overall result a valuable one. On the basis of such a conclusion, the teacher who intends to alter his instructional approach by emphasizing critical-thinking skills can do so with considerable assurance that he will not be sacrificing the acquisition of factual information on the part of his pupils.

Most studies dealing with critical-thinking skills assume that reflection is inextricably linked with problem solving or that the reflective skills can be improved only by direct use of problems. But McGarry (1961), in a doctoral study at the University of Minnesota, hypothesized that greater gains in reflective thinking would result if the process of determining meaning were made the primary goal of instruction. He assumed that the process through which the learner achieves understanding is synonymous with the determination of meaning through an analysis of generalizations or basic social concepts.

Using the course "Man in Society" at the university's general college, McGarry designed his study so that the control sections concentrated on understanding through the mastery of pertinent data. The experimental sections, on the other hand, focused on the understanding of selected social concepts or generalizations, like universal education, freedom, and responsibility. While the control group sought solutions to problems based upon fact, the experimental group attempted to pursue understanding through logical investigation of these fundamental social concepts.

Based on the results of pre- and post-testing with the *American Council on Education Test of Critical Thinking in Social Science,* McGarry found that both groups achieved significant gains in critical thinking, though the experimental sections consistently demonstrated greater gains.

Critical-thinking skills are, like all mental operations, complex and many-faceted. A skill which is described and tested inceptively in one experiment as an ability one uses in ordering his own thinking may operate receptively in another instance as the individual is taught to assess the thinking of someone else. For example, the ability to trace logical implications inceptively in order to test one's own hypothesis may be utilized receptively in detecting a speaker's bias. Thus, Devine (1961) attempted to determine whether certain critical-listening abilities can be developed in students. By means of a survey of expert opinion, he selected the following critical-listening abilities as the basis of his study:

1. Recognize the speaker's bias.
2. Recognize his competence.
3. Distinguish fact and opinion.
4. Recognize inferences.
5. Distinguish reportive and emotive language.

Devine then recorded a series of ten lessons that attempted to teach these abilities. The population of his experiment consisted of 614 ninth-grade pupils in three communities. He found that the experimental group, which had the benefit of the series of ten specially prepared lessons, did make a significantly greater gain in critical-listening abilities at the .01 level. However, the lessons did not significantly improve students' general listening comprehension, and both the experimental and control groups gained significantly and equally in their ability to think critically. But he also found that the lessons purporting to teach critical-listening abilities were effective with students of all levels of mental ability. Perhaps the clue to Devine's successful experiment was that each lesson was designed to develop proficiency in a specific listening skill.

The relationships among these four aspects of the findings of this study are especially amenable to interpretation. For example, they might suggest that there is, in fact, a difference between the abilities to listen and think critically, inasmuch as the students' improvement in the two was not equivalent. By a similar deduction, general listening comprehension is something different from each of these others. But perhaps of most immediate importance to the classroom teacher is the finding that the effort to improve critical-listening abilities was effective at all levels of intelligence. Experimental innovations are often reserved for those with higher mental abilities. Teachers will insist that a new practice will work with their high-ability students, but not with their low-ability students. But within this sample of over 600 students of varying abilities, the efforts to improve these skills were effective at all levels.

Just as the ability to deal critically with materials and propositions is demonstrated in different degrees by different persons, so does creative ability vary. Some researchers have suggested, in fact, that these two phenomena are related positively. That is, the person who is creative is likely to be highly capable in critical thinking.

At least one researcher has tested this supposed positive relationship. Gilbert (1961), in a doctoral study at the University of Buffalo, looked at the relationship of creativity to critical thinking and to performance in the social studies classroom. Gilbert defined creativity as a constellation of factors—adaptive flexibility, spontaneous flexibility, associational fluency, ideational fluency, originality, redefinition, and penetration—and hypothesized, therefore, that the creative person would perform better on critical-thinking tests and achievement tests. She further hypothesized that such a person would not fare so well on teachers' marks or in assignment to honors' classes.

In this study 597 eleventh-grade students in two high schools in an industrial city were given a battery of tests to measure these variables. Also examined were teachers' marks and the assignment of students to ability groups. Gilbert found a significant correlation between the total creativity score and the critical-thinking score, with intelligence held constant. This finding supported her hypothesized relationship between creativity and critical thinking. She also found that the highly creative and proficient thinkers do not receive academic rewards commensurate with their endowments. She found, furthermore, a significantly greater relationship between creativity and achievement than between creativity and teachers' marks.

The implication is that the schools operate with hidden assumptions deleterious to the creative and critical-thinking student. For example, the creative student may develop sound ideas which seem to vary from those of the teacher; or the same student may question, on valid grounds, statements made by the teacher. Further, the creative student may question the work assigned, especially if such work is designed merely to keep students busy. Thus, the creative and critically-minded student, even though he uses skills and abilities that appear as a stated objective of education, finds that he is penalized as far as his grades are concerned. In other words, schools seem to assume that the good student agrees with and follows the directions of the instructor. This implied indictment is a severe one if the schools intend to encourage achievement beyond the usual and the traditional.

School people also seem to assume that academically talented students will think reflectively whether or not they are taught explicitly to do so. However, most of the researches conducted regarding reflective thinking and problem solving indicate that students who are taught specifically to use critical-thinking skills become more proficient than those who undergo no explicit instruction.

The skills identified in these researches can be categorized into a pattern, which correlates with the patterned behavior indicated in the previous section of this chapter.

1. The skills of understanding
    a. Ability to summarize
    b. Sensitivity to new, ambiguous, or specialized words
    c. Ability to detect bias
    d. Ability to assess competence
    e. Ability to judge the validity of data and their sources
    f. Ability to identify strong and weak arguments
    g. Ability to develop analogies
    h. Ability to distinguish fact and opinion
2. The skills of hypothesizing or stating problems
    a. Ability to perceive possible solutions and state them as tentative generalizations
    b. Ability to detect material or intellectual problems in social studies materials
    c. Ability to develop and identify different types of generalizations
3. The skills of exploration
    a. Identification of assumptions
    b. Ability to develop valid inferences and trace logical implications
    c. Recognition of dogmatism or emotion in statements
    d. Ability to seek and utilize evidence
4. The skills of concluding
    a. Ability to accept, modify, or reject a hypothesis
    b. Ability to develop solutions and consensus on solutions
    c. Ability to test a generalization

This listing, though far from definitive, gives some indication of the skills examined in the above studies and an approximation of how they were employed. Obviously, many of the skills are not discretely classifiable and can in operational settings assume importance in more than one category. The major point to be considered is that reflective thinking is a particular, systematic approach to learning and to knowledge that requires the teacher to manage the classroom discourse so that the discussants move from one frame of mind to another. Reflection is necessarily a holistic conception inasmuch as it proceeds sequentially from doubt to a supported conclusion. However, many of the skills involved in reflection can be used to improve various styles of teaching. The reflective thinking skills of distinguishing fact and opinion and developing analogies, for example, are useful even if the teacher purports to do nothing more than promote the acquisition and understanding of facts.

FACTORS IN CRITICAL-THINKING SKILLS

Rust, Jones, and Kaiser (1962) worked with a number of critical-thinking skills with a different kind of categorization in mind. Their intent was to determine how many different kinds of abilities are actually represented in the variety of critical-thinking skills identified in a critical-thinking test; or at least to determine whether some of these skills are closely enough allied to be considered as a single factor. Taking the scores made by 587 subjects involved in the 1954 Illinois Critical Thinking Project, the investigators used the Pearson Product Moment Correlation to compute coefficients for 21 subscores. They found three basic factors. Factor A was identified as a general reasoning factor; factor B was identified as logical discrimination or application of logical principles; and a somewhat weaker factor, C, was called semantics. On the basis of this analysis, the investigators concluded that the "factor pattern was truly the result of differences in the kinds of abilities, skills, and knowledges required to answer the items correctly." The difficulty of items for most of the questions or the fact that subjects' beliefs and opinions were involved in answering some of the items did not influence the factor pattern.

Since Rust's earlier attempt to factor analyze these tests using item scores had been fruitless, this group concluded that the grouping of items affects the apparent factor content of a test. They suggest that in future tests, test constructors might experiment with grouping items in a variety of ways.

There is an apparent discrepancy between the results of Rust's previous attempt to discover factors through an item analysis and the findings of this study. If the general factors of reasoning, logic, and semantics are operable, or detectable, only in relation to significant portions of critical-thinking tests, then perhaps the skills should be taught in isolation. That is, the general factor of logical discrimination would best be strengthened by teaching each of the logical skills involved. Similarly, the general reasoning factor would be strengthened by identification and teaching of the reasoning skills independently. Had the general factors been detectable by means of Rust's previous item analysis, on the other hand, the teacher could expect the student's mastery of each skill involved in a general ability to be improved as he deals with the whole ability, or with any part of it.

THE LOGICAL OPERATIONS OF TEACHING

Two groups of investigators have begun the laborious process of describing the teaching act by means of an analysis of the logical operations of teachers and students. The attempt here is to infer from the language employed in the classroom the multidimensional character of teaching and to identify the entire range of logical constructs which comprise the dialogue of teaching.

The studies differ partially in the extent to which the experimenters establish norms for what they consider the "best" kind of teaching. Smith and Meux (1962), for example, appear to say that their classificatory system represents an exhaustive taxonomy of the logical operations employed in all didactic classrooms, while Oliver and Shaver (1963) imply that certain kinds of linguistic behavior and logical operations are characteristic of a preferred "style" of teaching.

Oliver and Shaver started by distinguishing (1) the *affective area,* which sets up a continuum reaching from friendly, pleasant exchange to hostility and constraint; (2) the *procedural area,* which refers to the amount of structure and organization utilized in the group for purposes of control of agenda, communication, and labor; and (3) the *task area,* which stipulates a measure of productivity that includes the quantity and quality of work done, such as the number of ideas and solutions considered within the classroom dialogue.

They then logically analyzed this affective, procedural, task trichotomy into a number of more specific dimensions presumed to be minimally adequate as a conceptual model of the act of teaching.

THE TASK AREA

Within the task area they proposed to analyze the teacher-student dialogue at four different levels: (1) statement posture, (2) discussion posture, (3) statement types, and (4) logical or intellectual operations. Statement posture refers to whether the teacher or student is making a positive assertion, asking a question, questioning or challenging a previous statement, or expressing doubt. Discussion posture, a somewhat broader category, indicates the speaker's overall attitude toward, or his way of handling, information. If the teacher regards the content of the subject area as problematical without definite right answers, the discussion posture would be considered *dialectical.* But if he regards the content as definitive truth, the discussion posture would be *descriptive.*

The discussion posture may also be either *substantive* or *analytic.* An analytic posture attempts to find new ways of looking at or structuring problems. The third level of analysis concerns the specific type of statement used, such as general or specific values, general or specific legal claims, and generalizations or specific factual statements. Oliver and Shaver's fourth level of analysis deals with the logical or intellectual operations performed by the teacher or student. Logical operations refer to such tasks as problem differentiation, relevance testing, and dialectical strategies.

It is at this point in the description that the Oliver-Shaver and Smith-Meux studies make the firmest contact. Their strategies are not identical, but the results of their analyses are compatible.

Smith and Meux restricted their study to an examination of the types of statements that are made in the classroom. They grouped these statements into categories of definitions, explanations, and evaluations. In order to deal with these categories, they divided all verbal behavior in the classroom into units called episodes and then analyzed these episodes logically.

They defined an episode as a unit of discourse involving a verbal exchange between at least two individuals. It passes typically through three phases: (1) an initial or opening phase, called an entry, (2) a sustained or continuing phase, called a response, and (3) a terminal or closing phase. An elaborate series of statements describing all of the categories of remarks served as the criteria for identifying episodes. A further analysis was made of the logical relations between an ideal response to an entry and the actual response to an entry.

Since the investigators assumed that the act of performing a logical operation is rule-guided behavior, they chose to develop rules of correctness as a means of differentiating subcategories. Some of these rules concern logical validity, and others concern truth. The investigators believe that the teacher who can operate by these rules is freed from the traditional authority of the textbook.

Smith and Meux's major categories are listed below. The extensiveness of their logical analysis is indicated by the fact that each major category may include as many as eight subcategories.

1. Defining episodes
2. Designating episodes
3. Classifying episodes
4. Comparing and contrasting episodes
5. Conditional-inference episodes
6. Explaining episodes
7. Evaluating episodes
8. Opining episodes

THE AFFECTIVE AREA

Oliver and Shaver extended their analysis of the teaching act beyond the description of statement types and intellectual operations. They also indicated an emotional dimension in the interacting of students and teacher. This affective area looks particularly at the positive or negative feelings communicated in the interaction process. They believe it is possible to discriminate at least two different types of affective expressions: support vs. antagonism and tension vs. tension release. Tension release may be indicated in the classroom by certain types of laughter, while the presence of tension may be inferred from such actions as pencil tapping or nervous laughter.

THE PROCEDURAL AREA

Furthermore, both groups of researchers have identified a non-logical area related to management and control of the classroom. In this area the teacher may give directions for the conduct of a discussion, may make assignments, or may handle a discipline problem.

TEACHING STYLE

In order to test their normative hypothesis that one kind of teaching is preferable, Oliver and Shaver defined two particular styles of teaching. They trained teachers to play the styles and attempted to observe to what extent various dimensions of teaching were affected by the different styles. Furthermore, they have attempted to determine the relationship between style and student learning.

The two general styles defined in this research were *recitation teaching* and *Socratic teaching*. In recitation teaching, the teacher characteristically assumes definitive control of information. Correct information is fed to the student by the teacher or by the textbook. The student's learning in this situation is measured by the exactness with which he can respond to questions regarding the information previously given him.

Socratic teaching, on the other hand, is clearly adversarial. That is, most discussions in such a classroom are of controversial topics. A Socratic teacher requires the student to take a position on the issue, to state the position, and to defend it. The emphasis is not only on knowledge utilized as background for the discussion but on the process by which the student finally arrives at a decision about the issue.

With reference to the dimensions they developed, recitation teaching assumes the statement posture of stating and question asking, while Socratic teaching shows a high frequency in "questioning" responses. The discussion posture of recitation teaching is largely descriptive, while the Socratic style is clearly dialectical.

The recitation teacher and the Socratic teacher make use of the same intellectual operations in the classroom. Intellectual episodes in the Socratic classroom are more complex, however, than they are in the recitation classroom. So the Socratic teacher tends to use more of these operations in dealing with controversy. Within the affective dimension, the Socratic discussion tends to be highly charged with negative affect, largely because of the open controversy engaged in in the classroom.

Oliver and Shaver suppose that by defining a number of dimensions of teaching we can identify more precisely the characteristics of teachers who are student-centered, democratic, or the like. Second, researchers can begin to identify the variation in teaching styles that may significantly affect student learning. They suggest a number of research questions emerging from their investigation. (1) Can an individual teacher use more than one style? (2) What are the variations that occur within a single style? Do styles overlap? (3) Do style differences result in learning differences? (4) What is the relationship between characteristics of students, styles of teaching, and the personality of the individual teacher? (5) Can observational instruments be devised to measure style or complex intellectual processes? (6) Can teachers be trained to operate consistently from a particular teaching style?

CLASSROOM APPLICATION

Both of these research groups made extensive use of tape recordings of classroom situations to arrive empirically at their logical and analytical descriptions of the act of teaching. They differed, however, in their eventual use of these descriptions. Oliver and Shaver, perhaps prematurely, have judged that the prescribed employment of these intellectual operations can result in one of two identifiable styles of teaching. They are careful, however, to explain that the learning or assuming of one style or the other on the part of a teacher is now only a testable hypothesis. Also, the existence of a relationship between the style chosen and the kind of learning which takes place is largely an untested hypothesis.

While we admit sympathy with the classification of opposed styles as conceived by Oliver and Shaver, we feel that their descriptions are highly selective and largely judgmental. That any constellation of acts and operations necessarily constitutes a "style" is doubtful in itself. That only two such constituted styles exist or can exist is unthinkable.

On the other hand, there appears to be a distinct advantage in creating such patterns or styles in order to implement a testable hypothesis. Oliver and Shaver's study, which is based on a hypothesis, may yield more immediately useful results than Smith and Meux's, which is not based on a hypothesis. Though the two studies are not legitimately comparable on this score, the finding of Oliver and Shaver—that the *Socratic* style of teaching is more productive in dealing with controversy—offers an immediately replicable pattern for social studies teachers. Smith and Meux's study, described by them as an analytic and descriptive one in the natural history sense, is an attempt to look at the teaching act from a supposedly hypothesis-free viewpoint— simply by observing, recording, and categorizing linguistic performance in terms of logical models. (Whether this or any other significant observation can be made without a controlling hypothesis of some kind is a question to be raised here also.) The profession as a whole may find these descriptions of logical operations very useful in future studies and in the preparation of teachers, but their immediate utility in the operation of the classroom is not explicit. We cannot say, of course, that these observations have been unproductive, since they *have* revealed a clear, more systematic description of a portion of the teaching act. There is the danger, however, that teachers and future researchers alike may make inappropriate inference about the logical units. That is, to infer that the whole of teaching is comprised of one isolable and logically analyzable episode after another, is reductionistic, to say the least. Smith probably does not intend to imply that teaching is this and only this.

MENTAL SETS THAT AFFECT LEARNING

A few studies have examined the way in which irrelevant emotional factors influence critical thinking. Such studies assume a dynamic relationship between personality and the way a person thinks.

For the most part, these studies have looked specifically at open and closed mindedness, rigidity, and dogmatism as they affect the way a person can make judgments.

The studies in this area assume importance for the social studies—both because of memory factors involved in learning social science facts and data, and because of the emphasis on the more abstract critical skills entailed in dealing with these data. The findings of these studies seem to show that certain mind sets related to dogmatism and rigidity have adverse effects on most learning processes—especially those of a more abstract nature or those requiring the entertainment of a number of alternatives or the creation of new hypotheses.

Kemp (1960) compared a sample of five hundred male and female freshmen in an attempt to discover the relationship between dogmatism and critical thinking. One hundred fifty students who ranked high on the *Dogmatism Scale, Form B,* were compared with a like number who ranked low on this scale. Kemp discovered that those with relatively open systems were superior in critical thinking to those with closed systems. He concluded that the highly dogmatic person cannot tolerate ambiguities and is impelled toward premature "closure" of problems.

Kemp (1961), in another investigation, examined the conditions conducive to open and closed mindedness and the improvement of critical thinking. In this study, eighty college freshmen were divided into control and experimental groups matched on open and closed mindedness, intelligence, and critical-thinking ability. The experimental group was divided into five subgroups of eight persons each. Four persons in each group were judged to have relatively closed systems, and four were judged to have relatively open systems. Each subgroup had ten 1-hour meetings that were designed to teach critical thinking. Both the experimental and control groups were enrolled in the same class and had the same lesson material other than those special meetings. The open-minded students in both groups did better than the closed-minded students. None of the control group improved, however, in critical-thinking ability. The closed-minded persons in the experimental group improved, but not significantly, in their ability to think critically. The open-minded in the experimental group improved significantly. Kemp concluded that the permissive, "safe," small-group situation may be the way to improve the learning of critical thinking, inasmuch as the small permissive group involves low threat to the student and intensive training in thinking skills.

In an attempt to test the ability to overcome mental sets, Rokeach (1960) devised ingenious problems involving "miniature cosmologies" whose basic principles differed from those known by the subjects. In "Introduction to Psychology" at Michigan State University, 109 students were given the *Gough-Sanford Rigidity Scale* and the *Dogmatism Scale, Form C*. Dogmatic thinking was defined as the total configuration of beliefs organized into a closed system, while rigidity was defined as the difficulty in overcoming single sets of beliefs or in learning a specific. Therefore, the rigid thinker has difficulty analyzing; the dogmatic thinker has difficulty synthesizing.

Rokeach found that persons who were low and high in rigidity differed in their ability to analyze but not in their ability to synthesize. On the other hand, he found that persons low and high on the dogmatism scale differed in their ability to synthesize but not in their ability to analyze. Rokeach also found that persons high in dogmatism and rigidity had more difficulty in memorizing data unrelated to their own sets and systems. The experiment also showed the inefficiency of "party-line thinking," which relies on uncritical acceptance of authority.

These studies appear to indicate that some mental attitudes of the learner, which he can, perhaps, control but little and his teacher not at all, are simultaneously crucial to learning and impervious to methodological strategies. The implications of these findings are most destructive when the social studies are seen as emphasizing analysis, synthesis, and critical thinking. Kemp's conclusion that low-threat, small-group situations may offer ways to deal with these factors is at least hopeful.

Some related inferences may be drawn from studies conducted by Bloomfield (1961) and Weinick (1960) on the effectiveness of small-group tactics. Weinick compared an essentially nondirective, group-centered method of teaching a course in psychology with a traditional, lecture-instructor-centered method. He found that both methods were equally effective in the acquisiton of psychological knowledge, but that the group-centered method produced significantly better gains in self-concept and acceptance of self as measured by the *Bill's Index of*

Judgment and Values. Weinick concluded that the permissive classroom produces superior attitudinal and personal adjustment.

Bloomfield looked at the effect of discussion grouping upon shifts of pupil opinion. Specifically, he attempted to assess the effects of loosely knit and closely knit discussion groups on the shifting and the polarizing of opinions. He applied the analysis of variance to the decisions made about school problems by discussion groups in thirteen classes of seventh- and eighth-grade students. The analysis showed that potentially cohesive groups shifted their opinions more easily toward *yes* or *no* decisions. He concluded that friendship groups will yield more polar decisions on problems.

Such findings of Kemp, Bloomfield, and Weinick present the kind of strategy that may prove useful in any number of classroom situations. Although Kemp found that the small-group situation is especially promising in dealing with dogmatic and rigid students, both Weinick and Bloomfield found evidence that persons not in these categories are also positively affected by group arrangements. The social studies deal continuously with problems related to mind sets, self-concept, and decision making. Group techniques found effective in all these areas are recommended to the social studies teacher by these studies.

INSTRUCTIONAL TECHNIQUES THAT PROMOTE REFLECTIVE INQUIRY

In recent years two promising instructional techniques have been developed and informally investigated. These two techniques are the "case-study" or jurisprudential approach to civil liberties and a technique designed to introduce students to the rationale of the social science disciplines. Due to the lack of well-structured research, these statements are based largely on judgments of teachers as they utilized these ideas in actual classroom situations.

THE CASE-STUDY TECHNIQUE

The case-study technique, utilized most frequently in the study of civil liberties, the Constitution, and Bill of Rights, was studied thoroughly by Davis (1955) in a doctoral dissertation. In analyzing the cases used in medicine, law, sociology, psychology, and educational administration, he arrived at the following definition of a case:

The use of a verbal stimulus or utterance (case document), one or more paragraphs in length, which reports the experience of a person or group of persons in a situation or a series of situations to a group of students in order that through analysis of the document, and in the discussion which follows the analysis, the students will acquire increments of verbal learning in the discipline or profession in which they study, and will undergo certain attitudinal changes resulting in greater understanding of themselves and others (p. 8).

Starr (1959), reporting on his use of the case method in connection with civil liberties, states that the purpose of the case is "to get under the skin of the student." Oliver and Baker (1959), reporting a short, well-structured study, state that the case method challenges the student to make personal decisions about important social problems.

The purpose of the case method, then, is to place before the student a real or hypothetical situation in which there are value conflicts, and to encourage the class to engage in a discussion whereby each student can arrive at what he believes to be "good," "right," "wrong," or "bad" in the particular situation under consideration. The discussion should clearly establish what the controversy is—that is, it should define the values in conflict and should indicate on what basic assumptions or grounds one position or another can be taken. As students become skilled at recognizing the grounds on which various beliefs are based, they may be challenged to question the value positions they hold.

Oliver and Baker (1959) utilized the case method as they taught classes engaged in studying the history of the labor movement. Two groups of slow students took part in this study—one a seventh-grade class, the other an eleventh-grade class. The teachers first presented cases that dealt with five basic understandings about the history of labor movements. Following the reading of the case, the teacher would structure the discussion so that students taking various "sides" would feel that the teacher had some empathy with them. The teacher then became a balancer in that he would pit one student's ideas against another's, ask probing questions, and provide additional information when needed.

This unit lasted nine days. Evaluation was based on impressionistic observations and the results of objective tests which were administered before, immediately after, and one month after the experiment. The objective tests were designed to measure facts, the ability to distinguish opinions from facts, and students' attitudes toward the working man. The researchers found that the seventh-grade students had some difficulty with the cases, possibly because of their length or the pupils' lack of background in basic human experiences necessary to understand certain concepts about the working man. They also noted that the lack of definite answers bothered the younger students, while the eleventh graders enjoyed working with conflicting value positions.

They found that both groups made striking increases in knowledge of facts; both groups increased in their ability to distinguish facts from opinion; and the attitudes of both groups shifted from a slightly anti-labor position to a slightly pro-labor position. Oliver and Baker suggest that future cases be designed to deal with smaller problems and be shorter in length.

Starr (1959), although not reporting a structured study, has made extensive use of cases dealing with the Bill of Rights and civil liberties in general. He uses short, one-to-two-paragraph briefs of Supreme Court cases as a primary source. Oliver and Baker suggest the Carrie Chapman Catt Fund as a source of case materials. Starr's (1959) bibliography is an excellent source of case materials, and he (1961) (1962) has written a series of case reviews for *Social Education,* which provide excellent, although somewhat complicated, case studies.

Parker and Econopouly (1961) believe the Constitution to be an indispensable part of teaching civil liberties, but they also take the position that local conflicts of interest are very important. They have experimented in writing a series of case histories, into which they build the particular issues they wish to discuss. They have also written cases in which several value conflicts are presented. After using these materials, they conclude that they cannot be certain whether attitudes have changed, but they are convinced that the students are interested, want to explore the problems in depth, and are fair-minded about the conclusions reached in the classes.

Graham (1960) utilized the case approach when she had students play the roles of those involved in value-centered conflicts. For example, she cites the following melodrama.

A teacher was needed in a school corporation. After viewing credentials, the superintendent called the man decided upon, and confirmed the hiring during their telephone conversation. A few days later the teacher reported to the superintendent's office. He was a Negro. The superintendent was upset because there had never been a Negro teacher in the corporation and he had assumed he was hiring a Caucasian. Since the teacher by this time had received his contract, the superintendent wanted him to resign because of his color.

THE STRUCTURES
OF THE SOCIAL SCIENCES

Another area requiring methodological implementation is that which attempts to teach the rationales of the social science disciplines as well as their substantive content. In 1959, Wronski made a plea for such a program, anticipating the current move. Two books, *The Social Studies and the Social Sciences* (Harcourt, 1962) and *High School Social Studies Perspectives* (Houghton, 1963), are more recent attempts to provide insights into the nature of the various disciplines. They attempt to answer such questions as "What is history?" or "How does a historian arrive at the generalizations he makes?"

Doyle (1963) reported a study carried out at the Peabody Demonstration School, in which the students used the methods of the political scientist as they studied the development of our constitutional rights. They examined copies of original documents, such as the Magna Charta, the English Bill of Rights, and the Mayflower Compact. Further, they analyzed case situations which involved civil liberties. These students, utilizing the methods of historical research, not only hear and know the historians' works; they also come to understand why certain liberties are preserved in writing.

Doyle (1963) also reported that students at the Francis W. Parker

School in Chicago are required to observe campaign headquarters during election years and write descriptive analyses of their observation. Park (1959) applied the principles of historical investigation in requiring junior high school students to write their own colonial newspaper. The students had to search for much more information than that contained in a textbook, select what was pertinent, arrive at generalizations, and then write the articles. In developing this newspaper, the students were, in an immature fashion, actually learning how written history comes into existence.

Halsey (1963) reported the work of a secondary school history committee in Amherst, Massachusetts. This group has developed materials specifically designed to teach the method of history as well as history itself, while avoiding the pitfall of "covering ground." Students utilize as many original sources as possible and arrive at their own generalizations on an inductive basis. They then test these generalizations deductively as they attempt to apply them to situations other than those from which they were developed. At the time of Halsey's report the college committee and the high school teachers involved were pleased with the results of the endeavor.

SUMMARY

The studies reviewed here purport to make a contribution to the theory and the practice of the social studies. The supposition is that these two areas are interrelated and that they support each other. Hypotheses about teaching must be proved in the harsh arena of practice. What is practiced in the classroom should be justifiable in the body of theory that describes the discipline of the social studies.

It is in this context of theory and practice that the authors' basic criterion is clearly stated. As stated in the introduction, the *nature of the teaching-learning situation* is believed by these reviewers to be the most important aspect of the social studies classroom. The use of the term *nature* at the beginning of that phrase and the term *situation* at its end is intended to wed the theoretical and practical. As the reader has progressed through the selected reviews contained here, he may be ready to entertain with these reviewers an additional assertion. Not only are the studies in critical thinking important because they are defensible in their design and conduct and useful for teachers in the management of their classrooms, but they are important because they most clearly unite theory and practice. In theory, the social studies ought to focus on inquiry into meaning, purpose, and predictability in social behavior. In practice, reflective thinking is the method that most nearly establishes the classroom climate, intellectual posture, and emotional commitment necessary for this inquiry. So, from this point of view, the reviewers claim a warrantable preference for reflective thinking as *the* method of the social studies. (In so doing they acknowledge the support of such authors as Hullfish and Smith (1961), who make an even broader claim for reflective thinking as the method of education.)

The Indiana studies claim that reflection in the classroom is best developed in terms of patterned behavior where a phase model is replicated. Several studies demonstrated that critical thinking skills are teachable in a variety of ways without disparagement of the acquisition of factual knowledge. Rust *et al.* explored the possibility that the many critical-thinking skills actually represent only a limited number of abilities—possibly only three; and Gilbert found a close relationship between creativity and critical thinking.

Rokeach and Kemp showed that mental sets are important factors in the teaching-learning situation and, in particular, that dogmatism and rigidity in students must be dealt with very sensitively by the teacher.

Oliver, Shaver, Smith, and others have begun to analyze the teaching act in terms of the logical operations of teachers and students. While Smith's work has been largely taxonomical, Oliver and Shaver have defined certain clusters of these operations as styles of teaching. Their research supports the adversarial Socratic style as the preferable one in dealing with controversy.

Starr and others have devised techniques, such as the use of cases in dramatizing value dilemmas, which show great promise in promoting the critical appraisal of issues in the social studies classroom.

These reviewers believe that, taken together, these studies begin to describe an emerging discipline of the social studies. No longer the pedagogical stepchild of the social sciences, the social studies presents itself as a discipline in its own right, involving its own theory and methodology of inquiry and synthesis, a unique focus and application, a growing body of literature, and a group of practitioners who have disengaged themselves from identification with the separate analytical disciplines of the social sciences. From this point of view, the social studies is seen as something different from the social sciences simply adapted for pedagogical purposes. In no way does it alienate itself from the social sciences, however. They remain the life blood of the social studies. They provide the facts and evidence, and in some cases the hypotheses and generalizations, that must be used in this further inquiry. The social sciences establish limitations and offer guidelines, but they do not *determine* the nature of the inquiry engaged in by the social studies.

Granted, this researching is as yet incomplete—and probably can never be completed. Yet to be described adequately is a reflective model that can be taught to teachers and students alike. We are not certain, for example, that all teachers can teach reflectively. We have some evidence that some students, at least, can operate at this intellectual level only in an emotionally protected climate. We do not know what kind of teacher-education program would best prepare social studies teachers to assume this changed role in the classroom. Moreover, although there appears to be a growing recognition of the social studies as a separate and legitimate field of study, the differentiation of the social studies and the social sciences remains obscure and vague.

The above statements merely suggest some of the major unresolved questions in the social studies. Some of these, obviously, the classroom teacher cannot deal with effectively. He can exert only minor influence on teacher-education institutions as they begin to redirect (or retrench) their social studies teacher-preparation programs. He may not contribute much to the dialogue which purports to deal with interdisciplinary relationships in the social studies. Neither of these statements is necessarily a judgment of the classroom teacher's ability to make these contributions, but both reflect the structure within which these problems will likely be attacked.

The classroom teacher, on the other hand, can serve in unique ways in answering some of these questions: At what age should reflective thinking be introduced to the school child? Are some school subjects in the present social studies curriculum more amenable to reflective inquiry than others? What changes in the curriculum will be necessary in a total reflective-thinking program? Would a partial program be effective? If so, which parts should remain untouched? How long can reflective thinking be sustained? That is, are there psychological or emotional factors that make it unproductive after a certain time in a single class session? Do other factors delimit its usefulness in an extended unit of work of, say, two or three weeks? Do age and mental ability play a part in reflective thinking? Can the process survive extensive employment over a period of years from elementary to high school? Are there aspects which can be introduced to the very young, leaving other aspects to be added as the student progresses through school without over-simplifying or weakening the program in the elementary grades? Can the low-ability student learn to think reflectively? What kind and what amount of materials are needed in any classroom before an adequate level of instruction is achieved?

The list is really interminable; for as each question is researched, others more complex and more sophisticated are revealed. But the fact remains that the door is open to new and hopefully better methods in social studies teaching. The research imperatives are great and the rewards inestimable.

BIBLIOGRAPHY

Aiken, Wilford M. *The Story of the Eight Year Study*. New York: Harper and Row, Publishers, 1942.

Bayles, Ernest E. *Experiments with Reflective Teaching, Kansas Studies in Education,* VI, No. 3. Lawrence, Kansas: School of Education, University of Kansas Publications, April 1956.

Bloomfield, Jack S. "The Effects of Discussion Grouping upon Shifts of Pupil Opinion: A Study to Determine the Effects of Discussion Grouping upon the Shifts of Pupil Opinion on Selected Problems Posed to Seventh and Eighth Grade Pupils," Unpublished Doctor's dissertation, New York University. Abstracted in *Dissertation Abstracts,* XXII (1961), 498–499.

Cottle, Eugene. "An Experiment in World History with Selected Pupils: Some Implications for the Improvement of Teaching with Motion Picture Films." Unpublished Doctor's dissertation, Southern Illinois University, 1960.

Cousins, Jack E. "The Development of Reflective Thinking in an Eighth Grade Social Studies Class." Unpublished Doctor's dissertation, Indiana University, 1962.

Cox, C. Benjamin. "A Description and Appraisal of a Reflective Method of Teaching United States History." Unpublished Doctor's dissertation, Indiana University, 1961.

Davis, Russell. "Exploratory Study of the Case Method." Unpublished Doctor's dissertation, Harvard University, 1955.

Devine, Thomas G. "The Development and Evaluation of a Series of Recordings of Teaching Certain Critical Listening Abilities." Unpublished Doctor's dissertation, Boston University, 1961. Abstracted in *Dissertation Abstracts,* XXII (1962), 3546–3547.

Dimond, Stanley E. *Schools and the Development of Good Citizens: The Final Report of the Citizenship Education Study, Detroit Public Schools and Wayne University.* Detroit: Wayne University Press, 1953.

Doyle, Casteel. "Utilizing the Methods of the Political Scientist in the Social Studies Classroom." *Peabody Journal of Education,* XL (1963), 219–227.

Elsmere, Robert T. "An Experimental Study Utilizing the Problem-Solving Approach in Teaching United States History." Unpublished Doctor's dissertation, Indiana University, 1961.

Gilbert, Janet Maude. "Creativity, Critical Thinking, and Performance in Social Studies." Unpublished Doctor's dissertation, University of Buffalo, 1961.

Graham, Grace. "Sociodrama as a Teaching Technique." *Social Studies,* LI (1960), 257–259.

Halsey, Van R., Jr. "American History: A New High School Course." *Social Education,* XXVII (1963), 249–252.

Hullfish, H. Gordon, and Philip G. Smith. *Reflective Thinking: The Method of Education.* New York: Dodd, Mead & Company, 1961.

Hunt, Maurice P., and Lawrence E. Metcalf. *The Teaching of High School Social Studies.* New York: Harper & Row, 1955.

Kemp, Clarence Gratton. "Effect of Dogmatism on Critical Thinking." *School Science and Mathematics,* LX (1960), 314–319.

————. "Influence of Dogmatism on Counseling." *Personnel and Guidance Journal,* XXXIX (1961), 662–665.

Massialas, Byron G. "Description and Analysis of a Method of Teaching a High School Course in World History." Unpublished Doctor's dissertation, Indiana University, 1961.

————, ed. *The Indiana Experiments in Inquiry: The Social Studies,* XXXIX, No. 3. Bloomington, Indiana: Bulletin of School of Education, Indiana University, May 1963.

McGarry, Eugene L. "An Experiment in the Teaching of Reflective Thinking in the Social Studies." Unpublished Doctor's dissertation, University of Iowa, 1961.

Metcalf, Lawrence E. "Research on Teaching the Social Studies," in *Handbook of Research on Teaching,* ed. N. L. Gage. Chicago: Rand McNally and Company, 1963, pp. 929–965.

Oliver, Donald W., and Susan Baker. "The Case Method." *Social Education,* XXIII (1959), 25–28.

————, and James P. Shaver. "The Development of a Multidimensional Observational System for the Analysis of Pupil-Teacher Interaction." American Educational Research Association, in adaptation from the report based on Cooperative Research Project No. 551, 1963.

Park, Frances Hauser. "The Liberty Speaker: A Class Project." *Social Education,* XXIII (1959), 23–24.

Parker, Donald, and Nicholas Econopouly. "Teaching Civil Liberties by the Case Method." *Social Education,* XXV (1961), 283–285.

Peters, Charles C. *Teaching High School History and Social Studies for Citizenship Training: The Miami Experiment in Democratic, Action-Centered Education, DAC.* Coral Gables, Florida: The University of Miami, 1948.

Robertson, James E. "The Effectiveness of a Selected Set of Books in the Study of a Unit in Twelfth Grade American History." Unpublished Doctor's dissertation, The Pennsylvania State University. Abstracted in *Dissertation Abstracts*, XXIII (1963), 3819–3820.

Rokeach, Milton. *The Open and Closed Mind*. New York: Basic Books, Inc., 1960.

Rothstein, Arnold. "An Experiment in Developing Critical Thinking through the Teaching of American History." Unpublished Doctor's dissertation, New York University, 1960.

Rust, Velma I., R. Stewart Jones, and Henry F. Kaiser. "A Factor-Analytic Study of Critical Thinking." *The Journal of Educational Research*, LV (1962), 253–259.

Smith, B. Othanel, and Milton O. Meux. *A Study of the Logic of Teaching*. Urbana, Illinois: Bureau of Educational Research, University of Illinois, 1962.

Smith, Eugene R., and Ralph W. Tyler. *Appraising and Recording Student Progress*. New York: Harper and Row, Publishers, 1942.

Starr, Isidore. "Teaching the Bill of Rights." *Social Education*, XXIII (1959), 373–378.

―――――. "Recent Supreme Court Decisions: Double Jeopardy." *Social Education*, XXV (1961), 185–188.

―――――. "Recent Supreme Court Decisions: Censorship of Films." *Social Education*, XXVI (1962), 19–22.

Weinick, George David, "The Comparative Effectiveness of Two Teaching Methods in Attaining Specific Course Objectives: An Evaluation of Two Different Methods of Teaching a Course in Psychology with Respect to the Students' Acquisition of Course Content and Changes in Personal Adjustment," Unpublished Doctor's dissertation, New York University, 1960. Abstracted in *Dissertation Abstracts*, XXI (1961), 2996.

Wronski, Stanley P. "A Proposed Breakthrough for the Social Studies." *Social Education*, XXIII (May 1959), 215–219.

5

THE TREATMENT OF CONTROVERSIAL ISSUES IN SOCIAL STUDIES INSTRUCTION

John P. Lunstrum
Indiana University

"Controversial issues" as used in this chapter are the recognizable components of larger social problems, in which real and meaningful alternatives are presented for critical decision. An effort has been made to include not only studies derived from the conventional sources of educational research but also from reports on both theoretical and empirical studies in related fields of the social sciences. The major criteria in the selection of material have been: relevance to the problems of social studies instruction, quality of reasoning, and adequacy of research design. Nevertheless, in order to provide a wide range of significant professional opinion, it has been necessary to include some studies which cannot satisfy all of the criteria. In any case, a primary concern of this review has been the inclusion of studies reflecting the various schools of thought that have been influential in shaping attitudes toward education.

SCHOOL AND COMMUNITY RELATIONSHIPS

Fear of the results of granting intellectual freedom to teachers often causes local communities to deny autonomy in the field of social

121

studies to the schools. Myron Lieberman (1960) thinks this tendency of communities to protect their students from contact with controversial topics is due to the fact that American education is locally controlled. While dominant points of view vary from community to community, this diversity—he contends—does not alter the fact that the various schools are all compelled to subscribe to some form of dogmatic education. Were it not that the student is exposed to conflicting ideas through the various mass media, there would be nothing to offset this parochial outlook of the local school systems.

On the other hand, a more optimistic finding is offered by Coan (1961), who discovered that the parents of school children in a Kansas community were generally agreeable to the inclusion of controversial topics in the social studies program. On the basis of his survey of the opinions of selected teachers and parents, Coan concluded that social studies instructors have more latitude in the treatment of controversial issues than they realize. Nevertheless, he did concede that certain special-interest groups might oppose the discussion of certain topics. In addition, he recognized that some people might question the methods utilized in the presentation of controversial data.

There is some disagreement indicated in research concerning the extent to which the teacher still reflects uncritically the dominant beliefs of a particular community. To determine the influence of social position on the perception of the public school teacher's role, Drabick (1960), a sociologist, constructed a model of the teacher's role from the responses of selected laymen. He then compared it with the activities actually recorded by teachers in a Pennsylvania community. Observing a relationship between social position and the ability to perceive the teacher's role, the investigator also found that teachers acquiesce in the norms of the community and adjust the performance of their roles according to the expectations of members of the community. On the other hand, Bardwell (1960) in Wisconsin and Hernandez (1962) in Florida compared the responses of teachers and citizens with those of teachers and parents to statements about the task or function of the school. Both reported basic disagreement between teachers and citizens, although Bardwell did not find any statistically significant difference between the two groups in a rural community.

In assessing community attitudes toward the school, Levine (1963) attempted to classify respondents on a questionnaire concerning educational viewpoint in terms of two dimensions of liberalism-conservatism—economic and social.

In order to relate views on education more precisely to economic and social orientations, he first classified the respondents (according to a scale previously validated) as: conservative on both economic and social problems, conservative on economic problems but liberal on social problems, liberal on economic problems but conservative on social problems, and liberal in both aspects. According to Levine the responses, particularly to the scale dealing with the treatment of controversy in the social studies, demonstrated that both economic and social liberalism are related to acceptance of freedom of inquiry, but that social liberalism is somewhat more closely related.

It may be true, of course, that teachers are offering only a perfunctory verbal support to ideas or conceptions of education which might not be recognized by the community. This particular tendency of social studies teachers has been noted in several earlier studies. In two inquiries conducted by Hall in Ohio (1953) and Deam in Virginia (1957), teachers appeared to be willing to endorse the principle that controversial ideas should be presented in the classroom; but they readily submitted to pressure to prevent discussion of certain topics that were taboo in local areas.

Concerning the presence of restraints on freedom of inquiry in local communities, the opinions of teachers also conflict with research findings. In an NEA Research Division study (1962), most of the secondary school teachers questioned reported that they encountered little or no opposition to teaching about Communism and the United Nations. A markedly greater proportion of elementary teachers (21.7 percent) reported varying amounts of opposition to teaching about Communism in local communities. This report differs substantially from the alarm voiced in the U.S. Office of Education's Conference of Education for Freedom and World Understanding (1962) and the claim of McMurrin (1962) that standing firm for the "preservation of intellectual freedom is now one of the great tasks of those in academic life" (p. 37). In support of McMurrin's claim, a study of book selection and censorship in

California by Fiske (1960) reported that 29 percent of school librarians consistently refrained from purchasing controversial material and that 82 percent of the 91 circulating units covered in the study placed restrictions on the circulation or distribution of controversial books. The Fiske study (based in part on 204 interviews with school administrators and municipal, county, and school librarians in 46 senior high schools and 48 municipal and county units in 26 California communities) sought to identify and explain the various factors that affect the selection and distribution of controversial materials in libraries.

There also appears to be a dearth of instructional materials on the United Nations Educational, Scientific, and Cultural Organization (UNESCO). Feldman (1960) sought information from city school superintendents in a nationwide sample regarding instruction about UNESCO, and, discovering little utilization of UNESCO materials, he concluded that the widely publicized Pasadena controversy over teaching about this agency might have contributed to the paucity of teaching materials on UNESCO activities. Fiske's (1960) findings offer some support to Feldman's conclusions with reference to the removal of UN, UNESCO, and other controversial materials from California school and public libraries. (In the wake of the Pasadena and Marin County controversies, eighteen of the twenty-six communities studied adopted restrictive measures.) The search for evidence of interference with academic freedom is further complicated because teachers and administrators seem unable to recognize or evince concern about some of the forces that restrict their actions in classrooms. First identified by Beale (1936) and confirmed by the NEA Committee on Tenure and Academic Freedom (1951), this tendency has been noted in an inquiry into the elementary school by Cooper (1959). In the latter study (which utilized a sample of eight representative school systems in second- and third-class Indiana cities), questionnaires and interviews were employed to discover what educational pressures were felt by superintendents, elementary school principals, and teachers. In this connection the investigator noted that differing interpretations of external pressures on the schools were expressed by teachers, principals, and superintendents and that, on occasion, all three failed to perceive the pressures which influenced both the curriculum and teaching.

An examination of professional literature suggests an increasing interest on the part of teachers and administrators in the development of local and organizational policies to encourage the rational discussion of controversial issues, although adequate empirical data regarding the direction and impact of this movement are lacking. From the National Education Association (1961) have come reports that an increasing number of schools are operating under specific written policies which guide the teaching of controversial subjects. In support of this claim, seven models of written policy statements are set forth in this publication to demonstrate the approach taken in local school systems, professional organizations, and state boards of education.

Some school administrators, however, apparently do not share the enthusiasm of the NEA for the development of written policies on controversial issues. Lunstrum (1962) reported that 90 percent of the administrators of 38 Indiana school corporations surveyed (encompassing about 40 percent of the state's total school population) were opposed to, or undecided concerning, the recommendation that policies be developed in written form. Most frequently advanced by superintendents and social studies supervisors were the beliefs that "no serious problem existed," and that their teachers were generally "discreet" or "diplomatic." After limited examination of selected school policies, Lunstrum concluded that teachers are seldom involved in policy development; and that the policies deal in ambiguous, contradictory terms with such an issue as the teacher's right to express a personal opinion in his discussion of controversial topics. Also, in Nebraska, Riggs (1960) observed an apparent disinclination to involve teachers in the process of formulating written policy manuals. In his analysis of the policies of 160 schools, Riggs discovered that lay citizens other than school-board members were seldom invited to assist and that members of school faculties assisted in less than 50 percent of the cases.

The opposing pressures exerted on the schools by certain groups often complicate the problem of establishing policies to guide the teacher in dealing with controversial issues. Maloney's case study (1958) of the "Lonesome Train" incident in Levittown, New York, reconstructed a crisis in school and community relationships and described the involved pattern of events and personalities which culminated in a climate of hostility and suspicion, drastically reducing the morale of the teaching staff. A controversy over the use in Levittown schools of a recording that allegedly contained communist propaganda—the recording was of a cantata on the subject of the movement of Abraham Lincoln's funeral train ("The Lonesome Train")—eventually involved the New York State Department of Education. The recording became the subject of conflicting policy recommendations and an issue in two school board elections.

Drawing upon the concepts developed in several recent studies, Getzels (1963) emphasized the vulnerability of the educator to demands and constraints which are not only numerous but also contradictory. In one study conducted by Gross (1958), involving 105 superintendents and 508 school-board members, there was evidence that board members and administrators differed sharply on certain definitions of the superintendent's role. For example, 66 percent of the school-board members felt that the superintendent should keep the personal life of teachers under surveillance; only 26 percent of the superintendents agreed with this proposition. Seventy percent of the superintendents and 29 percent of the school-board members believed that the superintendent should defend teachers under attack for the objective treatment of controversial social and political issues. In a related study of the same population, Gross (1958) found that school-board members and superintendents agreed that the free-enterprise system, democracy, and Communism should be treated objectively; but, at the same time, they felt that the teachers should convey an understanding of the "superiority of the American way of life in all things" when these topics were studied. He also found evidence to support the claim that school-board members are more often on the management side rather than the labor side on economic issues. A substantial majority of both school-board members and superintendents favored the use of business-supplied materials, while the support for use of materials supplied by labor unions was noticeably smaller, particularly among school-board members.

Another inquiry (cited by Getzels), based on detailed interviews with forty-one teachers representing four school systems in two states, suggested that teachers are unsure of their roles in the community. This insecurity derives from: (1) a socioeconomic clash between teachers' expectation of middle-class living standards and inadequate salaries, (2) a discrepancy between privileges accorded other responsible citizens and the restrictions placed upon political activity on the part of teachers, and (3) the difficulty teachers have in maintaining a professional position because of the tendency of communities to dictate to teachers on matters of content and procedure in their classrooms.

In general, the studies in this section have largely been concerned with the elaboration of a theory or the measurement of opinions or attitudes toward critical issues, although some inquiries have encompassed both elements. Overgeneralization about conditions or qualities from limited data or isolated cases appears to be a perennial problem for some investigators.

Nevertheless, some of the designs offer interesting possibilities for further investigation. The employment of Levine's sensitivity to the varying levels of conservatism and liberalism and their impact on educational viewpoint emphasizes the desirability of case studies of community conflicts similar to Levittown's "Lonesome Train" incident. Carefully prepared case studies of the origin and method of resolving community or state conflicts over academic freedom might also help to show how there can be recurring efforts to limit freedom of teaching in the community when surveys have shown that most citizens sanction the presentation of controversial issues in the classroom. In this connection, Fiske's (1960) unique and exacting study offers some interesting hypotheses. She found that complaints from library patrons were more likely to receive institutional review or discussion in communities where extremist groups were found and noted that school and public libraries were more successful in warding off attacks in those communities where both the local press and the school administration supported their freedom to choose materials.

Unfortunately, the image of the superintendent and principal which emerges from the research of Gross, Fiske, and others is far from reassuring. The studies suggest that these administrators do not comprehend the rationale underlying the treatment of controversy in the classroom and are indifferent to substantive issues involved in the selection and distribution of controversial materials in the library. The extent to which the presumably nonintellectual orientation of school administrators conflicts with the teacher's perception of the role of controversy in social studies instruction and contributes to the erosion of academic freedom can only be determined through more extensive examination. Deam's (1958) competent study of the opinions of Virginia teachers, administrators, and school-board members raised some interesting questions in this field and should be duplicated in other states.

INFLUENCE OF ORGANIZATIONS AND MOVEMENTS ON TEACHING AND LEARNING

Frequently, local conflicts over freedom of inquiry are influenced by the educational programs of organized special-interest groups operating on the state and national levels. Nelson and Roberts (1963) have demonstrated that, during the late nineteenth and early twentieth centuries, a variety of special-interest groups, including Civil War veterans, labor unions, public-utilities lobbies, and political-party leaders, achieved some degree of success in influencing the content of textbooks and the behavior of teachers in the classroom. During the 1960s, these investigators suggest, there has been a resurgence of organized efforts to censor textbooks, particularly in the social studies; and some publishers and school systems have yielded to the demands that changes be made in certain textbooks.

The reportedly bland, sterile content of social studies textbooks has recently stimulated a number of inquiries by scholars. *Economics in the Schools* (1963), a publication of the American Economics Association's Special Textbook Study Committee, confirmed the prior findings of Krug (1960) and Alexander (1960) in an analysis of the four leading high school textbooks used in the fields of economics, social problems, and United States history. The appraisal was based on the assumption that "minimal economic understanding" is necessary to good citizenship—a formula set forth more precisely in the National Task Force Report *Economic Education in the Schools*. "The approach to economic matters should be essentially analytical," postulated the Committee as one criterion, "though larded heavily with factual and descriptive material on economic institutions and their development" (p. viii). The Committee concluded that value judgments in the texts are only infrequently clarified and that, in terms of available evidence, both sides of significant controversies usually receive equal treatment, regardless of the intellectual merit of the conflicting arguments.

Several educational leaders and writers, including Stocker (1962) and Roberts (1963), have identified the "far right" or the ultraconservative groups as spearheading the drive for censorship of textbooks and intervention in the classroom. One historian, Clark (1963), contends that the extreme left and extreme right are equally dangerous to the schools, although no evidence is offered in support of this thesis. Yet, Iverson (1959) after an extensive inquiry could find little or no communist influence on educational philosophy, methods, or materials. This historical examination of efforts of communists to influence American education—based on a study of government documents, reports of professional and political organizations, communist literature, and personal narratives and interviews—disclosed that the most notable example of communist penetration of a sector of education was the infiltration of a New York City Teacher's Union. The organization later expelled its communist leadership and assumed a strong anti-communist orientation.

The proposition that the American tradition has also contained the elements of political and social intolerance is supported by Bell (1962), who emphasizes the inclination of some Americans to explain setbacks or reversals as "conspiracies." Accordingly, the term "extremist" as applied in this discussion to individual or organizational activities denotes "alienation" from the mainstream of American tradition and, as Lipset (1963) indicates, a rejection of the fundamental rules of a democratic society. "The ideological extremists (of the left and right)," writes Shils (1956) ". . . because of their isolation from the world feel menaced by unknown dangers" (pp. 231-234). It seems logical, to regard the educational pressures—from the far left or far right—which impair freedom of teaching and learning as "extremist."

To regard the radical right as merely another manifestation of the irrational but harmless lunatic fringe may be a serious error. Ellsworth and Harris (1962) found in their analysis of the publications of the radical right that moderates were beginning to support the extremists whom they had formerly disregarded. This conclusion appears to be based upon an examination of a vast amount of literature—chiefly periodicals and newsletters purporting to depict rightist philosophy; however, it is not clear what periods of time were covered or what precise standards of judgment were employed to discriminate between "rightist" and "non-rightist" literature. Under the banner of the right wing, Ellsworth and Harris would enroll all persons "who share the conviction that the relationship of government to the individual should be severely limited"—a dubious standard. In contrast, Westin (1963) links extreme right-wing educational activity (particularly in the form of "anti-Communism") with small or medium-sized business enter-prises in specific areas of the South, Midwest, and Southwest rather than with large, executive-managed corporations. In addition, Wolfinger's survey (1963) of 308 persons attending the anti-communism school of Schwarz's Christian Anti-Communism Crusade disclosed the distinctly right-wing points of view of the Crusaders, but at the same time emphasized that most held responsible positions in their community and were active in various civic and religious activities. The Crusaders in this sample could not be regarded as social deviates or irresponsible fanatics. This exploratory but significant study used mail questionnaires and personal-interview schedules containing questions taken principally from previous national studies by the Michigan Survey Research Center, Samuel Stouffer, and Martin Trow; it thus provides useful data for purposes of comparison. Unfortunately, the hostility and suspicion of the Crusaders made it impossible to use systematic sampling techniques. Other characteristics of the school observed in this research were: (1) a tendency to regard intellectuals—teachers and students—as highly vulnerable to communist propaganda, (2) an indication that holders of Protestant fundamentalist beliefs were sympathetic to the right-wing doctrines exemplified by the Crusade, and (3) the failure of the school to attract members of the Democratic Party.

It is not clear to what extent minority groups have been able to curtail academic freedom. According to Nelson and Roberts (1963), in the study previously cited, the National Association for the Advancement of Colored People and the Anti-Defamation League of B'nai B'rith have screened the content of textbooks for objectionable material, although on the national level both organizations have appeared reluctant to proscribe books. However, the state and local divisions of these groups appear somewhat more militant on occasion. For example, the Michigan Department of Public Instruction in its publication "The Treatment of Minority Groups in Textbooks" (1963) contends that social studies texts deal inadequately with minority groups and "human relations." Although the documentation in the latter publication is fragmentary and the criteria for evaluation vague, the Michigan publication recommends to publishers that "historically-documented facts be re-evaluated in terms of what is worthy of inclusion in a basic text." Publishers are also advised that in all textbooks "pictures of the American scene should show Negroes and Orientals shopping in our large urban centers, enjoying parks and recreational facilities, attending schools, working at productive jobs, etc." (p. 6). It is conceded that not every illustration or picture "need be integrated" (p. 6).

Business and patriotic organizations also exercise marked influence on curriculum decisions. Selakovich (1962) examined the techniques used from 1945 to 1960 by the following organizations in shaping the teaching of American history and government in the secondary school: (1) the American Legion, (2) the Daughters of the American Revolution, (3) the Conference of Small Business Organizations, (4) Friends of the Public Schools, and (5) the National Economic Council. All of the organizations criticized textbooks during the period, utilizing as their principal technique the charge of subversive intentions or disloyalty. They charged those who disagreed with their social and economic positions with disloyalty. An historical analysis of the programs and activities of veterans groups by Minott (1962) supports findings by other investigators that citizenship education advocated by veterans is dogmatic and narrow. Nevertheless, the record contains evidence of substantial material aid provided communities by veterans' projects. Moreover, Minott finds hope in the shift by some veterans' groups away from provincialism and toward a more mature conception of Americanism.

Since state legislatures reflect the conflicting demands of educational "pressure" groups, the influence of legislators on the curriculum has become a logical object of inquiry. Jordan (1961) and Samalonis (1962) examined the impact of state legislation on curriculum. Jordan's study disclosed that Indiana statutes include an unreasonable number of requirements in the field of curriculum, thus relegating the State Department of Public Instruction to the role of a regulatory agency, instead of a source of professional leadership. A study of the existing laws in all fifty states led Samalonis to the conclusion that most state legislatures follow the common practice of prescribing subject matter by statute, without clearly expressing objectives or intent. Legislatures showed their greatest tendency to specify time allotments and grade placement in the fields of social studies and physical education.

In the light of public knowledge about the rise of extremist groups and attempts to interfere with teachers' classrooms, it seems reasonable to assume a close relationship between the tensions of the Cold War and preoccupation with questions of internal security and the status of academic freedom. Studies such as Nelson's and Roberts' have marshalled extensive evidence to support the belief that there is increasing censorship of textbooks, but there are inadequate investigations of the extent to which teachers encounter limitations on their professional freedom. The tendency of teachers to engage in "voluntary censorship," i.e., to refrain from introducing topics into class discussion which might touch off controversy, as noted by Chandler (1960) has probably tended to complicate research in this field. Robinson (1962) described the types of harassment employed by superpatriotic groups, particularly in the Southwest and in the West, and found that the attack on a counselor in Fullerton, California, was organized. In such a climate of opinion the teacher, in Robinson's words, "becomes a victim of the war of nerves and is incapable of devoting his whole energy to teaching" (p. 187). A more precise inquiry was made by Lazarsfeld and Thielens (1963), who conducted lengthy interviews with 2,451 social scientists representing 165 colleges in the spring of 1955 to determine to what extent academic freedom had been impaired during the so-called "McCarthy period." In the 165 schools 1,000 incidents involving a variety of charges were studied. Although Lazarsfeld and Thielens did not find that morale had collapsed, they did conclude that morale was beginning to suffer a decline. More than half of the respondents seemed to have withdrawn from the community intellectually—i.e., they were reluctant to make speeches to local groups on sensitive topics or to write articles on controversial issues in nonprofessional periodicals. A substantial number had avoided participation in the meetings of political parties.

Only infrequently can a teacher who feels that his academic freedom has been interfered with have recourse to a court of law. According to Fellman's (1960) interpretation of selected significant decisions, academic freedom rests upon administrative procedures and understandings and is not covered by the official body of legal rights. Even though a teacher suffering an arbitrary loss of a position or an unreasonable infringement of freedom to teach does have the right to appeal to the United States Supreme Court on the basis of an issue involving due process, his chance for a favorable judgment is slight. In such cases, the Court has appeared quite reluctant to place limits on the power of the state over the qualifications of teachers. Moreover, in the case of *Barenblatt* v. *United States*,[1] the Court upheld in broad terms the power of Congressional committees to make investigations in the field of education. In an analysis of the 1960 Supreme Court decision in the case of *Shelton et al.* v. *Tucker et al.*,[2] Starr (1961) traced the litigation over a 1958 Arkansas law which required teachers to divulge the names and addresses of all organizations with which they had been affiliated in the past five years. This law was passed in a state in which teachers were not protected by a recognized system of tenure; furthermore, the law made no stipulations concerning the confidential nature of the information divulged. Facing the Court was the issue of a loss of the teacher's right to "personal, associational, and academic liberty," a right protected by the Due Process Clause of the Fourteenth Amendment. Although the Supreme Court ruled the Arkansas law unconstitutional its vote was divided five to four. From the implication in the majority opinion that the court might have sanctioned a more carefully constructed law, Starr concluded that "this decision cannot be considered a resounding victory for the teacher's right to freedom of association" (p. 360).

[1] 360 U.S. 109 (1959).
[2] 364 U.S. 479 (1960).

In view of the varied nature of the studies treated in this section it is impossible to categorize them in terms of the research techniques employed. The Nelson and Roberts work, though prepared in a journalistic style, nevertheless drew heavily on the files of the NEA Commission on Professional Rights and Responsibilities and on interviews with individual scholars and publishers; accordingly, its conclusions are well-grounded. Some of the other works cited are largely statements of positions and derive their significance, as in the case of Stocker and Clark, from the influential roles of the authors and the hypotheses suggested for further inquiry.

Wolfinger, and Lazarsfeld and Thielens, although dealing with different subjects, have both formulated research designs which can be applied to the study of political intolerance and its effect on the schools. For example, Wolfinger's contention that the absence in some states of a vigorous political-party organization has facilitated such radical rightist activities as the harassment of teachers and librarians should be verified by further research. Intensive studies of the roles of state departments of education and legislatures in determining local school policies are suggested by the research of Jordan and Samalonis. These issues are highlighted by a recent controversy in Indiana arising from the state-wide distribution by the Veterans of Foreign Wars of a Fred Schwarz broadside to all high school juniors with the endorsement of the State Superintendent of Public Instruction. The whole question of how much access to the schools should be allowed to influence-wielding groups—whether they are patriotic, business, or labor groups—should be extensively investigated by objective researchers. Policies that have developed in various states and local systems concerning the distribution of sponsored materials should be carefully assessed to determine their effectiveness.

THE SOCIAL ROLES OF THE SCHOOL AND THE SOCIAL STUDIES TEACHER

Recent philosophical and historical inquiries reveal increasing interest in the relationship between conflicting assumptions about the function of education and the degree to which freedom of teaching and learning are promoted. Related literature indicates a wide range of views on these two important questions. Alexander and Saylor (1959) expressed the traditional thesis that "by the very nature of its origin and controls, the structure, organization, program, and methods of the school must inevitably conform to the dominant concepts and beliefs of those who control the school . . ." (p. 167). This "basic thesis" is somewhat modified by the admission that the school "may bring about a change in the value patterns, ideals, traditions and aspirations of a society" (p. 167). Nevertheless, it follows that the teacher, in order to provide education acceptable to his fellow-citizens, must discover what basic beliefs, values, and traditions the large influential majority want to have transmitted to students.

Rossiter (1962) contends that the school has always been a conservative influence in American society and that its attempt to teach liberalism has meant the uncritical treatment of a tradition rather than the presentation of a viable political system. As public institutions, schools must teach beliefs and facts that reinforce the existing order rather than ones that undermine it. On the other hand, Brameld (1961) pointed out that in the past, as a result of pressure from various special-interest groups, American schools have engaged in indoctrination to support the *status quo*. He therefore called for a conception of education which would develop institutions and values essential to a period of rapid change.

Thayer's (1960) analysis revealed two opposing traditions which have influenced American schools: conformity and freedom of inquiry. The educational tradition of conformity appears to have been the result of the colonial desire to inculcate particular religious doctrines, the need to bring about the assimilation of numerous immigrants from foreign countries, and the reliance on an authoritarian psychology of learning. The educational tradition of freedom of inquiry is derived in part from liberal English political beliefs and institutions, the westward movement, increasing diversity of religious views and ethnic backgrounds in America, and a growing faith in the concept of an "open society."

Two studies attempted to discover a relationship between the treatment of controversial issues and the type of philosophical orientation held by the teacher. Pounds and Bryner (1959) traced the implications of the following philosophies: neo-humanism, social evolutionism, realism, experimentalism, and reconstructionism. They concluded that more emphasis would be placed on controversial topics in the curriculum by experimentalists, reconstructionists, and some realists; the neo-humanists might defend academic freedom, but they would not emphasize areas of conflict in their proposed curriculum. In an analysis of the role of the social studies teacher in the treatment of controversy, Lunstrum (1960) examined five opposing conceptions of the social function of education: (1) the conservation and unchanged transmission of the cultural heritage, (2) the neutral function of imparting truth, (3) social regeneration by a return to earlier virtues, (4) critical transmission of the cultural heritage in a transitional era, and (5) the revolutionary function of establishing a new social order. After tracing the logical implications of each hypothesis or conception of the social role of the school, he found number four, the critical transmission of the cultural heritage, more compatible with the tested ideals and goals of education in an American democratic culture than any of the others. The idea of critical transmission, which involves the process of examining and choosing intelligently among conflicting values and beliefs, derives substantial support from an analysis of the contemporary pluralistic culture of the United States. Lunstrum also noted that inadequate provision for inevitable change was made by the other conceptions of the school's social role. These conceptions employ the following strategies of evasion: (1) cultivation of the illusion of security by an orientation toward the past, (2) an unwarranted denial that the school is concerned with change or controversy, (3) an unsupported affirmation of the inviolable character of the existing order, and (4) an unreasoning faith in infallible schemes of salvation.

Muller (1960) and Brackenbury (1963) have related freedom of inquiry to the existence of a democratic society. An important element of democracy, according to Muller, is consent based upon reason and the recognition of alternatives. Brackenbury pointed out the inevitability of controversy in a democracy and concluded that teachers could not be neutral; he urged teachers, however, to defer discussion of controversial topics when the climate of opinion in the community is highly emotional.

How the social function of the school in the nineteenth century was limited and shaped by various cultural influences has been set forth in Mason's (1960) historical analysis. Among the influences which limited the earlier conceptions of the school as a significant moral force, he listed: (1) the anti-intellectualism of Jacksonian political thinking, (2) the revivalistic religious institutions of the frontier, which encouraged an emotional approach to problems, (3) sectarian rivalries inevitably leading to a position of religious neutrality in the schools, (4) the organization of schools by grades, thus facilitating *memoriter* learning, and (5) the philosophy of the Enlightenment and the German idealism expressed in Horace Mann's and Henry Barnard's emphasis on the impartial search for the truth as a function of the schools.

Other studies have focused on the teacher's role in the examination of controversial problems and the related problem of indoctrination. Fraser (1962) endorsed the treatment of controversial issues in the elementary social studies program and designed certain criteria to guide the teacher in this task. The teacher is advised to refrain from indoctrinating students in his own views although he may be permitted to express his opinions judiciously in the cause of critical thinking. The climate of opinion in the community must be assessed, however, before undertaking extensive treatment of areas of conflict. On the basis of his study (previously cited) Mason concurred with Brackenbury and others that in view of the normative character of education and the presence of conflict in American life, neutrality is impossible for the teacher. This assumption has been challenged by Ennis (1959). He found that the use of expressions such as "neutrality" and "taking a position" implied purpose in teaching and hence the logical extension of the thesis of "impossibility of neutrality" would lead to the untenable conclusion that the school could be held accountable for supporting one view or another in every controversy.

Fadden (1962) evaluated prevailing concepts of indoctrination in American education. Noting the diversity of opinion and the tendency to identify indoctrination with "brainwashing" or excesses of propaganda, he categorized the various positions as "extremes" and "qualified." The extreme position maintained by experimentalists assumed that all indoctrination meant the inculcation of absolutes and hence was hostile to the democratic process; the qualified position recognized that the process of indoctrination was inevitable on certain levels (i.e., the transmission of parental values to children) but opposed the general application of the process. Fadden concluded that: (1) the extreme position was in itself a dogmatic expression of "scientism" and would encourage a form of indoctrination, and (2) the qualified position frequently resulted in inconsistent teaching practices, at times leading to indoctrination for the attainment of certain "good" ends.

The question of indoctrination has also been raised with regard to the educational activities of the American Armed Forces. Boyer (1963) studied the educational documents of the military services to find out if any ideology had emerged and what method of teaching had been endorsed. He concluded that there is evidence that the Armed Forces have sanctioned a monolithic conception of American social philosophy; moreover, in his view, the selection of materials and instructions referring to teaching methods implied the acceptance of indoctrination as the method of teaching in the Armed Forces.

One recent inquiry has dealt with the approach to the treatment of controversy commended to future social studies teachers in methods textbooks. Ballinger (1963) examined fourteen texts used in social studies methods classes to determine what guidance was given to the prospective teacher in the teaching of subject matter dealing with serious conflicts in values. He found that, with only one exception, the texts failed to provide insight into the social foundation of controversy and to discuss concisely the theoretical and practical problems involved in the presentation of controversial materials in the classrooms. (There were, of course, the usual broad but vague affirmations of faith in the suitability of teaching about controversial issues.) Furthermore, Ballinger found that, with only two exceptions, the methods textbooks failed to recognize the role of values in treating controversial issues—a characteristic of most influential writing by social studies educators on the subject of "critical thinking" or "skills."

While some theoretical or philosophical inquiries have served to clarify the conflicting conceptions of the social role of the school and the function of the teacher, many others are purely speculative, failing to relate such concepts as indoctrination or neutrality to American culture.

Boyer's study of the educational activities of the armed forces points up the need for further inquiry concerning the influence of the military in shaping attitudes in high school R.O.T.C. programs. Equally far reaching are the implications of Ballinger's exploratory study, which has suggested certain serious shortcomings in the popular treatment of critical thinking by social studies educators—i.e., as a process seemingly removed from value judgments. If, as Ballinger suggests, there has been a cleavage in professional education between social studies specialists and philosophers, departments and schools of education should seriously consider reorganizing the traditional programs of advanced graduate study.

THE LEARNING PROCESS AND THE TREATMENT OF CONTROVERSY

A number of writers recently have reconstructed Dewey's concept of "reflective thinking" and related it to the task of dealing with controversial topics in the classroom. Park (1960) has hypothesized that inquiry stems from a condition of confusion and proceeds through various stages: formulation of hypotheses or tentative explanations, the rigorous testing of hypotheses, and the revision of hypotheses in the light of evidence to the taking of a position. The acceptance of such a process of inquiry would be, in Park's view, to intellectualize or discipline controversy. Hullfish and Smith (1961) have elucidated a theory of reflective thinking and emphasized its function in the testing of beliefs and examination of values.

Some investigators have reported that the use of a reflective method or problem-solving approach has been more effective than traditional methods in the rational treatment of controversial topics. Cox (1963) and Massialas (1963) experimented with reflectively-oriented procedures in U.S. history and world-history classes respectively. In appraising outcomes of the inquiry-centered classes—as distinguished from those with a relatively traditional approach—they used a number of evaluative instruments, including tape recordings, a "log" of daily activities, and objective tests. They reported that their reflectively-oriented classes were characterized by ". . . the free debate of divergent points of view, the open-endedness of the propositions under discussion . . . and a respect for each individual's considered comments" (p. xiii). Elsmere (1963) conducted an investigation in a U.S. history course in which the problem-solving method functioned as an independent variable. From his classes Elsmere selected matched pairs of students and appraised their comparative performance in terms of the acquisition of historical information and problem-solving ability. He concluded that when taught by the problem-solving method, students not only acquired more factual information but also employed a more rational approach to controversial issues.

According to Metcalf (1963b), controversial topics which lead to a clash of personal beliefs make for greater motivation of students in social studies classes. In support of this hypothesis, he cites the recent findings on learning, (expressed in the theories of "cognitive dissonance,") that suggest that a student confronted by meaningful, contradictory propositions or beliefs will seek to resolve the discrepancy. Festinger (1957), one of the leading advocates of the theory of cognitive dissonance, has concluded that students may be motivated by being presented with contradictions between two or more fixed beliefs and values. He cites the results of various experiments to prove that a "principle of congruity" operates to reduce disagreement.

In the past social studies educators have justified the inclusion of controversial issues in the curriculum by pointing to their contribution to the improvement of critical thinking. Similarly, after a summary of recent experimental research dealing with "open" and "closed" systems of thought, Kemp (1962) found that rigidity and dogmatism militate against critical thinking, particularly when they are applied to an unfamiliar problem. Threats and dependence on authority were also characteristic of students having "closed belief systems." "Partyline thinker" is a phrase used to denote not only the individual who shows resistance to change, but also the one who can shift easily to new positions in response to authority. Kemp concluded that the research already completed suggests that critical thinking might be improved by using small groups in which the individual may feel greater security.

In an experiment conducted by Fitzgerald and Ausubel (1963), an effort was made to measure the influence of intellectual and emotional factors on the learning and retention of controversial material. For the purposes of the experiment, 264 junior students from a Midwestern high school were asked to read a Southern interpretation of the causes of the Civil War, which severely criticized the Lincoln administration and dealt with Northern acts of violence during the War. Hence the students were confronted with the problem of comprehending material which interpreted generally known data in a manner that was both unfamiliar and controversial. All groups were tested on attitudes and verbal reasoning ability, and the experimental group was given an explanatory, introductory passage setting forth the major differences between the Northern and Southern positions. The "organizer" or introductory passage for the control group discussed in a general way the background of conflicting Civil War interpretations. Subsequently the students studied the material and completed tests covering the points of difference in the Northern and Southern interpretations. One week later the subjects were tested for retention of the material.

The findings revealed that the experimental group had learned more than the others and that retention was clearly facilitated by the use of the introductory passage. Challenging earlier findings, the investigators concluded that the use of such introductions improved learning and retention of controversial subject matter, and that, when adequate controls are employed, the learning and retention of controversial materials are related positively to the cognitive rather than the affective aspect of attitudes.

Some of the recent conclusions concerning the political socialization of children raise pertinent questions about the utilization of controversial issues in the classroom. In an exploratory study of the political world of children by Easton and Hess (1962), drawing on a national sample of 12,000 elementary school children, it is emphasized that the critical years for the formation of political beliefs appear to be from three to thirteen. This inquiry also points out that prior to the eighth grade, children have acquired relatively fixed political views and values. The attitudes about American government held by children when they reach the seventh and eighth grades were found to be quite favorable but largely unsupported by a body of knowledge. That the attitudes of children suggest a romantic and idealistic view of American politics is a fact readily conceded by Easton and Hess, who also point out that the results of their inquiries thus far indicate that students are capable of accepting the vigorous partisanship and conflict of presidential campaigns without giving way to cynicism. They consider this experience with controversy a significant factor in the child's process of political socialization—a process which emphasizes the stability of government. Easton and Hess found that formal instruction about government and politics in high school exercised little influence on the students' previously formed values and attitudes.

Massialas (1962) has succinctly stated a problem faced by experimental research in the area of reflective or critical thinking: In their traditional preoccupation with the comparison of "subject-centered" and "reflectively-centered" methods researchers have failed to recognize that these methods may lack a common basis for comparison. This equating of the two methods is illustrated by the willingness of investigators who are concerned with critical thinking to accept the results of standardized tests of factual recall as a valid criterion of success in teaching critical thinking. Cox, Massialas, and Elsmere have rendered an important service, however, by their exploration of other methods of measuring learning in this field. They have suggested the development and utilization of new and varied strategies of inquiry.

While the theory of "cognitive dissonance" is still somewhat obscure, it does open up new avenues of investigation in the neglected field of motivation. The work of Fitzgerald and Ausubel, indicating that the notion that student bias hampers the retention of controversial materials may be incorrect, has direct bearing on social studies instruction. (The significance of carefully prepared introductions to highly controversial subject matter is readily apparent.) However, the conclusion of these investigators that cognitive dissonance may explain the fact that the more knowledgeable students (as determined by the pre-test) were susceptible to higher degrees of forgetting requires further examination.

Although the lines of inquiry pursued by Easton and Hess raise important questions about the efficacy of traditional instructional programs in both elementary and secondary school social studies in shaping attitudes, little information is available about the design of this research. It is perhaps ironic that the experience in dealing with controversy in a political campaign—deemed so important by the investigators—is not usually introduced by the instructor, but is rather imposed on the students by the mass media and popular enthusiasm.

THE COLD WAR AND EDUCATION IN ANTI-COMMUNISM

In recent months public preoccupation with the status of the Cold War between the United States and the U.S.S.R. has been reflected in increased demands for special courses about Communism, new techniques in instruction, and the preparation of new materials. Since the teaching of the subject of Communism has been by definition a controversial issue in American schools, an examination of recent studies of this trend appears relevant.

Metcalf (1963a), Mallery (1962), Schrag (1962), and Miller (1962) have studied the impact of militant courses and instructional materials in anti-Communism on the schools. Their findings testify to mounting pressures for vigorous indoctrination. Mallery has identified some of the procedures and suggested content currently being used to discourage or limit attacks on the schools. Noting the widespread appeal of anti-communist units and courses, Miller cites an unpublished study by the American Political Science Association that emphasized the inadequacies of the large majority of locally-prepared topics or units.

The question of what educational method to use in presenting controversial topics has been vigorously debated among teachers, professional educators, and academic specialists. Niemeyer (1962) and Hansen (1962) have unequivocally sanctioned indoctrination as an appropriate and inevitable method of instruction. "Thus with respect to communism," writes Niemeyer, "the problem is not so much to avoid indoctrination as to base indoctrination on the criteria of profound rationality" (p. 195). In contrast to these views, Petrovich rejects indoctrination as an undesirable form of education, and he advocates that teachers avoid the catechistic "know thy enemy" philosophy which is the antithesis of the Western tradition of liberal education. Martin (1962) charged that the current criticism of the alleged relationship of the right wing to Cold War educational programs was originally initiated by the General Secretary of the Communist Party USA and that this campaign against anti-Communism has been aided by national magazines, newspapers, television, radio, influential educational circles, and even government memoranda.

The response on the state level to public demands for more instruction on Communism has been studied by Gray (1964), who reported that only six states (of the 47 responding to a questionnaire) advised that they were making no special efforts to deal with the issue. Eight states either had statutory or mandatory state board of education requirements dealing with the subject of Communism; action on the state level in the remaining states may be described as follows: (1) schools are required to utilize recommended units or courses of study, (2) the state board has adopted a policy statement without recommended courses of study, or (3) units or courses of study are in preparation. (None of the seven Canadian provinces replying to the same inquiry indicated the use or preparation of programs in this field.) A further examination of the course objectives or "guidelines" provided by twenty-five states led Gray to the conclusion that while some programs employed a more temperate style than others, all seemed "clearly to aim at the indoctrination of youth with acceptable anti-communist views" (p. 80).

A significant and promising study was undertaken by Farrell (1963). He surveyed the attitudes of students toward their high school courses bearing on the U.S.S.R. and the communist challenge. On the basis of findings (in the pilot project), which are acknowledged as tentative, Farrell reported the appearance of certain categories of problems: (1) the tendency of administrations to evade requirements on Cold War education, (2) the re-direction or modification of courses by teachers to produce unintended results, (3) the presence of unsuitable course content or the presentation of inaccurate material or material inappropriate to a given grade level, and (4) expressions of hostility or indifference by students to excessively hortatory or dogmatic programs of Cold War education.

In spite of the fact that many of the studies dealing with the pressure on the schools to teach about Communism lack precision, it is clear that the present torrent of anti-communist literature poses a serious challenge to the autonomy of the social studies teacher. Much of the material has been judged miseducative or superficial by competent scholars, but, nevertheless, teachers continue to be under pressure to wage ideological warfare in the classroom. Strategies for meeting such pressures constructively are urgently needed. Various proposals, such as setting-up a "clearing house" for assessing materials on the basis of sound criteria, and teaching about the concept of totalitarianism (encompassing both the left and the right), rather than just about Communism, are constructive approaches which require implementation and evaluation.

Farrell's proposed research on the effects of Cold War instruction—when linked to present knowledge about the authoritarian personality and party-line thinking—presents social studies teachers with a challenging area for further inquiry.

SUMMARY

The following tentative conclusions are based on this survey of research bearing on the treatment of controversial issues: There is a marked unevenness in the quality of research in this field. In spite of the appearance of promising models of research, many so-called empirical studies suffer from the absence of an explicitly formulated theoretical frame of reference designed to lend significance to the results obtained. Some studies employ a highly technical style (appealing to the specialists in specific research fields) but fail to state any important implications for the curriculum. Some highly theoretical studies, on the other hand, make sweeping claims while paying little attention to the need for precision in the collection and interpretation of relevant data.

Nevertheless, certain approaches appear to have great potential value. In order to obtain valuable information about the interplay of forces at the community level, carefully constructed case studies might describe the decision-making processes derived from a study of significant clashes over academic freedom. Lazarsfeld, Fiske, Deam, Levine, and others have also shown the value of inquiries which explore in some depth the attitudes of teachers, librarians, and parents toward both the theory and practice of intellectual freedom. In examining the influence of controversy on learning, Massialas and Cox have pointed up the utility of observational techniques and the construction of models. Both Kemp and Farrell have directed the attention of researchers to important related questions concerning the consequences of dogmatic instruction in Cold War education and the characteristics of the "party-line thinker" or authoritarian personality in the classroom. Another crucial area of research emphasized by Wolfinger, Selakovich, and others is the expanding influence of anti-democratic extremist groups on American public education. The opinions of social studies teachers have not provided reliable information about the status of freedom of learning and teaching because teachers and school administrators, in general, appear to be unable or unwilling to recognize the forces in the community and nation which restrict freedom of inquiry.

Regarding the social role of the school and the function of the teacher in presenting controversial issues, the ambiguity and confusion revealed in earlier studies persist. In spite of the importance attached by educators to the task of bringing intellectual discipline to bear on the examination of crucial issues, teachers are frequently advised to postpone the treatment of such issues if the community is aroused. Thus, it appears that at the very moment when a rational, objective appraisal of a problem is desperately needed, teachers must submit to the dominant irrational mood of the community. This tends to support Lieberman's thesis that the totalitarian outlook is fostered by a system of local control, which apparently has no confidence in the professional abilities of its teachers.

It seems clear that vigorous, enlightened professional leadership is urgently needed, particularly in the field of policy development and implementation. The work of the NEA Commission on Professional Rights and Responsibilities provides a useful example, which might well be emulated by other influential groups of school administrators and teachers, who often seem unaware of the resources of this commission. Colleges and universities might cooperate with professional organizations on the state and local level in obtaining and disseminating reliable data on the methods of operation of extremist groups and techniques or policies for dealing with such groups.

The conventional social studies program has failed to measure up to the many sweeping claims contained in numerous statements of objectives. Indeed, the social studies still appear to be very much at the mercy of curriculum evangelism and powerful pressure groups. The professional social studies teacher seems to have little influence on the selection of content and the development of methods of instruction. This may, of course, be a reflection of the historically passive role played by the school in connection with the problems of social change. To what extent this situation may be altered by the growing militancy of teacher organizations is an interesting subject for speculation.

BIBLIOGRAPHY

Alexander, Albert. "The Gray Flannel Cover on the American History Textbook." *Social Education,* XXIV (1960), 11–14.

Alexander, William H., and J. Galen Saylor. *Modern Secondary Education.* New York: Holt, Rinehart and Winston, Inc., 1959, 765 pp.

Ballinger, Stanley E. "The Social Studies and Social Controversy." *School Review,* LXXI, (1963), 97–111.

Bardwell, Roger W. "Differences in Perception of Citizens and Teachers about Educational Issues." Unpublished Doctor's dissertation, University of Wisconsin. Abstracted in *Dissertation Abstracts,* XXI (1960), 1430.

Beale, Howard K. *Are American Teachers Free?* New York: Charles Scribner's Sons, 1936, 855 pp.

Bell, Daniel. *The End of Ideology.* New York: Collier Books, 1962, 474 pp.

Boyer, William H. "The Armed Forces as Educator," in *Proceedings of the Nineteenth Annual Meeting of the Philosophy of Education Society.* Lawrence, Kansas: School of Education, University of Kansas, 1963, 253 pp.

Brackenbury, Robert L. "The Case for Controversy." *The National Elementary Principal,* XLIII (1963), 14–19.

Brameld, Theodore. "What Is the Central Purpose of Education?" *Phi Delta Kappan,* XLIII (1961) 9–14.

Chandler, B. J. "Freedom of Inquiry Is in Jeopardy." *Phi Delta Kappan,* XLI (1960) 356–358.

Clark, Thomas D. "Serious Threats to American Education from Fanatic Fringes and Critics," Address given at NEA Convention, Detroit, Michigan, July 4, 1963. National Education Association, Washington, D.C., 8 pp. mimeographed.

Coan, Clark. "A Study of the Attitudes of Selected Social Studies Teachers and Parents of Kansas High School Students Regarding the Inclusion of Controversial Issues as Part of the Secondary School Social Studies Program." Unpublished Doctor's dissertation, University of Kansas, 1961. Abstracted in *Dissertation Abstracts,* XXII (1962), 2246.

Committee on Tenure and Academic Freedom. "The Freedom of the Public School Teacher." Washington, D.C.: National Education Association, 1951.

Cooper, John Elsworth. "An Analysis of Certain External Pressures Affecting Teaching and Curriculum in Selected Elementary Schools of Indiana." Unpublished Doctor's dissertation, Indiana University, 1959. Abstracted in *Dissertation Abstracts,* XX (1960), 3590–3591.

Cox, C. Benjamin. "A Description and Appraisal of a Reflective Method of Teaching United States History," in *The Indiana Experiments in Inquiry: Social Studies,* pp. 74–113, ed. Byron G. Massialas. Bloomington, Indiana: Bulletin of the School of Education, Indiana University, XXXIX, No. 3, 1963, 142 pp.

Deam, Calvin. "Opinion of Virginia Schoolmen Concerning the Treatment of Controversial Issues." Unpublished Doctor's dissertation, Indiana University, 1958, 357 pp.

Drabick, Lawrence W. "Perception of the Public School Teacher's Role as a Correlate of Social Position." Unpublished Doctor's dissertation, Pennsylvania State University. Abstracted in *Dissertation Abstracts,* XXI (1960), 2030.

Easton, David, and Robert D. Hess. "The Child's Political World." *Midwest Journal of Political Science,* VI (1962), 229–346.

"Economics in the Schools." *American Economic Review,* LIII, No. 1, supplement (1963), 1–27.

Ellsworth, Ralph E., and Sarah M. Harris. *The American Right Wing*. Washington, D.C.: Public Affairs Press, 1962, 63 pp.

Elsmere, Robert. "An Experimental Study Utilizing the Problem-Solving Approach," in *The Indiana Experiments in Inquiry*, pp. 114–139, ed. Byron G. Massialas. Bloomington, Indiana: Bulletin of the School of Education, Indiana University, XXXIX, No. 3, 1963, 142 pp.

Ennis, Robert H. "The Impossibility of Neutrality." *Harvard Educational Review*, XXIX (1959) 128–136.

Fadden, Joseph A. "A Critical Study of Current Concepts on Indoctrination in American Education." Unpublished Doctor's dissertation, The Catholic University of America, 1962. Abstracted in *Dissertation Abstracts*, XXIII (1963), 3187–3188.

Farrell, R. Barry. "Some Problems in Teaching about Communism," address given at the Conference on Cold War Education, Tampa, Florida, June 13, 1963.

Feldman, Edwin. "UNESCO and American Schools." Unpublished Doctor's dissertation, Stanford University, 1960. Abstracted in *Dissertation Abstracts*, XXI (1961), 2942–2943.

Fellman, David. *The Supreme Court and Education*. New York: Columbia University, Bureau of Publications, Teacher's College, 1960, 120 pp.

Festinger, Leon. *A Theory of Cognitive Dissonance*. Stanford, California: Stanford University Press, 1957, 291 pp.

Fiske, Marjorie. *Book Selection and Censorship*. Berkeley: University of California Press, 1960, 145 pp.

Fitzgerald, Donald, and David P. Ausubel. "Cognitive versus Affective Factors in the Learning and Retention of Controversial Material." *Journal of Educational Psychology*, LIV (1963), 73–84.

Fraser, Dorothy M. "Current Affairs, Special Events and Civic Participation," in *Social Studies in Elementary Schools*, ed. John U. Michaelis. Washington, D.C.: National Council for the Social Studies, 1962, 334 pp.

Getzels, Jacob W. "Conflict and Role Behavior in the Educational Setting," in *Readings in the Social Psychology of Education*, pp. 309–318, eds. W. W. Charters, Jr., and N. L. Gage. Boston: Allyn and Bacon, Inc., 1963, 350 pp.

Gray, Roland F. "Teaching about Communism: A Survey of Objectives." *Social Education,* XXVIII (1964), 71–72, 80.

Gross, Neal. *Who Runs Our Schools?* New York: John Wiley and Sons, Inc., 1958, 195 pp.

Hall, Truman L. "A Study of the Teaching of Controversial Issues in the Secondary Schools of Ohio." Unpublished Doctor's dissertation, University of Ohio, 1953, 253 pp.

Hansen, Carl F. "Teaching about Communism in the Schools," pp. 53–64, in *Education for Survival in the Struggle against Communism.* A Symposium Prepared for the Subcommittee to Investigate the Administration of the Internal Security Act and Other Internal Security Laws, Committee on the Judiciary, United States Senate, Eighty-Seventh Congress, second session. Washington, D.C.: U.S. Government Printing Office, 1962, 127 pp.

Hernandez, David E. "The Role of the High School as Perceived and Communicated by Parents and Teachers." Unpublished Doctor's dissertation, Florida State University. Abstracted in *Dissertation Abstracts,* XXIII (1962), 505.

Hullfish, H. Gordon, and Philip Smith. *Reflective Thinking: The Method of Education.* New York: Dodd, Mead & Company, 1961, 273 pp.

Iverson, Robert W. *The Communists and the Schools.* New York: Harcourt, Brace and Company, Inc., 1959, 423 pp.

Jordan, Kenneth Forbis. "An Analysis and Evaluation of Legislative Policy Concerning Public School Curriculum in Indiana." Unpublished Doctor's dissertation, Indiana University. Abstracted in *Dissertation Abstracts,* XXII (1961), 779.

Kemp, C. Gratton. "Critical Thinking: Open and Closed Minds." *The American Behavioral Scientist,* V (1962), No. 5.

Krug, Mark M. " 'Safe' Textbooks and Citizenship Education." *School Review,* LXVIII (1960), 463–480.

Lazarsfeld, Paul F., and Wagner Thielens, Jr. "Social Scientists and Recent Threats to Academic Freedom," in *Readings in the Social Psychology of Education,* pp. 291–308, eds., W. W. Charters, Jr., and N. L. Gage. Boston: Allyn and Bacon, Inc., 1963.

Levine, Daniel U. "Liberalism, Conservatism and Educational Viewpoint." *Administrator's Notebook,* XI, No. 9 (1963), 1–4.

Lieberman, Myron. *The Future of Public Education*. Chicago: University of Chicago Press, 1960, 294 pp.

Lipset, Seymour. "Three Decades of the Radical Right: Coughlinites, McCarthyites, and Birchers—1962 in *The Radical Right*, pp. 312–377, ed. Daniel Bell. New York: Doubleday and Company, Inc., 1963, 394 pp.

Lunstrum, John P. "An Inquiry into the Proper Role of the Social Studies Teacher with Reference to the Use of Controversy." Unpublished Doctor's dissertation, Indiana University, 1960, 410 pp.

—————. "Controversial Issues, School Policies and Reflective Thinking: Part II." *Social Education*, XXVI (1962), 224–227.

McMurrin, Sterling. "Education for Freedom in a Free Society," in *Education for Freedom and World Understanding*. Washington, D.C.: U.S. Department of Health, Education and Welfare, Office of Education, 1962, 62 pp.

Mallery, David. *Teaching about Communism*. Boston: National Association of Independent Schools, 1962, 72 pp.

Maloney, Joseph F. "The Lonesome Train in Levittown," Interuniversity Case Program. University, Alabama: University of Alabama Press, 1958, 19 pp.

Martin, Glenn R. "America's External-Internal Peril." *The Indiana Social Studies Quarterly*, XV, No. 2 (1962), 15–26.

Mason, Robert G. *Educational Ideals in American Society*. New York: Allyn and Bacon, Inc., 1960, 337 pp.

Massialas, Byron G. "Developing a Method of Inquiry in Teaching World History," in *The Indiana Experiments in Inquiry*, pp. 1–35, ed. Byron G. Massialas. Bloomington, Indiana: Bulletin of the School of Education, Indiana University, XXXIX, No. 3, 1963, 142 pp.

—————. *Research Prospects in the Social Studies*. Bloomington, Indiana: Bulletin of the School of Education, Indiana University, XXVIII, No. 1, 1962, 48 pp.

Metcalf, Lawrence E. "Anti-Communism: Education or Propaganda." *The Nation*, CXCIV (1963a), 215–216, 222.

—————. "Some Guidelines for Changing Social Studies Education." *Social Education*, XXVII (1963b), 197–201.

Miller, Richard I. "Teaching about Communism in the Public Schools." An address to the Annual Meeting of the Council of Chief State School Officers, November 21, 1962, Miami Beach, Florida.

Minott, Rodney G. *Peerless Patriots*. Washington, D.C.: Public Affairs Press, 1962, 152 pp.

Muller, Herbert J. *Issues of Freedom: Paradoxes and Promises*. New York: Harper and Row, Publishers, 1960, 170 pp.

National Education Association. Research Division. "Teaching Controversial Units." *NEA Journal*, LI (1962), 56.

Nelson, Jack, and Gene Roberts, Jr. *The Censors and the Schools*. Boston: Little, Brown and Company, 1963, 208 pp.

Niemeyer, Gerhart. "Problems of Teaching about Communism." *Phi Delta Kappan*, XLIII (1962), 193–196.

Park, Joe. "What Will You Have?" *Social Education*, XXIV (1960), 15–20.

Petrovich, Michael B. "Teaching about Russia and Eastern Europe," in *The Social Studies and the Social Sciences*, pp. 241–281, sponsored by the American Council of Learned Societies and the National Council for the Social Studies. New York: Harcourt, Brace and World, Inc., 1962, 303 pp.

Pounds, Ralph L., and James R. Bryner. *The School in American Society*. New York: The Macmillan Company, 1959, 518 pp.

Riggs, Wayne L. "The Utilization, Effectiveness, and Improvement of Written School Board Policies." Unpublished Doctor's dissertation, University of Nebraska Teachers College, 1960, 173 pp. Abstracted in *Dissertation Abstracts*, XXI (1960), 1444.

Roberts, Gene, Jr. "The Censors and the Schools." Address Given at the NEA Convention, Detroit, Michigan, July 4, 1963. Washington, D.C.: NEA, 1962, 7 pp. mimeographed.

Robinson, Donald W. "The Teachers Take a Birching." *Phi Delta Kappan*, XLIII (1962), 182–188.

Rossiter, Clinton. *Conservatism in America*. New York: Vintage Books, 1962, 306 pp.

Samalonis, Bernice Luch. "An Analysis of the Role of the State Legislature in Prescribing the Curriculum." Unpublished Doctor's dissertation, University of Illinois, 1962, 153 pp. Abstracted in *Dissertation Abstracts*, XXIII (1962), 499.

Schrag, Peter. "The True Blue Schoolhouse." *Commonweal,* LXXVI (1962), 226–228.

Selakovich, Dan. "The Techniques of Certain Pressure Groups Attempting to Influence the Teaching of American History and Government in the Secondary School, 1945–1960." Unpublished Doctor's dissertation, University of Colorado. Abstracted in *Dissertation Abstracts,* XXIII (1962), 1632–1633.

Shils, Edward A. *The Torment of Secrecy.* Glencoe, Ill.: The Free Press of Glencoe, Inc., 1956.

Starr, Isidore. "Recent Supreme Court Decisions: Freedom of Association of Teachers." *Social Education,* XXV (1962), 357–360.

Stocker, Joseph. *Thunder on the Right and Education.* Address Given at the NEA Convention, Denver, Colorado, 1962. Washington, D.C.: NEA, 1962, 7 pp. mimeographed.

Thayer, V. T. *The Role of the School in American Society.* New York: Dodd, Mead & Co., 1960, 529 pp.

"Teaching Controversial Units." NEA Research Division, *NEA Journal,* LI, No. 7 (1962), 56 pp.

"Treatment of Minority Groups in Textbooks." Publication 529, Lansing, Michigan: Department of Public Instruction (1963), 7 pp.

Westin, Alan F. "Anti-Communism and the Corporations." *Commentary,* XXXVI (1963), 479–487.

Wolfinger, Raymond. "Clientele of the Christian Anti-Communism Crusade," paper presented at the National Convention of the American Political Science Association, New York, September 4, 1963.

6

SELECTION AND USE OF TEXTBOOKS AND AUDIO-VISUAL MATERIALS

John R. Palmer
University of Illinois

This chapter has a threefold purpose: to list the topics on which research has been done in the last five years, to point up the implications of this research for social studies teaching and program development, and to indicate where additional research is needed. No effort has been made to present an exhaustive bibliography of recent research. In fact, some of the references can hardly be considered to be research at all, but their inclusion is justified because they are provocative and suggest questions that ought to be investigated systematically. On the other hand, many studies by authors who seriously attempted to "research" a problem have been excluded because the studies appeared to be concerned with trivial topics or very poorly designed.

TEXTBOOKS

Although the fact hardly needed further substantiation, Siemers (1959), in a survey of world-history courses in California schools, found that in over 90 percent of these courses a basic textbook was used. Half of the teachers used newspapers, periodicals, encyclopedias, and materials developed from other sources to supplement the basic text. Approximately one-fourth admitted that they never used paperbacks, one-third never used radio or TV, and over half never used other texts as sources for instructional materials; at the same time, more than one-third of the teachers in the sample considered poor instructional resources a major problem. These data indirectly introduce a paradox that runs throughout this section. Although the recent literature pertaining to social studies textbooks is severely critical of them, giving the impression that textbooks may shortly disappear from the social studies classroom, it is difficult to locate a social studies classroom without a textbook. While there are many dissatisfactions with textbooks, most teachers evidently do not like the possible alternatives or are unable to take advantage of them.

Although many teachers criticize social studies textbooks, they evidently fail to look elsewhere for basic materials to put in the hands of students. A textbook rarely is able to provide all the necessary content for a social studies class. Admittedly the search for other materials can be quite time-consuming, and it is a task that continues as long as one teaches; but it is a necessary part of the building and revising process that goes into every effective social studies course.

EVALUATING AND SELECTING A TEXTBOOK

Selecting a textbook for use in the classroom continues to be a necessary task. Brown and Brown (1961) and Massialas (1961) were among those who reported on the dimensions that should be considered in the selection process. They considered such matters as the readability of the material, the appropriateness of the material to the age of the student, the accuracy and completeness of presentation, and the handling of controversial issues. Such lists usually contain the following: a basic set of items that virtually everyone would agree upon, and a few items that determine whether or not the book is appropriate for developing the particular aims of social studies teaching accepted by the author of the list of criteria. These lists are primarily reports of the opinions of the authors with little empirical or theoretical justification to support them. While the approaches taken by Brown and Brown and Massialas appear to have been developed with particular care, in many instances the choice of one set of criteria rather than another is largely a matter of personal preference. Presentations of this sort are of limited assistance in selecting a social studies textbook beyond the avoidance of gross inadequacies. That even these gross measures are often overlooked was demonstrated by Lawrence (1961), who found that in a sample of California high schools 73 percent of the districts reported they had no stated guidelines for textbook selection. Many teachers and administrators stated that the textbooks selected had not been carefully examined, and that the selection process had little relation to the program of curriculum development. It is obvious that in most schools the textbook is second only to the teacher in shaping the curriculum. It should be chosen to fit in with the pattern of a carefully planned curriculum. When textbooks are not carefully chosen, there is apt to be much confusion, repetition of content year after year, significant gaps in the knowledge of the students, and a general lack of direction in the total social studies program. Before selecting a textbook, teachers should clarify the objectives of the course, the role of the textbook in the development of these objectives, the teaching methods or strategies that will be employed, and the characteristics of a textbook that will serve these ends. At present some subjective judgments will be involved because techniques for assessing many aspects of textbooks have not been developed. This is particularly true of the areas of critical thinking, problem solving, and the normative content of textbooks, which includes the treatment of controversial issues.

READABILITY LEVEL AND READING DIFFICULTIES

There is considerable evidence that many students may be unable to read the social studies textbooks they are assigned. Berry (1961) found that the vocabulary load of a fourth-grade state-adoption text in geography was too heavy for the average fourth grader. Millis (1959) selected terms from the social studies textbooks being used by fifth graders and tested the students' comprehension of those terms. A significant number of the terms were not understood by most of the students. Sloan (1959) used the popular Dale-Chall formula to test the readability level of social studies textbooks for grades four, five, and six. Approximately half of the books were inappropriate for the grade level assigned by the publisher. The readability of questions, activities, and projects was particularly questionable. There was little continuity within and between textbooks in a given series offered by a publisher. Haffner (1959) introduced into his analysis elements of particular significance to the social studies. In addition to establishing the reading grade level of the fifth- and sixth-grade textbooks he analyzed, he compiled a list of concepts having social significance, determined the social concept "burden" of each book, and developed an objective method for comparing the social concept "burden" of two or more textbooks. He concluded that the fifth- and sixth-grade books in his sample contained excessive vocabulary loads and concept burdens.

While these findings are significant and perhaps even disturbing, as Arnsdorf (1963) is careful to point out readability formulas are very limited in scope. They are statistical devices that are not sensitive to variations in meaning among words and larger thought units. In evaluating a textbook for a particular classroom, a number of other factors—such as the place of the text in the total learning situation, the attention given to vocabulary development, the teacher, and the ability and experience of the learner—need to be considered. At the same time that the charge is being made that the content of the social studies has been "watered down" and is lacking in substance, these studies show that many textbooks presently in use are in certain respects too difficult for an appreciable portion of the student population.

One purpose of each successive exposure to any school subject is to increase the student's level of concept development and understanding. Those who would like to see textbooks made more difficult point out that there is little to be gained from presenting material that does not push students beyond their present level of understanding. The teacher must assume some responsibility, however, for assisting the student in this process of advancement. He should make use of the excellent remedial-reading books available, which include very specific suggestions, many of which are supported by research, for helping the poor reader use a textbook. Each of the subject fields represented within the social studies has a unique vocabulary. The social studies teacher must assist the student, whether he is a good reader or not, in comprehending a textbook that requires a specialized vocabulary, as well as specialized skills in reading maps and charts. Vocabulary development is primarily a matter of introducing and teaching concepts. These concepts are necessary for reading social studies material with understanding; they also form a major part of the basic knowledge to be taught in the social studies. In this sense, improving the students' reading comprehension involves nothing less than teaching part of the essential knowledge of the course. When viewed in this manner, vocabulary development takes on great significance; for concepts are basic tools of thought, essential to all problem solving and further learning in general.

Another reading skill—critical appraisal of what is read—has been reported by Lourie (1960). Disturbed that many students regard a textbook as an authority beyond reproach, Lourie has tried to teach them to apply the skills of critical reading to textbook study. Although there is no evidence of a research design, Lourie's problem is an important one, and his suggestions seem appropriate for classroom use. The basic approach is one of textbook reading under the teacher's guidance. Appropriate passages are subjected to very careful scrutiny by students in order to determine the meaning of concepts, to evaluate the interpretations made by authors, to check the author's facts against other sources, and generally to clarify the meaning of the passage. The ability to evaluate written or spoken communication is a particularly necessary element in the common experience of members of our society because of the constant assaults upon logical thinking put forward in the mass media.

CRITICAL ANALYSES OF TEXTBOOKS

No textbook has been or ever will be satisfactory to everyone. This is particularly true in the social studies, in part because much of the content appeals to the emotions and stirs the patriotic, religious, racial, or moral fervor of the reader. The pace of criticism has undoubtedly quickened in recent years. Much of the current criticism may come from special-interest or patriotic groups interested in furthering their particular set of values or ideas. An effort has been made to eliminate them from this summary.

A number of commentaries on social studies textbooks have expressed general dissatisfaction with their nature or content. Occupying an administrative position in a major city school system, Alexander (1960) was required to read and evaluate much of the social studies material presently available. Although he acknowledged that the newer textbooks are "attractive, voluminous, profusely and arrestingly illustrated," he was highly critical of the content and scholarship they displayed, noting that they remain "strangely dull, lifeless, and bear striking resemblance to each other." Furthermore, he found that the authors of these books demonstrate undue caution and are generally unwilling to take firm stands on controversial issues.

Bragdon (1962), although focusing primarily on the broad problem of social studies curriculum, made frequent references to inadequacies relating to text materials. Too often, geography consists of "learning inert facts about climate, topography, and resources," United States history includes a "strong dose of patriotic indoctrination," and civics deals with the structure of government but very little with the process. Bragdon suggested that there is need for a unifying body of concepts and ideas and a definitive structure in the social studies. These would undoubtedly require very different textbooks from those now in use.

In another general appraisal of the curriculum, Patterson (1962) concurred in Alexander's contention that history textbooks appear to dodge controversy and as a result are "tiresome, mechanical, and shallow."

It is difficult to assess the validity of the comments made by writers such as Alexander, Bragdon, and Patterson. Their reactions are representative of a host of similar commentaries that have been published or spoken recently. Although most of these people have not set out to study textbooks in a systematic fashion and have not developed explicit evaluative criteria, they are authorities in the social studies and they do continually read and work with textbooks. Although, on these grounds, it seems reasonable to give serious attention to their comments, the usefulness of these comments proves to be limited because they give little insight into the basic flaws in history textbooks.

Other, more explicit, studies typically focus on one or more specific aspects of social studies material, e.g., treatment of controversial issues, inclusion of sociological concepts, consideration of non-Western areas, development of critical-thinking skills, etc. Textbooks currently in use in the schools have been analyzed in detail and evaluated for their treatment of the aspects in question. Again, there is the danger that the researcher was only trying to lend support to a belief about textbooks that he had already accepted. In many instances, the weight given the findings must be based on an evaluation of the writer's competence and integrity as a scholar rather than on a clearly developed plan of textbook evaluation.

Krug (1960, 1961a,b) made a series of studies of textbooks. His basic conclusion was that our textbooks do not reflect the changing objectives of the social studies or take into account new research and insights into the learning process. He agreed with Patterson, Alexander, and others that many significant social and political issues are glossed over in an exaggerated effort to be objective. One result of this glossing over of significant issues is that little critical or clear thinking is permitted. In Krug's view, this soft-pedaling of controversial issues amounts to the avoidance of "a clear-cut commitment to the fundamental democratic rights and to the obligation to work for the betterment of our democratic society." Although he believes that much text material is well written and well chosen, the treatment of controversial issues is not only deplorable, it is a threat to the future of our society. Krug's investigation of textbooks appears to have been highly personal in design and execution. He has given little indication of his research design, and he has not clarified some of the basic concepts employed in his study, such as "clear thinking" or "the learning process."

Krug has also claimed that at very crucial points many textbooks include something less than the truth as it is seen by the best scholarship now available; "best scholarship" is again defined on the basis of personal criteria mainly derived from historical method and material. What Krug and others fail to discuss, however, is the role of the teacher in the teaching of crucial social issues, a role which is determined in part by the social-emotional nature of the students, the community of values and mores, and the teacher's own ethical commitments. Noah, Prince, and Riggs (1962) examined eleven popular United States history textbooks and came to the same conclusion as Krug; that is, instead of making use of recent historical research, most textbooks continue to include stereotyped or chauvinistic accounts of events in our past. The researchers looked carefully at the treatments of the Revolutionary period, the Civil War, and the Cold War and found all wanting. They concluded that the students are being dangerously "brainwashed" by the perpetuation of myths. This inadequacy enormously increases the task of the teacher, who must attempt to counteract the harmful effects of these textbooks by presenting more defensible interpretations.

Robbins (1961) was particularly concerned about the treatment given Asia in geography and history textbooks. He gained three main impressions from a detailed investigation of a very limited sample: (1) the space devoted to Asia was inadequate; (2) the most crucial problems of contemporary Asia—poverty, hunger, political instability, economic weakness, vulnerability to Communism, and the population explosion—were either overlooked or poorly handled; and (3) the general impression left in the mind of the reader—of inevitable progress and a bright future for all of Asia—was at least misleading, if not demonstrably false. The historical sketches were accurate, although occasionally inconsequential; but the description and analysis of the contemporary situation were extremely unrealistic and naive.

Bragdon (1962) and Patterson (1962) both expressed concern over the role of the social sciences, as distinct from history, in the total curriculum. They indicated that economics, sociology, anthropology, social psychology, and related fields have little place as yet in the curriculum and therefore in textbooks as well. The most extensive recent study of this problem has been reported by the Textbook Committee of the Committee on Economic Education of the American Economic Association (1963). Thirteen professional economists examined twenty-four popular high school textbooks in the fields of economics, social problems, and United States history to assess their economic content. They concluded "that the high school student whose knowledge of economics has been acquired through courses circumscribed by . . . [these] . . . textbooks . . . would be quite unprepared to cope understandingly with most problems of economic policy." More specifically, they found that (1) the emphasis is on understanding consumer economics rather than on understanding the functioning of an economic system; (2) much that is significant is omitted, much that is included is relatively unimportant; (3) routine descriptions of how the economic system operates are more common than analysis of cause and effect relations, etc.; (4) when value judgments are made, they are not identified or examined as such; and (5) some errors of fact and analysis are present. In sum, descriptive and narrative material dominated the textbooks to such an extent that little opportunity was given for critical thinking, understanding, or the developing and testing of hypotheses.

Other studies have tried to ascertain the extent to which geographic generalizations are presented in world history, American history, and geography textbooks for use in grades seven through twelve. After reviewing forty-three such books, Langhans (1961) concluded that world history and United States history textbooks include few direct statements of geographic generalizations, although the United States history books did make considerable reference to social geographical generalizations.

Hanvey (1961) was concerned about the same shortcomings of social studies texts but on somewhat different grounds. He found that the textbooks were not making use of the analytical and explanatory devices now available. The explanation of historical events and human behavior was clearly inadequate and gave the reader little opportunity for examining and understanding the complexities of social action. Palmer (1960) noted similar shortcomings in a study of the explanations of social change given in a large sample of history textbooks. The analysis of human behavior from concepts and generalizations developed in the several social sciences was very frequently absent or poorly presented. As a result, the student has little opportunity to gain understanding of the processes of social change and historical development. He is forced to conclude that somehow things just happen or that some unseen and unknown force is at work moving men and nations.

There continues to be an interest in the manner in which textbooks treat other cultures, although the most recent studies merely confirm earlier findings. Smith (1959) analyzed the treatment of other cultures in 406 stories included in basal readers for the elementary school to determine how well they realized the objective of acceptance of world neighbors. A number of distortions and inadequacies were apparent: minority groups with picturesque customs were more often portrayed than others; many illustrations and examples were not true or realistic; some stories portrayed countries as they never have been; many had children in other cultures act like American children; and past and present realities were often confused.

Provincialism and cultural bias continue to be problems at all levels of schooling. Attempts to simplify the subject matter and to arouse the student's interest are undoubtedly at the root of much of the difficulty. There is a temptation to stress the quaint and the startling in other cultures in order to stimulate students to read and discuss social studies material. Distortions are apt to creep in when an effort is made to cover many nations or geographic areas in a relatively short time. The result is that a very complex subject is dealt with quite superficially. There is a further possibility. The teacher may not be aware that his own understanding of other cultures is inadequate and inaccurate. Few social studies teachers have been or are being prepared to teach any cultures except those in the Graeco-Roman—Western European stream of development. Teachers generally have little to add to the text materials concerning non-Western cultures. There is need for inservice training programs, intensive individual study, and revision of teacher-training curricula to alleviate this situation.

SUGGESTIONS FOR CHANGING TEXTBOOKS

The UNESCO *Handbook for the Improvement of Textbooks and Teaching Materials* (1949), while not new, remains one of the most useful overviews of the subject of textbook revision. A significant recent development has been the emphasis on social science generalizations in social studies teaching and materials. (A generalization is a statement of a relationship between two or more events or phenomena.) Many teachers apparently believe that generalizations are difficult to grasp and therefore are out of place except at the advanced levels of education. Very few standardized or teacher-constructed tests evaluate the students' understanding of or ability to use generalizations. Beaubier (1962) attempted to teach sixth-grade students three relatively sophisticated generalizations. Although it is possible the Hawthorne effect was at work, Beaubier's study showed statistically significant differences between the experimental group, which emphasized the development of a set of generalizations, and the control group, which stressed the more typical descriptive, factually oriented approach. The findings showed that the experimental group had a better grasp of the material under consideration. He concluded that children at the sixth-grade level can probably understand more complex ideas and generalizations than we generally expect. In this particular experiment, the result was obtained through the use of a variety of instructional materials rather than a single textbook.

A number of research studies have been conducted on the assumption that generalizations are significant in the social studies and that they can and should be taught. Nash (1962), Weaver (1962), Geer (1959), Ross (1959), and Hofstrand (1959) were among those seeking to ascertain what generalizations could be formulated to make up the content of the social studies. Using a jury technique, Nash got wide consensus on the value of a set of sociological generalizations in achieving the commonly accepted goals of the social studies. Ross conducted research on the problem in the field of geography, Weaver in United States history, Geer for the topic of conservation of human and natural resources, and Hofstrand for the material dealing with creating tools, technics, and social arrangements. In many of these studies the crucial logical and linguistic dimensions for generalizing about social phenomena have been overlooked or poorly understood. Considerable assistance in these matters has been provided by Nagel (1961), Hughes (1960), Metcalf (1962), and Gottschalk (1963).

Implicit in the current interest in social science generalizations is the assumption that knowledge that is potentially capable of serving as a guide to action and influencing behavior—i.e., most likely to transfer from the learning situation to other situations—is *knowledge that is general*. Functionally, in the decision-making process, it appears that the use of the social studies requires generalizations, concepts, values or attitudes, and techniques. There must be common factors in past, present, and future situations if social science knowledge is to be useful in the daily life of the citizen. Generalizations make these common factors explicit and point the way to appropriate behavior in the light of these factors.

Social scientists and historians do not agree on the importance of generalizations in their fields. Many social scientists see the development of generalizations as one of their primary research objectives. Historians, however, although they use generalizations extensively, do not define their research activities in such a way that the formation of generalizations is one of their aims. However, in order to construct a narrative and relate events sequentially, the historian does use generalizations about life in society, ranging from the traditional truisms to theorems and abstract models of the social sciences.

There is little place at present in the social studies for universal truths, generalizations that may be stated in the form "If and only if . . ." We must recognize, and learn to be emotionally content with, probabilistic generalizations that are subject to revision and the possibility of exception. We must accept the fact that causal associations are tentative, open-ended, and subject to continuous analysis and reconstruction.

Once a social studies teacher understands the nature of generalizations and the role they play, he has the further problem of dealing with them in the classroom. When, at what age level, is it appropriate to introduce generalizations? How does one teach an understanding of a generalization? What is involved in the testing of a generalization? How much time should be devoted to the teaching of generalizations in relation to the other cognitive elements taught in the social studies? Very little empirical research is available on these matters.

The attention now being given to the structure of the social sciences and history will undoubtedly be very profitable. However, it may be that expectations are unduly high for quick and revolutionary results. Many basic concepts in the social sciences are as yet not clearly defined; research techniques and other fundamental methodological dimensions have been developing rapidly, but there is not wide agreement on them; and the scholars in the several fields not only talk past each other, they often have little respect for one another. While much will be learned in grappling with the idea of structure, the end result may be quite different from that envisioned by some enthusiasts at present. The social studies teacher would do well to keep in touch with the research in this area. It is possible that the investigations into generalizations and concepts in the social sciences will result in a complete overhaul of the curriculum. If this occurs, it will mean very different textbooks and other resource materials.

The criticisms of textbooks presented earlier in this chapter also point toward possible changes. Recent research has emphasized three areas where change is particularly needed: (1) more extensive use of the content of such social sciences as economics, sociology, anthropology, and social psychology; (2) more scholarly, up-to-date, accurate, and realistic text materials; and (3) frank and direct consideration of controversial issues. Although some of the newer textbooks have been responsive to these criticisms, there is also evidence that powerful forces are at work to preserve the *status quo* and prevent significant changes in textbooks in the directions indicated. This means, of course, that the teacher interested in promoting these trends will have to introduce supplementary content into the classroom and not rely entirely on a textbook.

A number of influences prevent more attention being given the social sciences as distinct from history: (1) history has traditionally been the dominant subject in the social studies, and therefore it need not justify its presence; (2) most social studies teachers have been trained primarily in history, they are psychologically committed to history, and they quite naturally wish to teach what they have been prepared to teach; (3) the curriculum is already overcrowded, so that it is extremely difficult to make room for a new course or different content; and (4) experts in the several social sciences have been reluctant to devote their energies to the preparation of materials for use in the schools. As a result, little high-quality material is available.

It is difficult to be certain where the blame rests for the inaccuracies and lack of up-to-date scholarship in textbooks. In part, these defects appear to be the fault of the demands placed on authors by some publishers, but it certainly reflects the unwillingness of university scholars in the subject fields to assist in the preparation of school textbooks. The very nature of social studies courses—the effort to cover ground, the demand for exposure to a traditional set of events or facts, the survey approach—makes it very difficult to avoid cursory textbook presentations that are almost certain to be superficial and full of half truths. There is the further difficulty of the controversial and highly emotional nature of some social studies content. Public agencies in the United States frequently attempt to avoid offending any section of the population. Authors of textbooks used in public schools strive to achieve ethical neutrality by "sticking to the facts." In the process, of course, they avoid many very pertinent facts and present to the reader a distorted picture of social reality. As Lawrence Metcalf and others have pointed out, it is impossible to teach students social understanding and engage them in critical analysis of social issues if certain social truths are kept from them. Of course, a textbook which presents a distorted picture can be very useful in teaching if the teacher is aware of the distortion and knows how to capitalize on it in the classroom. Certainly it is stretching things a bit to rationalize the adoption of unscholarly, distorted textbooks on the grounds that, in the hands of a skilled teacher, some benefit can be derived from such material. The very minimum requirements for a social studies textbook are that it be up-to-date, accurate, and reflect sound scholarship.

There is now considerable speculation about the future of the textbook, at least in its traditional form. Teacher and student may soon be provided with a system or articulated set of instructional materials which employs a great variety of media for presenting ideas and information to the learner. In such an approach, the place of the textbook would be greatly diminished.

THE PROGRAMMED TEXTBOOK AND AUTO-INSTRUCTIONAL MATERIALS

The most obvious challenge to the traditional textbook has developed from the spectacular growth of machined and programmed instruction. Self-instructional materials are a crude form of the Socratic question-and-answer method of teaching. They proceed in small steps of graded difficulty, so that concepts, understandings, and skills are gradually mastered as the learner works through the program. A great quantity of material on auto-instructional learning has been published within the last five years. Although the method in its present form is quite new, a number of books, articles, and bibliographies provide educators with a general introduction to the theory and practice of programmed instruction. Lumsdaine and Glaser (1960) and Rigney and Fry (1961) are excellent examples. It is not our purpose here to repeat or attempt to improve upon these extensive treatments of the subject. It may be appropriate, however, to review certain aspects of research in programming that are particularly pertinent to the social studies.

One preliminary general observation seems in order after reviewing the research. Many fundamental issues have not been satisfactorily clarified. Generally, given the rather narrow teaching objectives that most classroom experiments have set forth, auto-instructional devices "work," but little is known as to why we get the results from them we do. Even more disturbing is the problem of broadening the learning objectives to include all significant categories. At present, programmed instruction may be giving us a false conception of knowledge and its uses. Knowledge, in the form of items of information and association, is emphasized, but other forms of knowledge and the various roles of knowledge in intellectual endeavors are neglected. Intuitive or creative thinking and the various forms of reflective thinking are generally not evaluated.

The problems just raised may be more disturbing to social studies teachers than to most other educators, because the production and use of programmed materials in the social studies lags far behind most other major subject fields. In 1962 only seven programs were available from commercial publishers. Of the schools using programmed materials in 1963, 61 percent were using them in mathematics while 3 percent were using them in social studies. Typical subjects are "How a Bill Goes through Congress," "Parliamentary Procedure," and "The United Nations." The potential buyer is not told who was responsible for the frames, how many children were tested, or who was involved in the experimentation. Apparently the high standards that have been developed for the preparation of standardized tests have not been transferred to the preparation of programmed materials, although they could potentially influence millions of students.

As might be expected, there have been few experiments conducted on the use of programmed materials in the social studies. Those noted below appear to have been well done within the present limitations of such research. Wood (1962) compared groups of ninth-grade geography students: one group received a combination of programmed material and teacher-led instruction; other classes received only teacher-led instruction. The students using programmed materials learned factual material significantly better than those entirely under the direction of the teacher. Although students in the experimental group scored higher, there was no significant difference in the ability of pupils to apply factual knowledge. Wood suggested that the use of teacher-led activities to learn factual material may be unnecessary and inefficient. The question remains, however, as to how much and what sorts of learning can be effectively programmed.

Ingham (1962) experimented with two types of self-instruction in eighth-grade United States history. One group of students used a programmed text, work sheets for use with filmstrips and viewers, and work sheets for tape-recorded presentations. Another group combined these same experiences with small-group teacher-pupil conferences. A third group employed "conventional" classroom practices with a textbook and teacher-led discussion. The differences in instructional effects of the methods employed in teaching the three groups as evaluated by an objective achievement test were not statistically significant.

The American Institute for Research (1962) attempted to find the best of several possible ways of combining programmed instruction with standard classroom procedures. The experiment dealt with a one-month unit on "The Structure and Function of the Federal Government." The experimenters concluded that students were enthusiastic about the new materials and that their use substantially increased the amount of learning that took place. However, the evaluation instruments were primarily measures of information acquired rather than understanding.

The great number of "no-significant-difference" findings in the research on programmed instruction raises the possibility that the critical variables have not been isolated. The results of many studies comparing the use of conventional methods with programmed instruction are confusing and conflicting. It is often very easy to question the research design. Often, very short programs are administered to small groups of highly motivated students who viewed the program as a test. There is particular need for tested materials, for greater attention to the retention rather than merely the acquisition of learning, and for a greater emphasis on specifying the behavioral goals of education.

Many theoretical and practical problems remain, but the eventual gain from the intense current interest in this type of instruction may be appreciable. Programming has drawn attention to the details of the stimulus series in teaching and to its internal logic. Programmed materials must, therefore, be exceptionally lucid and well structured. Regardless of what form research may eventually demonstrate to be best for presenting knowledge to the learner, learning outcomes will probably be more effective because of the experience of preparing auto-instructional materials.

AUDIO-VISUAL MATERIALS

For purposes of this review, the term "audio-visual aids" has been restricted in meaning to such special kinds of communication devices as motion pictures, filmstrips, television, radio, recordings, graphic illustrations, and models. Because the research dealing exclusively with audio-visual materials in the social studies is quite limited, considerable reference will be made to research which has implications for the social studies as well as other subject areas. Particular attention is given to research directly involving social studies materials where this is available. The framework and conclusions suggested by Allen (1959) have been relied on for the organization of much of the material that follows.

TEACHING FACTUAL INFORMATION

Motion pictures, television, filmstrips, and slides can teach arbitrary associations at least as effectively as conventional classroom techniques over a wide range of subject matter, age levels, abilities, and conditions of use. Retention appears to be at least as good as for conventional teaching. Wendt and Butts (1960) tested a series of 54 world-history films in grade nine in seven schools. Experimental classes saw the films while the control groups did not. The classes using films completed the course in one semester while the control groups took two semesters. A test primarily of factual information given immediately after instruction showed no significant difference between the two types of instruction. Cottle (1960) used the same design but on high and low achievers. The experimental materials were equally effective for both groups. McBeath (1961) used twenty matched sixth-grade classes to test four ways of presenting a social studies lesson: (a) a silent captioned filmstrip, (b) a captioned filmstrip with a recorded narration, (c) a 16-millimeter sound filmograph, and (d) a sound filmstrip with a filmograph sound track. Information tests given immediately after the showing and after some lapse of time showed no significant difference among the four groups.

Little useful research in teaching of information has been conducted with other media such as radio, recordings, still pictures, graphics, stereographs, and models. A few interesting attempts have been made, however, and some go beyond the teaching of factual information. English (1961) found that in the fields of science and arithmetic at the second- and fifth-grade levels there was no significant difference in the amount of learning from black and white as compared with colored instructional materials. (The production costs of colored instructional materials is nearly eight times that of black and white materials.) Georgiady (1959) identified the effect of the use of motion-picture films, filmstrips, and other projected pictures on vocabulary growth in social studies for grades six, seven, and eight. Control groups used certain audio-visual aids but nothing that projected pictures. The results demonstrated that the careful use of projected pictures in several forms significantly increased vocabulary growth. Devine (1961) developed and evaluated a series of recorded lessons designed to promote growth in certain critical listening abilities in the ninth grade: recognizing a speaker's bias, recognizing his competence, distinguishing between statements of fact and opinion, recognizing a speaker's inferences, and distinguishing between reportive and emotive language. Ten recorded lessons were developed and given to large experimental groups. The growth in critical listening abilities was statistically significant for the experimental groups. Goodman (1962), on the basis of trials and with the assistance of expert observers, prepared a handbook of suggestions for the use of sound-recorded dramatic episodes in cultivating the ability to understand social interaction. Thus, there is some evidence that films and other media can develop concepts and teach critical thinking, but much more research is needed.

INFLUENCING ATTITUDES, OPINIONS, AND MOTIVATIONS

From the limited research on the ability of various audio-visual aids to influence attitudes, opinions, and motivations, only tentative conclusions can be made. There is evidence that motion pictures, television, and radio can influence attitudes, opinions, and motivations if the messages they carry stimulate or reinforce existing beliefs of the audience. However, audiences probably require repeated exposure to prevent them from returning to their previous position. Change probably will not result if the messages are contrary to the existing beliefs, personality structure, or social environment of the audience. Although the subject matter was only indirectly related to social studies, studies by Merrill (1962) and McAshan (1962) on the effectiveness of films on safety appear to have significance in this field. Both studies, which were concerned with the value of films on safety in actually changing the viewer's attitudes, were carefully designed and executed. Merrill's procedure was designed to measure the shift in saliency and the change in the cognitive component of attitude structure of those who viewed one of two types of films on safety. The experiment was not conducted in a classroom situation. A content analysis of the films used suggested that they did not directly change the affective component of attitude structure. The initial result of the viewing of an attitude film appeared to be a change in the cognitive component. Such films are often dramatic in form, and when they arouse strong fears in the viewer, defensive avoidance (of the affective component) occurs.

This mechanism prevents attitude change. McAshan was interested in developing a predictive instrument which would assist in analyzing films for their potential to change attitudes. The successful completion of this sort of research could be very helpful in the social studies, for while many teachers attempt to change students' attitudes, they have little knowledge of what materials and procedures are most likely to be successful. The problem of assessing the impact of film content on viewer behavior was spelled out in detail by Twyford, McAshan, Messier, and Rowley (1959). They sought to determine what factors induce changed behavior and how these factors can be manipulated. While their research is not definitive, it is worthy of extended treatment because of the cognitive dimensions with which it deals.

Twyford and associates combined a careful theoretical analysis of the problem of effecting changes in behavior with a series of experiments using a highway-safety film to test their hypotheses. They listed every fact presented in the film and analyzed the facts to determine how much learning could be expected for various target audiences. The facts were placed into four categories: background, unimportant, learnable, and behavioral. Background and unimportant facts were those not intended to be learned, so they could be ignored as factors in behavioral change. The two remaining categories consisted of the information which the film purported to transmit to the viewer. The most important of these were the behavioral, for it was assumed that these at least had the potential of bringing about a behavior change in the viewer.

The reactions of the viewers were also analyzed. How a message was received depended on the previous experience of the viewer and on the facts he brought to bear on the message. Twyford found that people just learning to drive were prone to accept information given them as correct and final, while experienced drivers were much more selective with regard to the information given them because of the information they already had dealing with the subject under consideration.

After experimenting with five safety films, Twyford concluded that very little behavior change could be attributed to them. The critical factors in effecting a change in behavior appeared to be the personal judgment of the viewer and his observations of other people's behavior.

There was a great difference in the effect of films on groups with varying amounts of experience. New drivers learned a great deal and
responded with correct behavior, but very frequently they changed
again as the result of observing incorrect behavior on the part of others.
The effect of safety films on experienced drivers was negligible.

The investigators speculated that, because most films must be sold
nationwide and must conform to standardized norms of behavior,
the behavior pattern they recommend deviates radically from actual
behavior, and, hence, the information provided has little impact. Viewers tend to see the desired behavior as ludicrous or unrealistic. Similarly,
the many studies done in the armed forces show that attitudinal films
have little or no effect on behavior.

Many statements of social studies teaching objectives place
changed behavior as the ultimate aim of the program. It is a truism that
no learning has taken place if changed behavior has not resulted. The
research now available indicates that, worthy as the goal of changing
behavior may be, we are presently operating largely at the level of
hunch and conjecture when it comes to planning for achieving this goal.
The information that is available tends to be largely negative—it
indicates that many of the experiences we use to bring about behavior
change apparently miss the mark rather badly. The basic need is for
experimentation to establish cause-and-effect or functional relationships
between various learning experiences and the resultant response on the
part of the learner. Twyford's study offers assistance in planning the
needed research.

INSTRUCTIONAL USE OF
AUDIO-VISUAL AIDS

Considerable attention has been given to techniques of using the
various media in the classroom. There is adequate research in support of
the following classroom practices: (1) preparation of the class on the
part of the teacher for the audio-visual materials to be used; (2) student
participation in conjunction with audio-visual lessons; and (3) the
exposure of students to the communication two or more times. These
findings imply that audio-visual materials are only teacher aids. A few

experiments have demonstrated that motion pictures and television can completely take over the teaching role with no loss of information gain.

Some of the most important factors contributing to audio-visual effectiveness lie in the characteristics of the audience. In this regard a few principles have been demonstrated: (1) the ability to learn from visual materials develops with increased exposure; (2) the predisposition of the learner toward the subject influences his acceptance and interpretation of it; and (3) the student's learning ability is not a significant factor. Cottle (1960) investigated the efficiency of teaching procedures involving motion-picture films in high school world history. He found that the amount of learning that takes place is influenced by the way a film is presented, the teacher's enthusiasm, the appropriateness of the film, and the time at which it is shown.

Some articles, usually the ones based on classroom trial-and-error procedures rather than controlled experiments, report ideas for using paintings, music, maps, microfilms, and a great variety of other materials to increase motivation and learning in social studies classes. The limits to the ingenious ways one can make use of audio-visual aids in the classroom are set only by the far reaches of the human imagination. One issue of an audio-visual journal, for example, was devoted to a number of reports of ways to use the overhead projector. The social studies teacher can refer to any of the following journals for suggestions: *Educational Screen and Audiovisual Guide;* the monthly feature, "Instructional Materials," in *Social Studies;* the column "Sight and Sound in Social Studies" in *Social Education;* the features entitled "Films" and "Geographic Materials Received" in the *Journal of Geography*. However, these lists of materials and "how-to-do-it" suggestions have very limited purposes. It is unusual to find any research evidence to assure the teacher that any particular audio-visual item or way of using audio-visual materials will actually improve classroom learning. Usually we have no evidence at all that approach "A" for presenting a particular idea is superior to approach "B." Too often, choices of audio-visual materials are made on the basis of familiarity with the equipment, accessibility of materials, personal preference, or habit. The monthly features in social studies and audio-visual journals generally do not report research; they merely list new materials or describe them briefly. Critical analysis of methods or materials is seldom included.

TELEVISED TEACHING IN THE SOCIAL STUDIES

Although many of the research findings cited thus far are also applicable to television, its current prominence demands that it be given special attention. A number of specialists have recently reviewed the research which has accompanied the great interest in and expenditure of money for televised teaching. Schramm (1962) gave a particularly comprehensive overview of the available research. Schramm had access to many studies that have not been reported in the literature. He found that of 74 comparative studies of televised teaching in the social studies at all grade levels, 16 reported significantly better learning gains from television, 5 reported that conventional methods were better, and 53 found no significant difference between television and conventional methods. Most students like television in the classroom, and the television teachers like it. Classroom teachers tend to be suspicious of it at first, but most approve after some experience with it. There is no longer any doubt that all types of students learn information efficiently from instructional television.

According to Williams (1962), about 90 percent of the gross comparisons between the information gain of students taught by television and those taught in more traditional ways have indicated no significant differences between the two methods. She does not feel that these findings warrant the assumption that the two conditions of communication are equal. A number of points need to be considered: (1) The television teacher, who is chosen because of his excellence, is provided with every possible teaching aid, including extensive time for preparation. The control groups have typical teachers and facilities. (2) Evaluation usually is a measure of information gain so narrowly conceived as to assess little more than the learner's ability to recall specific facts. Other learning outcomes, as well as concomitant learning, have generally been ignored. (3) The short duration of most experiments does not allow us to assess the effectiveness of instructional television.

Many questions of significance for the social studies teacher remain unanswered. There is little doubt that television has much to contribute to education, but precisely what does television do to improve learning? Improving learning does not mean the amassing of odd bits of information. What can television contribute to understanding cause-and-effect relationships? To identifying and clarifying social forces? To the shaping of attitudes and values? What can it do to develop intelligent and rational decision making? To resolve conflicts and facilitate social change? The needs for research and the theoretical considerations expressed in the remainder of this chapter apply to televised teaching as well as to other audio-visual instructional devices.

THEORETICAL CONSIDERATIONS AND NEEDED RESEARCH

It is clear that we do not now need more audio-visual materials nearly so much as we need substantial research to support the use of this or that kind of film or recording to achieve a particular teaching objective. Although the social studies has some problems of its own, the basic deficiency of research is present throughout the audio-visual field. Very simply, teachers have been encouraged to use audio-visual materials before there was sufficient research to show how and in what ways these materials aided the learning process.

Perhaps the most pressing need is for the development of a defensible theory of learning and teaching which can serve as the basis for the production and use of audio-visual materials. Meierhenry (1961), Porter (1962), and Snygg (1962) have dealt with this very critical problem. Learning theory has tended to describe how learning occurs in certain circumscribed situations and has explained only aspects of learning. Often these theories have had little to do with the problems of teachers. Investigators studying the psychology of learning have shown little concern with the problem of causing learning to occur or with investigating the optimum classroom conditions under which learning is ordered. However, most classroom teaching is directly concerned with the problem of presenting and sequencing material so that it will be most readily learned and transferred. The solution to this problem leads to a theory of instruction which would be of assistance in determining the best way of teaching a body of material. In what form should the knowledge be organized? What disposes the learner to learn? In what sequence should the knowledge be presented? What communication media are most appropriate? Answers to these questions would provide a more valid basis for the production and use of audio-visual materials than now exists.

Most audio-visual devices are relatively new, and additional ones appear frequently as part of the contemporary world's accelerating technological revolution. Hoban (1962) analyzed the role and impact of audio-visual instruction in the total educational enterprise. He pointed out that "all the new media reduce the area of permissiveness, impose order on events, require the exercise of a high degree of intellectual activity, establish new requirements for both teachers and students, and demand intense, prolonged, and detailed advanced planning." Although this is a technological age, many educators fear technology. It requires of them a good deal of unlearning as well as learning. To avoid too much change, they frequently make the new resemble the old or simply add it onto the traditional with little change in the latter.

Finn (1960) has contributed a very provocative analysis of the place of audio-visual instruction in the broad stream of the technological revolution. Although many difficulties and uncertainties in the use of audio-visual materials and other learning aids have been expressed in this chapter, the thrust of technology into education appears to be irrepressible and accelerating. As yet, educators have not developed a defensible point of view concerning the influence of technology on education. Technological development has bypassed education until very recently, and, now that it has begun to have great impact, educators are not prepared to deal with it. Ultimately, this may result in the technologist's usurping control of education.

As Finn points out, it is a gross error to think of technology exclusively in terms of projectors, phonographs, or other types of machines. Technology includes processes, systems, management and control mechanisms both human and nonhuman, and a pervasive attitude or way of looking at problems in terms of their potential for solution by technological means. While technology may influence every facet of education, our concern here is with instruction.

During the first half of this century, while it was transforming much of the rest of the culture, technology barely touched the instructional process. As Finn expresses it, instruction and education generally remained at the preindustrial stage. However, about 1955 the Ford Foundation provided the impetus that has resulted in rapid application of technological developments to education. The circumstances were advantageous for such a shift—teachers were in short supply, education was under severe attack, many of the basic machines and other technological apparatus were already developed and only waiting to be applied to instruction, the space race with Russia had become a national obsession, and large portions of the general public were clamoring for educational change.

The most sweeping change was the widespread use of television in teaching. The teaching profession in general and audio-visual specialists in particular were for the most part left out of the movement. Significant roles were played by administrators, board members, and influential opinion makers of all types. This trend is particularly important because it carries with it the potential loss of control of educational instruction by the teaching profession.

Finn noted two major trends that are now developing out of this technological revolution. The first is toward a mass instructional technology in the form of television or film systems that provide instruction for entire courses. The Midwest Program on Airborne Television Instruction, which carries telecasts of nearly complete courses to schools in several states, provides one example of this trend. Paralleling but in a sense in opposition to this trend is the one toward technology for individual instruction. This includes a variety of teaching machines for individual viewing and listening. An obvious next step, of course, is the combining of these two trends to provide total educational automation—group viewing of filmed or televised courses with supplementary individual instruction as needed. With the use of home television sets and public facilities such as libraries, it may be feasible to eliminate not only the teacher but the school system as well, at least at some educational levels.

There is pressing need for an assessment of the impact of this entire technological movement. Indications have already been given in this chapter regarding the limited evaluations of learning outcomes that have been made. Other basic questions must be answered. Who is to determine the curriculum? What is the role of the teacher? It should be clearly understood that the medium and those who prepare the materials control the message. This situation completely alters the traditional picture of the teacher and his pupils isolated for an hour from the rest of the world while sharing in a unique intellectual experience. The new conditions in the classroom were illustrated very clearly in the data obtained by Fritz and Massialas (1964) in a study of the reactions of social studies teachers to televised lessons. The teachers indicated that their role both on selected tasks and in the control of the curriculum was greatly diminished. Many appeared to accept these changes rather fatalistically. Almost three out of four of the 158 teachers completing the instrument reported a change in teacher role of considerable proportions. These teachers noted that the most obvious changes had been their loss of control over the pacing of content exposure, topic selection and emphasis, range of student activities, and opportunities to deal with individual differences. These are obviously matters of great importance in the total teaching-learning situation. However, when asked what recommendations they would make as to changes in the current program schedule or format (four televised lessons a week of thirty minutes or more each), most teachers found the existing situation acceptable. It is not clear whether their responses indicated approval or merely an assumption that they were powerless to change the situation. It should be noted that all teachers in this sample were receiving televised social studies lessons from the same source. Teachers working with other programs might respond differently.

Finn (1960) picturesquely describes our educational society as being "in the position of a backward underdeveloped culture suddenly assailed by the 20th Century engineer." Instructional technology is here to stay. The problem of the social studies teacher, as of educators generally, is how to control it so that the proper objectives of education may be served and the human being remain central in the process.

Technology has filled the future of instruction with uncertainties, but it has also provided more potential and a wider range of choices than ever before.

The problem of adopting new ideas and practices has been dealt with by Lionberger (1960). Lionberger has established five stages in the adoption process: awareness, interest, evaluation, trial, and adoption. Mass media are especially appropriate for the early phase of the process. The information necessary to get people to perceive the need for change is most efficiently disseminated through mass media. Group processes are effective for the intermediate phases, but direct, personal experiences are necessary for the final step. Lionberger's study suggests a number of possible reasons why there has not been wider acceptance of certain audio-visual aids and how this resistance might be overcome. It is to be hoped, however, that before these techniques of persuasion are fully developed and used, much more will be known about the production and use of audio-visual materials themselves. There is little point in convincing teachers to accept new methods of materials until there is research evidence which establishes their value.

Only a few particularly crucial research needs have been dealt with in this chapter. Specialists in the audio-visual field, such as Fleming (1962), Meierhenry (1962), and Allen (1959), have developed extensive lists that go into considerably more detail than has been possible here. Fleming spelled out the need for research on the nature and proper use of pictorial communication. What kinds of concepts are best communicated by pictorial language and what particular vocabulary would be most suited to each? What are the unique properties of pictorial communication? How can these best be incorporated into instructional materials of all kinds? Meierhenry and Allen considered the reasearch needs of the entire field of audio-visual aids. Meierhenry summarized the situation well when he stated that "to give teachers and administrators better recommendations for the use of specific media, much more needs to be known." Both he and Allen list most of the basic questions one might ask about audio-visual aids. While all these matters are of significance for social studies instruction, social studies teachers are particularly concerned that research deal with the possibility of using audio-visual aids in handling controversy, in developing effective thinking, in developing and testing social science generalizations, in problem solving, and in teaching the concept of culture.

SUMMARY

Teaching materials are extremely important to the teaching-learning process in all social studies classrooms. Teachers lean heavily on commercially prepared textbooks, films, slides, records, and the like to provide the content for their courses. This situation makes it imperative that these materials be as effective as possible in fulfilling course objectives. The selection of these materials is one of the most important tasks performed by a social studies teacher. Research indicates that this process of selection is a difficult task requiring the teacher to be highly selective on the basis of carefully developed criteria.

Many social studies textbooks have been found to be inappropriate for the intended readers in terms of vocabulary and reading difficulty. Others have been criticized because they were unscholarly, dull, bland, or failed to present the content necessary for the development of desirable social studies objectives. These objections are significant primarily in terms of particular theories of social studies instruction.

Strong currents are in motion for changing both the role and make-up of textbooks. Some of these reflect efforts to make adjustments in light of the criticisms just noted while others involve new conceptions of the place of the textbook in instruction. The teaching machine and the use of films and other substitutes for textbooks may require a substantial revision in the manner in which the textbook is used. While the application of the idea that structure rather than information should be the content of the social studies may not change the place of textbooks in the instructional process, it could require that they be completely rewritten.

Audio-visual aids are not as widely used as sources of knowledge by the average teacher as textbooks, and they are not as well understood. Research indicates that their influence on learning is also less certain. The areas of uncertainty and confused empirical evidence far exceed those of certainty and clear-cut research findings. It is clear that students can learn information as well if not better from films, television, and other sources than from typical teacher-led discussions or lectures. The social studies teacher, however, is interested in many other learning outcomes in addition to the acquisition of information, but at present there is little research to guide him in utilizing audio-visual materials for these ends.

While the application of technology to the learning process is proceeding and will not be stopped, much that is being done is not adequately supported by research findings. There appears to be real danger that the great educational potential offered by audio-visual devices may be distorted or largely lost because of a failure to determine when, where, and how they can be most effectively used. Despite these shortcomings, it is entirely possible that technology will soon revolutionize the instructional process. It is urgent that the changes that do occur lead to the realization of desirable educational outcomes. This seems possible only if more basic research is conducted in the field of educational technology.

BIBLIOGRAPHY

Alexander, Albert. "The Grey Flannel Cover on the American History Textbook." *Social Education*, XXIV (1960), 11–14.

Allen, William H. "Research on New Educational Media: Summary and Problems." *Audio-Visual Communication Review*, VII (1959), 83–96.

American Institute for Research. *Integrating Programed Instruction with Conventional Classroom Teaching*. Mimeographed, 1962.

Arnsdorf, Val E. "Readability of Basal Social Studies Materials." *Reading Teacher*, XVI (1963), 243–246.

Beaubier, Edward W. "Capacity of Sixth-Grade Children to Understand Social Science Generalizations." Unpublished Doctor's dissertation, University of Southern California, 1962.

Berry, Mary T. "A Study of the Vocabulary Load of *Geography of Many Lands,* an Alabama State-Adopted Text for the Fourth Grade." Unpublished Doctor's dissertation, University of Alabama, 1961.

Bragdon, Henry W. "The New Curricula in Social Studies." *American Behavioral Scientist,* VI (1962), 32–34.

Brown, Ralph, and Marian Brown. "How to Select a Social Studies Textbook." *Social Education,* XXV (1961), 391–397.

Cottle, Eugene. "An Experiment Using World History Films with Selected Tenth Grade Pupils: Implications for the Improvement of Teaching with Motion Picture Films." Unpublished Doctor's dissertation, Southern Illinois University, 1960.

Devine, Thomas G. "The Development and Evaluation of a Series of Recordings for Teaching Certain Critical Listening Abilities." Unpublished Doctor's dissertation, Boston University, 1961.

English, Marvin D. "A Comparison of the Influence of Colored as Opposed to Black and White Instructional Materials on the Acquisition of Learning." Unpublished Doctor's dissertation, University of Wisconsin, 1961.

Finn, James D. "Automation and Education: III. Technology and Instructional Process." *Audio-Visual Communication Review,* VIII (1960), 5–26.

Fleming, Malcolm. "Pictorial Communication: An Essay on Its Plight." *Audio-Visual Communication Review,* X (1962), 223–237.

Fritz, John, and Byron G. Massialas. "Instructional Television and the Classroom Teacher," *Audio-Visual Communication Review,* XII (1964), 5–15.

Geer, Owen C. "Social Science Generalizations for Use in the Social Studies Curriculum: Protecting and Conserving Human and Natural Resources." Unpublished Doctor's dissertation, Stanford University, 1959.

Georgiady, Nicholas P. "Vocabulary Growth in the Elementary Social Studies as Influenced by the Use of Selected Audio-Visual Materials." Unpublished Doctor's dissertation, University of Wisconsin, 1959.

Goodman, Earl O., Jr. "Procedures for the Use of Sound-Recorded Dramatic Episodes in Cultivating the Ability to Understand Social Interaction." Unpublished Doctor's dissertation, Columbia University, 1962.

Gottschalk, Louis, ed. *Generalization in the Writing of History*. Chicago; University of Chicago Press, 1963.

Haffner, Hyman. "A Study of Vocabulary Load and Social-Concept Burden of Fifth and Sixth Grade Social Studies, History and Geography Textbooks." Unpublished Doctor's dissertation, University of Pittsburgh, 1959.

Hanvey, Robert. "Augury for the Social Studies." *School Review*, LXIX (1961), 11–24.

Hoban, Charles F. "The New Media and the School." *Audio-Visual Communication Review*, X (1962), 353–355.

Hofstrand, John M. "Social Science Generalizations for Use in the Social Studies Curriculum: Creating Tools, Technics, and Social Arrangements." Unpublished Doctor's dissertation, Stanford University, 1959.

Hughes, H. Stuart. "The Historian and the Social Scientist." *American Historical Review*, LXVI (1960), 20–46.

Ingham, George E. "Comparison of Two Methods of Self-Instruction in Teaching a Unit in Social Studies." Unpublished Doctor's dissertation, University of Connecticut, 1962.

Krug, Mark M. "Needed: New Frontiers in the Social Studies." *Chicago Schools Journal*, XLIII (1961), 7–12.

——————. "On Rewriting of the Story of Reconstruction in the U.S. History Textbooks." *Journal of Negro History*, XLVI (1961), 133–153.

——————. "Safe Textbooks and Citizenship Education." *School Review*, LXVIII (1960), 463–480.

Langhans, Elizabeth J. "An Analysis of Current Social Studies Texts, Grades Seven through Twelve, in Terms of Inclusion of Geographic Generalizations." Unpublished Doctor's dissertation, University of Colorado, 1961.

Lawrence, John D. "The Application of Criteria to Textbooks in the Secondary Schools of Los Angeles County." Unpublished Doctor's dissertation, University of Southern California, 1961.

Lionberger, Herbert F. *Adoption of New Ideas and Practices*. Ames, Iowa: Iowa State University Press, 1960.

Lourie, Samuel. "Breaking the Textbook Strait Jacket." *Clearing House,* XXXIV (1960), 417–418.

Lumsdaine, A. A., and Robert Glaser, eds. *Teaching Machines and Programmed Learning: A Source Book.* Washington, D. C.: Department of Audio-Visual Instruction, National Education Association, 1960.

McAshan, H. H. "An Experimental Study of Traffic Safety Films." *Journal of Experimental Education,* XXXI (1962), 43–53.

McBeath, Ronald J. *A Comparative Study of the Effectiveness of the Filmstrip, Sound Filmstrip, and Filmograph for Teaching Facts and Concepts.* Los Angeles: Dept. of Audio-Visual Education, University of Southern California, 1961.

Massialas, Byron G. "Selecting a Social Studies Textbook." *Social Education,* XXV (1961), 237–238.

Meierhenry, Wesley C., ed. "Learning Theory and AV Utilization." *Audio-Visual Communication Review,* IX (1961), 3–87.

—————. "Needed Research in the Introduction and Use of Audiovisual Materials: A Special Report." *Audio-Visual Communication Review,* X (1962), 307–316.

Merrill, Irving R. "Attitude Films and Attitude Change." *Audio-Visual Communication Review,* X (1962), 3–13.

Metcalf, Lawrence E. "The Reflective Teacher." *Phi Delta Kappan,* XLIV (1962), 17–21.

Millis, George H. "Fifth-Grade Pupils' Understanding of Terms Encountered in Their Social Studies Texts." Unpublished Doctor's dissertation, University of Illinois, 1959.

Nagel, Ernest. *The Structure of Science.* New York: Harcourt, Brace and World, Inc., 1961.

Nash, John F. "A Study of the Relevance of Selected Major Concepts and Generalizations from the Field of Sociology to Commonly Accepted Objectives of the Social Studies in the Secondary School." Unpublished Doctor's dissertation, Syracuse University, 1962.

Noah, Harold J., Carl E. Prince, and C. Russell Riggs. "History in High-School Textbooks: A Note." *School Review,* LXX (1962), 415–436.

Palmer, John R. "The Treatment of Social Change in High School History

Textbooks." Unpublished Doctor's dissertation, University of Illinois, 1960.

Patterson, Franklin. "Social Science and the New Curriculum." *American Behavioral Scientist,* VI (1962), 28–32.

Porter, Douglas. "What Does Learning Theory Contribute to the Classroom?" *Audiovisual Instruction,* VII (1962), 13–16.

Rigney, Joseph W., and Edward B. Fry. "Current Teaching-Machine Programs and Programming Technique." *Audio-Visual Communication Review,* IX (1961), 1–122.

Robbins, John. "The New Asia and American Education." *Teacher's College Record,* LXII (1961), 339–347.

Ross, Mildred E. "Some Basic Geographic Concepts to which Elementary Students Can Relate Subsequent Knowledge." Unpublished Doctor's dissertation, Pennsylvania State University, 1959.

Schramm, Wilbur. "Learning from Instructional Television." *Review of Educational Research,* XXXII (1962), 156–167.

Siemers, Allan A. "World History in Selected California High Schools." Unpublished Doctor's dissertation, Stanford University, 1959.

Sloan, Fred A., Jr. "Readability of Social Studies Textbooks for Grades Four, Five, and Six, as Measured by the Dale-Chall Formula." Unpublished Doctor's dissertation, George Peabody College for Teachers, 1959.

Smith, Mildred M. "An Analysis of Basal Reader Stories with Cultural Settings outside Continental United States." Unpublished Doctor's dissertation, Indiana University, 1959.

Snygg, Donald. "The Tortuous Path of Learning Theory." *Audiovisual Instruction,* VII (1962), 8–12.

Textbook Committee of the Committee on Economic Education of the American Economic Association. "Economics in the Schools," *American Economic Review,* LIII, No. 1, Part 2, Supplement (1963), 1–27.

Twyford, Loran C., Hildreth McAshan, Paul Messier, and Philip Rowley. "Behavioral and Factual Analysis." *Audio-Visual Communication Review,* VII (1959), 182–192.

United Nations Educational, Scientific and Cultural Organization. *A Handbook for the Improvement of Textbooks and Teaching Materials as Aids to International Understanding.* Paris: UNESCO, 1949.

Weaver, Vernon P. "Basic American History Generalizations Necessary for the Social Studies Curriculum in the Elementary Grades." Unpublished Doctor's dissertation, Pennsylvania State University, 1962.

Wendt, Paul R., and Gordon K. Butts. *A Report of an Experiment in the Acceleration of Teaching Tenth Grade World History with the Help of an Integrated Series of Films.* Carbondale, Ill.: Southern Illinois University Press, 1960.

Williams, Catharine M. "Reexamination of 'No Significant Differences' that ITV Studies Report." *Audio-Visual Communication Review,* X (1962), 263–265.

Wood, Leslie A. "Programmed Textual Material as a Partial Substitute for Teacher-Led Classroom Procedures in Geography." Unpublished Doctor's dissertation, Stanford University, 1962.

7

SOCIAL STUDIES INSTRUCTION IN WORLD PERSPECTIVE

Byron G. Massialas
University of Chicago

This chapter is written on the assumption that the study and practice of educational theory in our society will become more meaningful if it is seen in international perspective. It attempts to summarize, interpret, and critically analyze studies and surveys in social studies education in countries other than the United States. The review is by no means exhaustive, but it strives to provide a starting point in this important area of research and scholarship. The following have been the major criteria for selecting studies to be reviewed: (1) The report must have relevance to social studies instruction. (2) The report or the study should have been written in the English language and should have been readily accessible in the United States. (3) The article or book must have been published in the United States in the last five years. The only exception is the inclusion of studies reported in the *Times Educational Supplement* of London and in selected UNESCO publications, and one or two reports in the *Year Book of Education*. Pamphlets and reports distributed by foreign governments through embassies or information offices were not considered. For the most part, current bibliographical indexes, such as the *Education Index* and the *Reader's Guide* were the source of the references used. (4) Each study or article under review should have presented and analyzed a problem in a logical, systematic, and consistent style. Historical and philosophical research, as well as research of an experimental nature, was included. In the case of the Soviet Union, about which material was more than abundant, the foregoing standards were more rigorously applied than elsewhere. Purely impressionistic, undocumented attempts at characterization of cultures or social studies programs were generally excluded.

The reviewer has considered different operational schemes in organizing, classifying, and interpreting the material at hand. A most fruitful approach is that followed by King (1962). It is based on major educational themes which, more or less, cut across cultures, such as policies concerning selection and differentiation of students, teacher recruitment and preparation, technological developments and ramifications in the society, and ideological conflicts which confront educators. However, the author has found it virtually impossible to apply the same methodological frame of reference for these reasons: (1) Educational writers concerned with social studies in foreign countries do not address themselves to the same issues. For example, postwar Japan is faced with educational problems of tremendous magnitude growing out of a society caught in a social dilemma—between the moral prescriptions of the past, including unquestioned devotion to the Emperor, and the unavoidable transition to a Western type of culture introduced by the occupying forces, which have stressed democratic ends and commensurate means. In England, the question still centers on problems emanating from the implementation of traditional curricula: What histories should be emphasized? What historiographical styles are more consistent with modern scholarship? Which interpretations of certain historical episodes are valid? This is not to say that there are no contact points among different cultures; there are many. The point is, though, that these central themes or connecting ideas have not been adequately explored in the literature—there are limitless gaps in the research. (2) With a few unrelated exceptions, there are no cross-cultural studies in the true sense of the word. Most of the research applies to one problem area within the national boundaries of a given state, often utilizing what Herbert Hyman called a "pseudo cross-national design," which assumes hypothetical criteria of comparison. In most cases very little indeed has been done to relate explicitly the educational context and practice of a culture to that of another.

For the purposes of this study and because of the restrictions outlined above, a regional approach, as suggested by the Division of International Education of the U.S. Office of Education (1960), has been accepted. This organizational pattern groups countries in five general areas: Africa South of the Sahara, Europe, the Far East, the Near East, and the Western Hemisphere. An attempt will be made to identify and discuss selected topics from a comparative point of view. A summary at the end will emphasize cross-national themes as they apply to the teaching of the social studies.

GENERAL SURVEYS

Some very informative general surveys of social studies programs in a number of nations have been conducted by UNESCO and its cooperating agencies. A report presented to UNESCO (1955) by the International Federation of Secondary Teachers summarized the findings of a questionnaire submitted to representatives of Egypt, France, Mexico, Sweden, the United Kingdom, the United States of America, and Yugoslavia. The survey was concerned with the status of the social sciences in the various secondary school curricula. With the exception of France and possibly Yugoslavia, the social sciences did not quite receive the attention and the interpretation suggested by the definition in the questionnaire. According to this definition, the social sciences aim at familiarizing students with scientific methods in the study of social issues. Social studies as a school subject is concerned with practical knowledge and the values associated with good citizenship. However, the two purposes are not really incompatible and are expressed in one way or another in all programs under study. Responsible citizenship was stressed by all respondents as a definite goal of the curriculum, but objectivity in dealing with social issues was also accepted as a value. It was stated that the method of teaching is as important in developing an objective-scientific approach as the subject in which instruction is given. It is interesting to note that educators from the United Kingdom stressed citizenship education and development of an interest in democratic institutions as the aims of secondary education. As we shall see later, however, the English syllabi and textbooks do not generally reflect this attitude.

With the exception of Yugoslavia, where emphasis was placed on exposition by the teacher and the use of printed material, there was a general tendency in all the countries studied to accept activity methods drawn from the pupil's own knowledge and experience. There was a feeling that children need to engage in their own research and draw their own conclusions about their political and social environment. A review of the syllabi indicated that certain topics are consistently found in the respective curricula—topics such as population, the family, property, genetics, humanitarianism, and crime and delinquency. This condition points to promising classroom encounters with ideas about mankind and about pressing human problems which are the concern of all. It would be most valuable to conduct a more thorough survey, incorporating many more countries and communities, in order to investigate the extent to which teachers deal responsibly with social themes that have world-wide implications.

Another UNESCO (1959) publication has provided a brief (in places, superficial) guide for teaching about the United Nations, human rights, and other cultures. Some reports of educational practice in teaching about other countries, often referred to as "experiments," suggest a growing preoccupation in social studies programs with a truly global view of social problems; i.e., one that includes non-Western cultures. Some titles of projects reported in the booklet reveal the scope and focus of the effort for mutual understanding: "Studying Japan in Switzerland," "A Project on Turkey in a British School," "A Study of Korea in Japan," "A Project in a French School on the History of Slavery." The suggested techniques of teaching and the means of evaluation, however, offer rather superficial solutions to many pressing educational problems. For example, very little is said about the role of the teacher with regard to controversial issues, such as slavery, which still exists in one form or another in many parts of the world; the ideological conflict between East and West manifested in crucial areas, such as Berlin, Vietnam, and Cuba; and the pressing issue of the equitable distribution of the natural resources of the earth. Which strategy in dealing with social issues and cleavages should the teacher accept: indoctrination, uncritical perpetuation of the status quo, ethical neutrality, or defensible partiality? Which alternative is compatible with the idea of understanding and appreciating cultures other than our own and providing the means for intercommunication and a cordial exchange of views? Which alternative is consistent with democratic goals?

A most interesting study which opens up new paths in cross-cultural research is the one reported by Lambert and Klineberg (1959) on national stereotypes among children. The major purpose of this pilot study was to develop and refine data-gathering and analytic techniques for future research. Approximately 40 to 50 students in three age groups, 6-, 10-, and 14-year-olds in English Canada, French Canada, England, Belgium, and Holland were interviewed. The children came from large urban communities, and factors of intelligence, socio-economic background, and attendance in public schools were considered. During the interview the respondents were confronted with questions such as "What are you?" and "What else are you?", and were asked to associate themselves with relevant categories. On the first question the study revealed patterns of local idiosyncracies (e.g., the Belgian reference to "white") on one hand, and cross-nationally stable categories (e.g., sex, child, and religion) on the other. The children's reference to themselves as boy or girl and child decreased through the age groups. It is interesting to note that the major sources of information about other nations or peoples were people and communication media, while books and trips were minor. This finding should provide the springboard for exploring the actual relationship between textbooks and images or "pictures" students have of people who belong to socio-economic and ethnic groups other than their own. When asked to name other peoples who were similar to their group and those who were not, the respondents indicated that they considered the English, French, and Americans to be "like us." Americans were judged "like us" by several Belgian and Dutch students. Chinese and Africans (or Negroes) were most consistently considered "not like us." As students grew older, they increasingly considered the Russians "not like us." The characterizations given to the four reference groups are also revealing. The

Americans were thought of in terms of "good, bad, similarities, differences, and wealthy"; the French in terms of "similarities, differences, and 'good' in general"; the Chinese in terms of "differences, good, and poor"; and the Russians were generally in terms of "aggression, differences, bad, and communist." It was suggested that "with age the images children hold of other peoples become less stereotyped." This preliminary study points out the need for reliable knowledge and means of examining commonly held beliefs of "other" peoples.

The study employs a reliable and sophisticated research design which may well apply to other studies of this type. The images that school children have of other nationalities as revealed in this investigation should offer several working hypotheses for executing cross-national investigations. It is desirable that future studies expand the sample to include more nationalities and age groups and that an attempt be made to examine the causes for the differences in national images. Teachers of social studies have numerous opportunities to destroy certain stereotypes and consider other people and nations in a more congenial and realistic context. However, it is important in changing popularly held images to consider the social-emotional level of students and the historic traditions of the community. As we will note later, an abrupt and forced transformation of values can create serious social problems.

A comparative study (Almond and Verba, 1963) of patterns of political socialization in the United States, Great Britain, Germany, Italy, and Mexico revealed that American respondents had the greatest expectations for participation in political decision making, at both the local and national levels, followed by English, Germans, Italians, and Mexicans, in that order. It was found that non-political participatory activities in the family, the school, and the job could be generalized and applied to politics. It was concluded that the more educated the person is the more he pays attention to elections and the more interested he is to discuss and participate in the governmental affairs of the country. It is also interesting to note that direct teaching about the political system in the United States, Britain, and Mexico has an impact on the individual's sense of political competence. This is not true, however, of Germany and Italy, whose educational systems were dominated over a relatively long period of time by anti-democratic theories. This finding suggests that the content of what is taught has much to do with expectations for political participation.

The evidence in the above study points to a strong relationship between classroom discussion and participation in class activities and political sensitivity, or feelings of political competence. The teacher should be aware that opportunities to participate in such activities should be given in class, along with formalized instruction, in order to help children become responsible political decision makers.

REGIONAL SURVEYS

THE FAR EAST

Research in this broad area is practically nonexistent. It is indeed strange that, with increasing American interest in and commitment to several states in Southeast Asia, such as Laos, Thailand, and South Vietnam, no major works on the teaching of social studies in this area have been reported in the literature.

Although the research on Communist China and Japan is rather sketchy, it points toward pressing issues and other topics which need to be investigated in depth. The growing interest in these two countries is expressed in writings reviewed here.

COMMUNIST CHINA. In the opening chapter of a book on Chinese education, Hu (1962) offers an excellent analysis of current practice in historical and cultural perspective. In earlier times education was based on Confucianism, and its goal was the achievement of universal tranquility through the cultivation of the quality of humanness or *Jen*. Under the traditional Chinese system, education was the means for the selection and perpetuation of an elite. A person was considered educated if he could memorize the classics; the idea that knowledge should be capable of being applied was generally absent. In the 19th Century, as China came under the influence of the West, liberal ideas were introduced but remained largely in the hands of a small group of Western-trained intellectuals who were divorced from the populace. Under Communism the cultural dislocation created by the rejection of

Confucian principles takes a new form. Two incompatible movements are introduced at the same time—liberal ideas from the West and "a partial reversion to traditional patterns." On the ideological front, Marxism-Leninism replaced Confucianism, and, although antithetic to it, "is equally pervasive." The exclusive concern of the Chinese communist state, like that of the Soviet Union, is the ideological reconditioning of its citizens. Drawing from an extensive bibliography, including Chinese and American publications, Hu offers a full description and explanation of the major philosophical premises underlying the political and educational tasks of the state, some of which are as follows: marriage of theory with practice (education should be connected with productive work); development of nationalism and stress on the cultural achievements of the state; emphasis on science and technology; educating the proletariat (by enlarging the base of education to include all citizens). The official pronouncements of educational goals as expressed by Mao Tse-Tung, Lu Ting-Yi and others are incorporated in the book under several headings, such as "On the Correct Handling of Contradictions among the People," and "Education Must Be Combined with Productive Labor." Furthermore, the goals of education are expressed in the outcomes of the Chinese Communist Party conference in 1958, and are reported by Chen (1961). Here three principles (the three "P's") are emphasized: politics, production, and party. Education must serve politics, it must promote production, and, under the guidance of the party, it must "serve the ends of proletarian society."

Both Chen and Hu emphasize the totalitarian aspect of Communist education—i.e., the attempt to include all phases of the human quest under the careful scrutiny and direction of the state. Family relations and subjects touching on personal matters can only be discussed from a point of view which is sanctioned by the Party. Consequently, political subjects such as "Dialectical Materialism" and "History of Chinese Revolution" are discussed not only in formal courses in the schools but in youth organizations such as the Young Pioneers and the Communist Youth League. Drawing from Ministry of Education reports published in newspapers in China, Chen (1960) reviews the state of teacher education in another article and concludes that political education in Marxist-Leninist philosophy plays an important part in the training of teachers. The 1957 anti-rightist campaign receives special attention in his article. Psychology professors came under attack at that time because they were neglecting politics and were discussing human nature. The attack was based on the assumption that the subject matter of psychology, which deals with generalizable patterns of human behavior, must be related to class origins. It was argued that psychology, like all the other sciences, must be put at the service of socialism.

Benton (1961), reporting an investigation of education in Red China purported to be based on government and private sources of information and interviews with refugees, corroborated the claims of deliberate thought control, but offered statistical evidence which suggests a conscious effort on the part of the government to combat mass illiteracy. Schools have increased dramatically from 350,000 in 1949 to 1,000,000 in 1961. Likewise, adult education programs have become very popular. The system has encountered many difficulties in raising the standards of schools and teachers and in indoctrinating the youth in communist beliefs. Benton's report is the only one which attempts to evaluate general educational outcomes in China. Surprisingly, none of the studies mentions the ideological split between the Russians and the Chinese and its implications in Chinese educational practice. From reports and analyses of the current educational system in China, it would appear that the new state has been concerned with raising the literacy level of its people at the price of individual freedom and self-respect. This situation points to the perennial social problem, observed by Alexis de Tocqueville in the mid-nineteenth century, of democratic decision making (where individual choices are respected and their expression is encouraged) versus the efficient management and administration of the state (where decisions are made arbitrarily by an elite group headed by a philosopher-king or a dictator). Is a government ethically justified in emphasizing efficiency and rapid social transformation without due respect for the historic and cultural traditions of a given people (e.g., the family unit as a base of social organization in China)? In what ways is it possible for a government to organize its human and natural resources productively and at the same time provide the conditions for individual initiative, human freedom, and the preservation and functioning of primary social institutions?

JAPAN. Moral education, a controversial topic in Japan, has been the subject of three recent reports. Oshiba (1961) traces its history, pointing out that the notorious *shushin* (moral education) which emphasized national legends and reverence of the Emperor had its roots in the West. In later years, the course was conducted with a solemnity similar to that accompanying religious services in the United States. After the storm of militarism in the 1930s, and especially during World War II, *shushin* was used by the Japanese as a means of inculcating loyalty and patriotism. The standard of patriotism was the willingness of the populace to sacrifice their lives for the Emperor. When Japan was occupied by the Allied forces, the courses in *shushin* were suspended and "social studies" was introduced into the curriculum. According to Adams (1960) the role of the school as interpreted by the American consultants was to provide the grounds for youth to participate in the formulation of new ethical imperatives. In accordance with the American tradition, it was assumed that morals were to be "caught" rather than taught through school instruction.

A controversy arose when the Ministry of Education reintroduced the course in *shushin* in 1958. Shimbori (1960), in a rather apologetic manner, lists the reasons for this governmental action. Social studies, American style, de-emphasized nationalism and patriotism, resulting in moral confusion, since democratic values were not yet known to the Japanese. In addition to moral degeneration, social studies instruction stressing problem-solving methods resulted in fragmentary knowledge of basic historical and geographical facts. This claim is evidently based on a survey of the Ministry of Education conducted in 1956 and 1957, which Shimbori mentions only in passing.

Although the separate course in moral education purports to provide a different content and orientation than that included in the *shushin* (in many respects it resembles the American "Problems in Democracy" course), there has been opposition to it from Japanese teachers and American advisers. That the course in and by itself will offset rising juvenile delinquency and major social conflicts among the youth is rather doubtful. On the other hand, the assumption that transplanting an American-patterned social studies program in a society with a rich and deep-seated historical tradition will solve the ills of contemporary Japan is equally untenable.

The three fairly-well-documented essays, unavoidably representing different points of view on the controversy, raise significant questions about the role of social studies instruction in a society in transition. (Some of the same problems are faced by educators in West Germany.) Perhaps, the next step would be to pursue studies which would systematically describe and assess the educational outcomes of the new course in the light of current social goals and aspirations, the educational objectives expressed by responsible leaders, and the prevailing cultural conditions.

Lifton (1962) has tried to identify some of the social contradictions and ethical dilemmas faced by Japanese youth. His report, based on intensive interviews with students, suggests as its main theme that the social-historical dislocation taking place in Japan today is due to the abrupt break with the past—there is the absence of a sense of connection. Japanese education has traditionally emphasized aesthetics, a subject which seems irrelevant to the demands of the modern world. Obligations to and harmony within the family, the local group, and the nation are now considered sources of embarrassment, rather than of strength and pride as formerly. The life story of a young man, as carefully narrated by the author, provides a vivid illustration of the different identification symbols and styles of life (filled with psychological contradictions) experienced by boys growing up in Japan during the war and postwar periods. At the age of twenty-five the young man is a *Sarariman* (salaried man), who identifies with his firm and acknowledges its contribution to the economic growth of the nation. At the same time he resents his new life, and he engages in fantasy—stealing money and then spending it in Europe and America amusing himself. In unguarded moments he would "go into tirades against the constricted life-pattern of the 'typical salaried man' . . ." (p. 177). Similar internal contradictions are present throughout his life: when he learns to hate the Americans but, later, as a student, becomes a convert to many aspects of American life and is baptized as a Christian; when he joins the *Zengakuren* as an activist embracing the ideal of "pure communism" and then becomes disillusioned with the organization during his third year at the university. It is claimed that the Japanese "have felt impelled to immerse themselves in Western ideas . . . and at the same time they have waged a constant struggle against being psychologically inundated by these same Western influences" (p. 179). How this conflict in values in Japan will be resolved remains to be seen. This same conflict, however, is evident in many societies which have come in contact with the West and which have a rich heritage of their own—e.g., India, Iran, Thailand.

Lifton's well-written and insightful report is one of the few which gives some tangible evidence of the social problems of modern Japan. His psychoanalytic frame of reference brings a new focus to and a reasonably sound interpretation of the conditions which contribute to personal ambivalence and feelings of alienation. Since cultural and psychological alienation of youth appears to be a phenomenon which also characterizes industrial societies in the West (Fromm, 1955), studies such as the one conducted by Lifton should be of great value in understanding the symptoms, the causes, and the consequences of the problems of our time.

Mitsuhashi (1962) made a good beginning in the systematic study of social studies education from a comparative viewpoint. The aim of her study was "to develop techniques for identifying the kinds of 'pictures' of the geographic world that people 'carry around in their heads'" (p. 142). Pupils in Tokyo and Chicago (100 fourteen-year-old ninth graders of each sex) were tested by an instrument developed by the investigator. The mean percentage of correct answers for all Japanese students was 71 and for Americans 47. On the average, boys in both countries scored higher than girls. On the fact questions, Tokyo students averaged 77 percent correct and the Chicago students 57 percent. On the "fact plus analysis" items the Japanese averaged 56 and the Americans 30 percent correct. On the "application of geographic techniques in interpretation" items the respective percentages were 80 and 58 for the two groups. The investigator suggests that Japanese students display more geographic aptitude than their American counterparts. From her findings, she also infers that, although there are significant differences in achievement, there are no differences in the kinds of geographic images formed as a result of growing up in contrasting societies. However, a number of flaws in the research design tend to weaken the study. For example, groups are generally treated as equivalent, notwithstanding the fact that very little is mentioned about controlling significant personality, intelligence, and socio-economic variables. Also, several claims are not supported by adequate evidence (e.g., "The pupils in the first and third Chicago schools, who are now taking geography, are not uniformly more knowledgeable than in the other Chicago schools"). A review of the fifteen sample test items used in the study points out that the instrument emphasizes physical geography. Had the stress been on cultural or political geography, the results might have been different, since geography in the United States, usually taught at the ninth-grade level, centers on historical, political, and economic conditions influencing man's behavior. The study has value if it is considered as a pioneer effort to develop defensible approaches in cross-cultural investigations. As studies of this nature multiply, it is expected that investigators will develop sophistication in carrying out the research procedure.

AFRICA SOUTH OF THE SAHARA

Recently, the emerging nations of Africa have attracted the attention of some American educators. Nothing has appeared in American literature with regard to the social studies field, however. A "functional reference survey" compiled by Ruth Sloan Associates and edited by Kitchen (1962) provides a general overview of forty-two educational systems in Africa. It claims that the educational systems of Africa mainly reflect the overall objectives of the colonial powers by whom they have, until recently, been controlled. Consequently, each country fits into a pattern and a philosophy developed by a colonial state. Under British rule it was understood that the overseas possessions might eventually gain autonomy; consequently, under the system of "indirect rule," local talent and initiative was respected and encouraged. British educational policy in the colonies generally reflected the foregoing political attitude. Under the French, all mission schools in

Africa conformed to a State model, requiring French as the medium of instruction. The objective of the system "was to create a political and professional elite of high intellectual quality—and in the French image" (p. 5). The educational goals of France were consistent with her colonial policy of assimilation. The Portuguese, in a much more direct manner, have attempted to indoctrinate the African tribes with their language and culture. This goal is in line with the governmental policy of imbuing the Africans under their control with Portuguese nationalism and insulating them "against the heretical doctrines of African nationalism" (p. 6). The Spanish policy has been much like that of the Portuguese, although they have adjusted the educational directives in preparation for any eventuality. Under Belgian paternalistic rule, "neither the elaborate educational system nor the country's political institutions were designed to produce or train personnel for leadership positions" (p. 5). The consequences of this policy have been felt in the now independent Congo, where there has been a dire need for trained people to occupy important positions in the new administration and its technical agencies. This sketchy survey, which includes statistical tables on school enrollments, fields of study, and types of schools, might be helpful as a general reference to the investigator interested in a broad statement of the problems faced by social studies teachers in developing nations which have come under the influence of the West. It would be interesting to see what major changes in the educational system have been brought about by the indigenous leaders since independence. More specifically, some of the questions that need to be asked are: In what way are social studies programs designed to provide a sense of connection with the past? What aspects and what periods of African history are emphasized? How is the West treated in textbooks and school syllabi? In what way does social studies instruction relate to problems associated with modernization and democratization? How does the school develop a common national mythology in the midst of numerous tribes (as in Nigeria), each one having its own language and identification symbols?

THE NEAR EAST

With the exception of the two studies reviewed here and some descriptive reports in UNESCO publications, no research of any significance on the status of social studies in the Near East has appeared in current literature.

After examining a number of representative history textbooks used in secondary schools in Israel, Krug (1963a) concluded that the question of the destruction of the European Jewry has been discussed with great thoroughness. The interpretations of the conditions under which Hitler was able to exterminate millions of Jews vary, however. There seem to be two major points of view on this question. The first one, which is popular among native-born writers, generally attributes Hitler's success in his grim task to the unwillingness of Jews to resist and the development of a "Ghetto psychology" among European Jews. As against this position other historians and writers hold that the very fact of Jewish determination to live, in Warsaw and elsewhere, under extremely adverse conditions created by the Germans and by the lack of cooperation of the native populations such as the Poles, indicated great heroism on their part. There is additional evidence to suggest that among high school students there is reluctance to explore the details of the period. Resistance to the study of this tragic chapter in human history, coupled with a feeling of contempt for European Jews, is often shown by Israeli students. This attitude is shared by some teachers. High school students are imbued with a spirit of confidence and love for Israel's recent glories in the battlefield; in this context it is extremely difficult to study objectively the darkest period in Jewish history. Germany and Japan face the same problem in attempting to account for the defeat of the Axis powers during World War II. The role of America in general, and of American Jews in particular, vis-à-vis the creation of an independent State of Israel is minimized in several books. Furthermore, there is the assertion that Jews in America are really second-class citizens and that their apparent affluency is deceptive; a satisfying life is possible only in Israel.

In another study Krug (1963b) examined history textbooks approved by the Ministry of Education and used in the high schools of the United Arab Republic. The analysis concerned controversial topics, such as the Zionist colonization movement in Palestine, and the dispute over the nationalization of the Suez Canal. With very few exceptions the textbooks under study very strongly disapprove of the attempt of the Zionist movement, backed by the West, to create an independent State of Israel. The writers feel that the main responsibility for effecting the partition of Palestine, which was accepted by the United Nations in 1947, and the ensuing problems in the Near East, lies with Great Britain, the United States, and the Jews of Palestine. President Truman is given major responsibility for American support of the movement. A most interesting aspect of the study is the part dealing with certain crucial issues as seen by Arab and Israeli historians. For instance, Krug finds very little similarity between Egyptian and Israeli textbooks on the treatment of the international situation, and the conditions in Palestine leading to the creation of a Jewish sovereign state. This example perhaps indicates that there is some validity to the proposition that histories are in the last analysis nationalistic because they always represent the national commitment and cultural background of the writer. On the other hand, Krug's plea for historical objectivity cannot be taken lightly in view of the growing interdependence of nations, the concern for mutual understanding, and a renewed faith in mankind. Krug's studies generally are well written and are based on original sources. His findings and conclusions would have had additional validity had he described his reviewing procedure and theoretical framework more explicitly, and had he considered the specific cultural context in which these highly controversial problems are discussed. The dimension of the learner (the psychological dimension), largely ignored by Krug, should be a criterion in future analyses of history textbooks.

THE WESTERN HEMISPHERE

It is ironical and paradoxical for a country such as the United States, located as it is in the Western Hemisphere, to exhibit so little concern with the practices of its neighbors in that hemisphere, especially in the domain of educational practice and research. This lack of interest can be partly explained by historical tradition—the fact that American scholars and educators have looked mostly to Western Europe for guidance and inspiration in "cultural" affairs and scholarship. Furthermore, the political isolation of America in the early part of the century, coupled with a deep-seated conviction that Hispanic America had very little in common with the predominantly white, Protestant, Anglo-Saxon America might provide other plausible explanations. The fact is that, with the exception of the studies reviewed here, there is virtually nothing in the national literature on the subject of social studies education in the Hemisphere.

Tavel (1963), on the basis of curriculum guides and programs issued by Ministries of Education and school authorities and some incidental interviews with teachers, attempted to give a broad picture of the status of social studies in Latin America. Acknowledging the condition of cultural diversity between and within nations, he proceeded to formulate some plausible generalizations on objectives, curriculum, method of instruction, and evaluation in social studies. He suggested that the main concern of the educational systems in question is the transmission of the cultural heritage. No effort is made to inculcate a critical attitude concerning social institutions. Objectives are expressed in terms of distinct bodies of knowledge, with special emphasis on history and geography. Since the content is thought of as subjects replicating the historical and social disciplines, no attempt is made to discuss pressing social problems. This philosophy of social studies education is reflected in teaching patterns in the classroom (lecturing is stressed) and in evaluation practices (measurement in terms of mastery of arbitrary associations). The report has limited value in that the cultural context in which social studies is taught and practiced is not given its due. Furthermore, the basis on which many "global" conclusions have been made can be questioned primarily because of limited samples and unwarranted concentration on official programs and syllabi.

A most thorough and methodologically defensible study, employing an interdisciplinary approach, of an emerging society evolving from a Hispanic past is that conducted by Brameld (1959) on Puerto Rico. His systematic investigation, based primarily on interviews with Puerto Ricans, and on relevant sociological studies, was concerned with the images that Puerto Ricans held of their own culture, especially of the educational system. His analysis of how the people look upon their history has many implications for the subsequent development of educational programs and the general orientation and tempo of cultural change. Primarily because of a "lack of fanatical fixation on bygone glories," and a rather "thin" national history, education pays attention to the present and the future. However, the history of a nation plays an important role in its social development, and its continued study was recommended by the majority of the respondents. Although there was no common agreement as to the central causes of insular historical development, Brameld's investigation showed that the drive for leadership and the economic and political system were considered very important. The majority of the teachers interviewed suggested more study of Puerto Rican history in relation to Latin American history as a whole. National leaders thought that high school students are capable of dealing with historical causation, the idea of progress, and similar topics. They stated that the development of these skills should be cultivated as early as possible in the schools.

Brameld, taking issue with some of the above suggestions and points of view, expresses doubt whether teaching more history will develop sensitivity to and concern with problems of a temporal nature. He points out that there is a definite need in education to relate the past to the present and the future. This need is seldom filled by separating historical resources into subject-matter areas. Nevertheless, this philosophy of social studies instruction is gaining momentum in the United States and is the one accepted by the writer. The point is that no single subject offers the necessary perspective and tools of investigation to enable the student to see man in a broad context. Better understanding and appreciation of other cultures and their current problems will take place when they are viewed from an interdisciplinary perspective. In accordance with his position favoring social reconstruction, Brameld makes an extremely valuable contribution to the field of social studies education by outlining and amply justifying a consistent philosophy of teaching history and the social sciences. Furthermore, his research technique (basically anthropological) has wide implications in the study of other cultures.

A descriptive study of the status of geography in Canada, based on questionnaires sent to directors of curriculum in the ten provinces, was conducted by Weir and Russell (1959). In five provinces (mostly the Western provinces) social studies implies an integrated or fused curriculum, primarily based on historical and geographical material. In the other provinces geography and history are treated as separate subjects; thus no violation of "the integrity of either discipline" is made. With the exception of Quebec, where geography and history are taught as "nearly equal courses," the main emphasis is placed on history. Since there is no explicit philosophical or psychological rationale to justify the authors' point of view that disciplines purportedly based on different philosophical considerations cannot logically be fused, the study has limited value unless considered as a purely descriptive account of existing programs in Canada. These authors are obviously in disagreement with Brameld, who makes a convincing and well supported case for the utilization of an interdisciplinary (not necessarily "fused") method in the study of society.

THE SOVIET UNION

In recent years the topic of Soviet education has been treated rather extensively in the national literature. Roughly speaking, there is more research and writing on the Soviet educational system than on any other system in the world. The caliber of the research ranges from thoroughly systematic and documented studies of major historical movements and educational theories to superficial accounts of educational "practice" by transients, travelers, and journalists. A number of general surveys such as those by King (1963), Bereday, Brickman, and Read (1960), and Bereday and Pennar (1960), which attempt to deal with broad educational problems, do offer the reader good background material. The most comprehensive and definitive work on the subject is that completed by DeWitt (1961). The book provides an excellent account of the pre- and post-1959 reforms in the aims and the structure of the schools, mostly based on original sources and documents and direct observation of the Soviet educational scene. DeWitt's main theme is that Soviet policy is best characterized by the term "functional education" for all, that is, education which effects a marriage between academic knowledge and productive labor. Now that Russia has emerged as a major industrial state, her educational goal is to allocate her manpower resources so that an optimum work efficiency and output will take place.

The major task of history and the social sciences, as expressed in the writings of scholars and the official pronouncements of the Ministry of Education, is to inculcate in youth an unquestioned loyalty to the Soviet system and the Marxist-Leninist ideology. This goal is reflected in the social studies curriculum and methods of instruction in the Soviet Union.

HISTORY AND PHILOSOPHY OF SOCIAL STUDIES INSTRUCTION. The most scholarly studies on this topic, based primarily on Soviet sources, have been conducted by Shteppa (1962) and Pundeff (1962). Shteppa, a Soviet historian in exile, traced Russian historiography since the Revolution and concluded that the period witnessed a movement toward the subjugation of all intellectual life to official Party doctrine. The period from 1918 until 1932 is dominated by the Pokrovsky school of thought, which emphasizes broad "sociological" themes and socialist theory, and deprecates Tsarist institutions and heroic deeds. Under Stalin, Pokrovsky is discredited and an attempt is made to justify, even canonize, the Russian past and glorify heroic exploits. The change in mood is vividly exemplified by excerpts from history books, written during and after Pokrovsky. For instance, under Pokrovsky Peter I is depicted as a vicious ruler, who came under the influence of merchant capitalism. After Pokrovsky's downfall, Peter is described as a wise and active young Tsar, who introduced many useful innovations into Russia. According to Pundeff (1962), under Stalin history emphasized Russian patriotism and created an atmosphere of hero worship which suited the latter's aim of self-glorification. The 1959 decree of the Central Committee of the Communist Party and the Council of Ministers of the U.S.S.R. sought to bring about a balance "between Pokrovsky's sociological schematicism and Stalin's stress on the great man" (p. 70). The objective was to understand the scientific laws of the evolution of society, form a conviction on the part of the students of the inevitability of the victory of Communism and the collapse of capitalism, and carefully disclose the important role of the masses and individuals in making history. Through history and other school subjects, the youth is to be reared "in the spirit of communist dedication to ideas and morality, intolerance toward bourgeois ideology, socialist patriotism and proletarian internationalism, and deep respect for labor" (quoted by Pundeff, p. 71).

THE CURRICULUM. Brief descriptions of offerings in the Soviet schools are presented by DeWitt (1961), Medlin (1960), and Pundeff (1962). The teaching of history is introduced early in the child's school life; it begins in grades two and three and continues through the last grade of the secondary school. Although history of the ancient, medieval, and modern periods is included, emphasis is placed on the history of the U.S.S.R. According to Medlin, this trend is reflected in the examinations at the end of the school program, where over 70 percent of the 30 questions asked deal with political and social events of the Lenin period. Pundeff identifies two "concentric" patterns of history teaching in the curriculum, one for grades 4–8 and the other for grades 9–11. In the first stage the subjects are treated in an elementary fashion, beginning with stories from U.S.S.R. history in the fifth and sixth grades, and terminating with U.S.S.R. history itself in the seventh and eighth grades, supplemented by work on the modern history of foreign countries. During the second stage (grades 9–11) U.S.S.R. history is "systematically" treated and is paralleled by a course in the modern history of foreign countries. In accordance with the principle of local area study, the history of the local union republic is taught either as an independent course or in conjunction with the course on the history of the U.S.S.R. A decree of the Central Committee in 1960 introduced a course on political education in the senior grades, stressing Marxist-Leninist theory. A course on the Soviet Constitution was reintroduced as a separate subject in the new program. Geography begins in grade five and continues through grades ten and eleven, where economic geography of the Soviet Union and of foreign countries, with heavy political bias, is offered.

A 1958 issue of the *International Social Science Journal*, entitled "Teaching of the Social Sciences in the Higher Educational Establishments of the U.S.S.R.," included articles, written by Soviet educators, descriptive of the social science programs on the university level. History, political economy, philosophy, sociology, logic and psychology, legal sciences, and pedagogy are among the fields mentioned. Sociology is part of the field of philosophy. Psychology is part of the formal training of teachers and is also offered as a specialized field in larger universities. The field is defined as "the science of man's mental make-up and of the objective laws governing mental activity." The concentration is on the works of preeminent Russian scientists and materialist philosophers, including Lomonosov, Radishchev, Herzen, Chernishevsky, Sechenov, and Pavlov. Medlin (1960) indicates that all teacher-preparation programs in history place a premium on subject matter. Universities, such as the University of Moscow, require that 45 percent of the total program be taken in history, including the history of the Communist Party of the Soviet Union, whereas pedagogical institutes require only 31 percent of the total hours to be devoted to history. The remaining hours are allocated as follows: universities—7 percent in pedagogy; 12 percent in language, literature, physical education, and elective subjects. In pedagogical institutes the distribution is 10 percent, 8 percent, and 51 percent respectively. Courses in pedagogy include methods of teaching history, history of pedagogy, psychology, supervised experience, extracurricular activities, and teacher training. In this respect the content of the program is similar to that of its counterpart in the United States.

Most illuminating reports concerning the fostering of atheism among students in the formal curriculum are those by DeWitt (1961) and Floridi (1960) and articles written by Soviet educators and translated into English in the journal *Soviet Education*. For example, Malkov (1961) suggests that in teaching the notion that religion is the opiate of the people the pupils should become familiar with the topic "The Great Patriotic War of the Soviet People against the Fascist Aggressor" and with the reactionary part that the Roman Catholic Church played under Hitler. Anti-religious propaganda enters all phases of school life. DeWitt (1961) reports that some universities (the University of Kiev, for example) have established permanent departments on the history and theory of atheism. All teachers in training are required to take a course in atheism. In developing the new Soviet man an elaborate code of socialist morality is offered to the youth—e.g., "Do not steal or destroy socialist property; but it is 'morally right' to rob a capitalist bank in order to foster the revolution" (p. 122).

TEACHING METHOD. The method of instruction is compatible with the political and educational aims of the Soviet regime. The "lecture" style, followed by "recitation," is generally espoused in the teaching of history and geography. Direct observations of American educators reported by Bereday, Brickman, and Read (1960) corroborated this claim. For every question in the classroom there was a "correct" answer—the authority of the teacher or the textbook was never disputed. However, in certain classrooms it was observed that some teachers allowed more leeway to their pupils than others—the personality and the psychological make-up of the instructor possibly made the difference. In the study of maps, the ability to locate places was stressed. History teaching, even Slavonic history, emphasized the means of production, the nature of property, the master-slave relationships of the Slavonic tribes. According to DeWitt (1961), Makarenko, one of the most popular spokesmen of the Soviet educational ideology, was the strongest opponent of Western influences. Upon his recommendation school discipline became strict, and official codes of behavior were promulgated. An elaborate system of rewards and punishments has been operative in the Soviet Union. Rewards are given by the teacher or the youth organizations; the names of the "good" students are posted in conspicuous places in the school. Although physical punishment is forbidden, group shaming or direct suspension are commonly employed practices.

The authors of articles in social studies published in current Soviet pedagogical journals, like many of their American counterparts, did not exhibit conceptual sophistication and systematic analysis in dealing with problems of teaching strategy. No experimental studies of a controlled nature are reported; theories of learning and their implications for curriculum development or measuring instruments are not considered in the treatment of method. For the most part, the articles relate the experiences of their authors in introducing a new course on political education, in connecting school work with life, or in educating school children in atheism. These articles are impressionistic and present a very narrow point of view in the location and treatment of educational problems. All of them have political and ideological undertones. Essays by Monosnon (1961), Nikishov (1960), and Potapenko (1960) are cases in point. It is also interesting to note some of the comments of Soviet educators after a visit to the United States in an article entitled "What We Saw in the Schools of the U.S.A." (1959). They observed that

American schools pay great attention to promoting patriotism among students. This is done through special courses in civics and pledging allegiance to the nation. The American flag is displayed in the most prominent places. Although they acknowledged the fact that the teaching of religion is absent from the American public school, they pointed out that religious education is realized in other ways. For instance, it was pointed out that in some places the school day would begin by singing a religious hymn.

TEXTBOOKS. The topic of Russian textbooks has been adequately treated by educators in the United States. Medlin (1959) critically examined history textbooks used before the 1959 reorganization act. The texts were examined in terms of topic coverage, approach in dealing with historical documentation, presentation, emphasis, and validity of interpretation. He concluded that 70 percent of the material concentrated on the history of Russia in the last 450 years. Only 6 percent of the total pages dealt with non-European cultures. The texts made liberal use of generalizations conforming to the official doctrine—e.g., "The class struggle between feudal lords and the enserfed peasantry constituted the basic feature of feudal society." A gross distortion of historical facts was reported in order to accommodate Marxist-Leninist interpretations. The modern history text "jumps from one revolutionary situation or one socialist pronouncement to the next, oblivious of major historical developments in other fields." Krug and Paper (1964) reviewed current history textbooks and concluded that nationalism and patriotism in Soviet education have been underestimated in the West. Major revisions in the texts were effected after Stalin's death. The idea of the cult of personality was discredited and the patriotic efforts of the Russian people were emphasized. America is presented as an imperialistic land where the masses are suffering under capitalist exploiters. Distorted pictures of American life frequently appear. The following quoted statement is representative of this image: "In America, not only are millions of workers deprived of their opportunity to work and to earn a living, but many physicians, educators, and engineers are also unemployed" (p. 79). Krug and Paper concluded that the content of history textbooks reveals strong hatred toward the United States on the part of Soviet leaders.[1]

Shteppa (1962) has written the most definitive work regarding history textbooks in the Soviet Union. The social studies educator will find his well-documented chapter on Anti-Americanism extremely valuable. Although Americans were considered exploiters of the proletariat during the prewar period, they were regarded by the Soviets with much admiration coupled with jealousy. America appeared to them as a fairyland. After the destruction of Nazi Germany, however, America was depicted as the main threat to Communism. Anti-American propaganda reached its peak during the Korean War. Attacks were directed against American military bases, the Truman Doctrine, and the Marshall Plan. American "colonialism" in Asia and Latin America was mentioned frequently. Shteppa suggested that the works and interpretations attributed to Americans by Soviet historians actually reveal the latter's "innermost thoughts." He pointed out that "in attempting to picture the actual situation of scholarship in America, or in trying to read between the lines of what is written by American scholars, they are only disclosing the relations and phenomena of the Soviet system as a whole and the condition and place in it of historical scholarship in particular" (p. 325).

An essay by Levit (1959) presents a careful and systematic analysis of a history text entitled *History of the U.S.S.R.: Epoch of Socialism (1917–1957)*. The collective work of twenty Soviet historians, the text is used in higher educational institutions. Levit made an effort to develop valid categories and themes which allowed him to classify the state-

---

[1] Krug and Paper state that through history programs the Soviet regime tries to imbue the youth with a hatred of America and Capitalism. Ironically, the same journal contains a survey of programs and courses of study on teaching about Communism issued by state departments of education in the United States which reveals that anti-Communist indoctrination is the most prevalent objective of the courses in question. The investigation concludes that none of the state programs or policy statements "really permits a scholarly or objective study of the subject of Communism." (Roland F. Gray, "Teaching about Communism: A Survey of Objectives." *Social Education,* XXVIII (February 1964), 71–72.) These findings reinforce Bereday and Stretch's claim that all countries, regardless of system of government and political ideology, engage in indoctrination.

ments and assertions in the book. The recording unit was the paragraph, and the data were presented in frequencies and percent distributions. Levit's analysis represents a beginning in the systematic and scientific examination of social studies instruction in other lands. Although the study is based on a single textbook, it introduces a valid approach to content analysis, being far superior to other similar endeavors reported in this chapter. The findings suggest a number of hypotheses about the operation of the Soviet political and economic system.

Levit found that the history textbook under investigation is primarily a political history. The distribution of the total space is as follows: 43 percent political history; 31 percent economic and social; 18 percent military; and 8 percent cultural. He observed that there is a major shift from attributing causes of historical events to economic factors (the forces and relations of production) to establishing relationships based on "superstructural" factors, such as the party, education, patriotism, and formal government. Party dissension is attributed to social class divisions in the early years (until about 1925) but "personal evil," "careerism," and "bureaucratic behavior" become the dominant factors in later years. In the period between 1917 and 1957 there is a substantial decrease of frequency of assertions that Great Russia is the leader among equals. During the same period statements about the danger of Great Russian chauvinism decrease.

EDUCATIONAL OUTCOMES. There are virtually no studies which attempt to survey and assess systematically educational outcomes in the Soviet Union. The studies available from American or Soviet sources either describe the content of the curriculum or identify goals of instruction expressed by political leaders and officially commissioned textbook writers. It would be most interesting to investigate the claims of the communists with regard to their accomplishments in education by actually surveying and appraising student beliefs and values on selected issues. The only study which merits review is the one conducted by Juviler (1961) on Communist morality and Soviet youth. Although the author disclaims sociological or statistical expertise, his investigation is analytical and opens up new approaches to the study of values. The report is based on personal observation and purports to measure the values of Soviet urban youth against the "yardstick of the major canons of 'Communist morality.'" Juviler demonstrates his points by presenting vivid interviews with university students and "jokes" which are expressive of the spirit of youth in modern Russia. Except for the political activists, young people seem to be much less preoccupied with their moral values than is the regime. When asked to define "Communist morality" they would cite examples demonstrating truthfulness, respect for women, and generosity toward one's fellows. Only a small minority espouse or even pay lip service to the moral code of the party. There is generally more devotion to "Soviet patriotism" than there is to Communism. Many other personal interests and values interfere with devotion to Communism. Among city youth the following points of conflict have been observed: "individual career goal vs. the obligation to work for the 'common cause' wherever the citizen is assigned and needed; creative drives and personal views of artistic or scientific truth vs. the party's version of truth; curiosity about the outside world vs. the continued relative isolation of the Soviet Union" (p. 23). According to Juviler the main reason for this state of mind among youth is the sterility of communist ideology and the fact that the Soviet Union has reached a period of normalcy which permits points of friction between youth culture and official doctrine to emerge. It would be erroneous, however, to conclude that young people do not take pride in the achievements of the fatherland or accept the basic idea that socialism is far superior to capitalism. Since Stalin has been discredited, there is more leeway in the expression of individualistic goals and aspirations. The main problem faced by the government is the conflict between individual interpretation of truth and Communist doctrine.

COMPARATIVE STUDIES. In a most interesting but undocumented essay Katz (1963) found similar patterns of growth in Communist and Western societies, despite differences in ideology. Both types of societies are concerned with basic human problems, such as those associated with the mastery of nature, socialization, and social control. The process of education in the Soviet Union, including the structure of the curriculum, the methods of instruction, and the role of discipline in the school, remarkably resembles that of Western countries. The main difference is that the Communist school has undertaken a program of polytechnization, whereas Western educational systems have retained the humanistic tradition and the Athenian concept of a liberally ed-ucated man. Both systems are concerned with the political accultura-tion of their youth through formal or informal means. The Octobrist, Pioneer, and Komsomol groups seem to be better organized to that end than their counterparts, Boy Scouts, Girl Guides, and YWCA. Although different interpretations are placed on political theory and its implications for the development of society, both the Western and the Communist countries are concerned with teaching youth a system of values that is in harmony with the political orientation of the society in which they live. The process of political socialization seems "to be identical in both types of society."

Katz's claims regarding basic similarities between the two systems are corroborated by a recent study of political education by Bereday and Stretch (1963). The investigators, after surveying school programs reported in both official and unofficial documents, concluded that the amount of political exposure in the schools of the United States is greater than in the Soviet Union. The total percentage of time devoted to political education (courses in language arts and social studies, and homeroom and school life activities) in grades 5–8 is 50 and 47, respectively. In grades 9–12, the percentage of time allotment is 41.9 versus 26.8. Total exposure to political education for grades five–twelve is approximately 46 percent for the United States and 38 percent for the Soviet Union. From these data it is obvious that confrontation with political and social ideas and issues in both countries decreases with age (more markedly, however, in the Soviet Union). It is possible that Soviet educators operate under the assumption, which is plausible and supported by recent findings (Easton and Hess, 1962), that the formative years in politics are those spent in elementary school—political and moral attitudes and beliefs are firmly established before children leave the eighth grade. Nevertheless, it should be understood that mere exposure, calculated on the basis of distribution of subjects in the curriculum, does not necessarily indicate the depth and intensity of treatment. As it was pointed out by several authors reviewed earlier, the content presented in the Soviet schools differs greatly from that of Western democratically-oriented societies. "But in extent of indoctrination, the Soviet Union presents little that is unusual. . . . All societies indoctrinate" (p. 1). All societies try to inculcate in their youth accepted values and norms and to mold their behavior into a socially relevant form. All countries make a conscious effort to imbue their youth with loyalty and devotion to their social institutions and to develop responsible citizenship.[2] To what extent they have been successful in realizing these objectives of social education is largely subject to conjecture since empirical data on the subject are not readily available.

One might question the exclusion of subjects such as biology, and even chemistry and physics, which, admittedly, have strong ideological undertones in the Soviet Union, from consideration in the study. Also, the role of youth organizations in political socialization, although difficult to assess, must be taken into account. According to the authors the seemingly startling differences (also, similarities) in political exposure between the two systems are reasonable since it takes "more time to elicit allegiance in a new, pluralistic, and free society, than in a more traditional . . . more monolithic . . . and more controlled society" (pp. 15–16). On the whole, the study suggests fruitful approaches to issues of cross-national interest, including the function and the effect of the school in enculturating and "politicizing" the youth.

EASTERN EUROPE

Educators in the West generally assume that the educational system in the U.S.S.R. provides the prototype for the East European Com-

[2] As mentioned earlier, a national survey of policy statements and recommended courses of study in the United States concerning units on teaching about Communism revealed that few states seem to be willing to allow a completely unbiased analysis of the subject. Most of them "contrast the darkest realities of Communism in the Soviet Union with the noblest ideals of American democracy," and there is a tendency to use emotive language and such loaded words as "slavery, menace, evil, threat, deadly, deceitful, dishonest," when they discuss the Soviet Union and Communism. It is also reported that most of the proposals and courses of study concentrate on the fallacies and failures of Communism, and completely ignore analytical works written by Communists. See Roland F. Gray, "Teaching about Communism: A Survey of Objectives," *Social Education.* XXVIII (February 1964), 71–72.

munist states. This reasoning perhaps partly explains the dearth of published material and research on this area. Hofmann (1962) and Lottich (1963) outlined some of the formal and informal educational practices undertaken in East Germany to transform the Nazi school into a socialist school. Lottich pointed out that of the 200,000 escapees from East Germany in 1960 one-half were under twenty-five years of age. Does this mean that the schools have not been successful in indoctrinating the youth? Or are the escapees in revolt against the social and economic conditions prevailing in Eastern Europe? Cekič (1958) gave a brief description of the goals and curricula of civics teaching and moral education in Yugoslavia. A course in civic education was introduced in 1953 and was accompanied by an official syllabus. The aim of social education is to bring about political cohesion and acquaint the student with a "scientific, dialectic-materialistic picture of the world." The course in world history deals with the conventional topics, including the achievements of the Chinese and Egyptians, Greco-Roman civilization, and the history of modern nation-states. The author's claim that "the teaching of history is free from nationalistic prejudice" is not consistent with reports on the degree of individual freedom under Tito. Another study in this area is that by Krug (1961), who analyzed history textbooks in East and West Germany. He found basic differences in the treatment and interpretation in the two countries of certain important events, such as Hitler's rise to power, the causes of World War II, and the fall of the Weimar Republic. He concluded that history textbooks in East Germany are designed to fit Marxist-Leninist interpretations of history and to incorporate the political aims and interests of the Soviet Union into the curriculum.

THE UNITED KINGDOM

It is difficult to explain the scarcity of studies available in America on social studies theory and practice in Western Europe. With the exception of recent reports on political education in West Germany, there is very little of any educational significance published by American educators. However, the interested reader can get an idea of current problems confronting the profession in England by leafing through recent issues of the *Times Educational Supplement*. A survey conducted by the Parliamentary Group for World Government (*Times Educational Supplement,* February 16, 1962) concluded that "Britain, compared with other countries, offers the more able of her adolescents between fifteen and eighteen far less world history and far less recent history than their contemporaries receive elsewhere." The survey included a comparison of syllabi in British Columbia, Western Australia, the United States, West Germany, East Germany, and the Soviet Union and revealed that children in non-Marxist countries do not have a frame of reference which would allow them to make sense of modern history. A recommendation was made that a course in basic world civics be offered—rather than a new academic discipline—which would stress human tolerance, and a sympathetic understanding of the problems of the contemporary world. Other commentators and authors have also been concerned with the inadequacy of history courses in giving a comprehensive and accurate picture of non-Western civilizations and in critically examining recent events. (*Times Educational Supplement,* January 22, 1960; February 19, 1960.) Krug (1963) compared history textbooks used in England and in America and concluded that British historians exemplify much more historical sophistication, subscribing to rigorous criteria of scholarship. The English textbook reflects the point of view that high school students are capable of dealing critically with crucial and problematic periods in history, and it plays down the need to make teaching and learning "easy" or appealing. The school curriculum in England, by and large, reflects a deep-seated tradition of humanism and academic learning.

On the whole, the educational writings of English authors do not indicate a genuine concern for including the dimensions of the individual and the society (largely the psychological and sociological aspects of education) when dealing with objectives and methods of teaching history and the social sciences. It is reasonable to expect that the British social studies program would not be successful if applied to all students because it fails to take into consideration the values, goals, and aspirations and cultural conditions of British society and the capabilities of individual learners. The British, in contradistinction somewhat to the Russians and Americans, may fail to emphasize these aspects of the curriculum because only a minority of children pursue an academic course of study.

WEST GERMANY

A subject of considerable controversy in educational writings is the extent to which the Germans deal in an intellectually honest way with their Nazi past and the degree to which democratic values have been accepted by students. Krug (1961) reviewed four textbooks, approved by the government and in use in the Oberschule or the Gymnasium. After carefully documenting his study, he concluded that the West German textbooks in current use completely omit an objective discussion of a decisive period of recent history. The decisive period includes World War I, the Treaty of Versailles, and subsequent developments in Europe, the creation of the Weimar Republic, and Hitler's rise to power, followed by persecution of minorities and World War II. It is asserted that the history textbooks contain inaccurate statements regarding the causes of both world wars and Germany's role in them. The vicious Nazi persecution and extermination of six million Jews is narrated in a detached manner. It is maintained that Hitler and other Nazi leaders were responsible for practicing genocide while the majority of the German people knew practically nothing about it. The issue of collective guilt is not properly treated. The books are critical of American decisions concerning the fate of postwar Germany and the establishment of the Nuremberg tribunal. Roosevelt, Truman, and Eisenhower are generally considered as villains responsible for the dismemberment of Germany. Following a similar line of inquiry, Bunn (1962) reviewed fifty-one history textbooks and selected eight books for study in depth. In order to get a representative sample of the books he applied four criteria—relative recency of publication date, inclusion of a cross-section of the various types of texts, popularity of the texts, and incorporation in the sample of texts adopted by major West German States in public elementary schools and in the Gymnasia. His careful identification of the selection process gives additional strength and validity to his findings. The criterion question was the treatment of Hitler's rise to power. His investigation revealed that the following reasons were given for the ascendancy of Hitler to a position of absolute authority: (1) The economic crisis of the early 1930s and its concomitant effects in society; (2) the common belief that National Socialism rather than Communism could improve the situation brought about by the inept government of the Weimar Republic; (3) the support given to Hitler by certain industrial and conservative elements; (4) the fact that the Weimar government did not receive support from the elite groups which blamed it for the unreasonable terms of the Versailles Treaty; (5) Hitler's consolidation of his authority and popularity once in power; (6) Hitler's ability to deal with problems of unemployment and his monopolization of the public information media. The investigator concluded that Hitler's rise to power was explained in terms of the immediate sequence of events, with little effort to examine critically the historic roots underlying the phenomenon of National Socialism. The books are rather narrow in their interpretations of the rise of National Socialism. Conant (1963), in a recently published essay on German textbooks, takes issue with Krug on the question of their historical objectivity in dealing with Nazi brutality. Her examination of ten widely used textbooks in West Germany reveals that there are few distortions of historical episodes in them and that they include a full description of the Nazi period. She claims that the books give "detailed accounts of the persecution of the Jews . . . including a heartbreaking photograph taken in the Warsaw Ghetto, a description of Auschwitz" (p. 53). The study is not adequately documented and footnoted, and the criteria upon which the review is based remain vague; her remarks, however, should caution future reviewers against superficial and subjective analyses of textbooks. The contradictory accounts of history textbooks presented by the foregoing authors (Krug, Bunn, Conant) might in part be explained in terms of the implicit and explicit criteria applied by the authors and the fact that Conant examined books of a more recent date. The studies suggest the need for a continuous appraisal of history textbooks by means of defensible methods and public, rather than private, criteria of content analysis.

Von Friedeberg (1962) summarized the findings of several studies concerned with political education in West Germany. The studies, based on questionnaires and interviews with students and teachers, presented empirical data which illuminate several issues confronting modern Germany. The Ellwein Report suggests that political education can be made meaningful when teachers become conscious of democratic ends and when democracy is practiced as well as taught. Among respondents it was widely feared that acceptance of democratic values would have a negative effect on "the performance of fundamental tasks" and on the authority of the teacher. Hilligen concluded that very little was done to give the pupils a clear understanding of the prevailing social and political processes in Germany. In a sociological study in Frankfort, no significant difference was found between students who had received instruction in civics and those who had not on questions such as knowledge of democratic institutions and willingness to participate actively in politics. The Becker and Teschner Study indicates that there is no reason to assume that a special course in civics had any "incisive influence on the political consciousness of pupils." [3] Some of these studies are described in more detail in a recent publication by Stahl (1961). In the opening essay Stahl presents data and statistical tables, contributed by the Institute of Public Opinion Research in Germany, to substantiate the claim that the people of the Federal Republic have begun to associate themselves with the values of Western democracies. Although some studies conducted by psychologists and sociologists are extremely valuable and illuminating, several articles imply an attempt (possibly unconscious) to rationalize the behavior and the values of present-day German youth. In one of the essays a change in teaching method from a teacher-directed classroom to one which invites pupil participation in discussion and inquiry is reported. It is claimed that this change reflects the spirit of modern Germany. Although there is some reluctance on the part of many parents and teachers to deal with the crucial epoch of the German past, recent history, including the Nazi period, is incorporated in the curriculum. Rolf Schoerken, on the basis of his survey, suggests that average German boys tend to associate certain incidents under Hitler's regime with similar attitudes held

---

[3] A recent study reported that there is very little or no relationship between courses in civics or government and the development of democratic attitudes. See H. H. Remmers, ed., *Anti-Democratic Attitudes in American Schools* (Evanston, Ill.: Northwestern University Press, 1963).

toward games and other familiar activities. Their attitude toward war is expressed in terms of support for the home team; in a match, the better team wins. If the team loses the contest, someone must have let it down, or there was unfair play on the other side. In the war against the Allies, the Germans were fighting against "unfair odds." "If both sides had had the same chance, we should have inevitably won." According to Matthewes, the question of war guilt is beyond the average boy. On the other hand, the intellectually able students move naturally from the historical and political level to moral issues. Shafer (1962) concludes that postwar American proposals emphasizing the study of current events and recent history are reflected in the State (*Länder*) syllabi. Teachers are teaching domestic and international politics, and matters relating to the rise of National Socialism. Her observation that the teacher transmits information, but rarely discusses controversial problems with his students, is not quite consistent with the studies conducted by German educators, where the emerging classroom climate is shown to be rather permissive and conducive to critical reflection of past and current social issues. Shafer's major theme is that the great impetus to courses on international affairs and recent history has come from American social studies advisors working together with German educational authorities. We will have to wait and see whether German educators will, in retrospect, have second thoughts about this type of social studies teaching, as did the educators in Japan.

Although most of the research on political and social beliefs and concomitant behavior in students is inconclusive, a number of studies completed or under way indicate that German and American scholars are determined to pursue the subject in depth. The use of empirical surveys of the sociological type is a very promising approach to research on political education in Germany, which might open new avenues for similar studies in other countries.

SUMMARY

This review of social studies theory and practice in other lands has been aimed at offering teachers and curriculum specialists a broader context within which their special inquiries may be extended. The following general remarks on social studies are based on the foregoing review:

1. The social studies curriculum provides a good indicator of the conditions and group aspirations of a given society. The content of social studies and the way the subject is organized and taught reflect the dominant social norms of the culture.

2. Regardless of the prevailing ideology or official doctrine, courses in social studies are used as an instrument of socialization. With varying degrees of intensity, rigor, and success among national systems, political and economic indoctrination takes place through history and social science courses. Outside the school, youth organizations play an important role in this indoctrination. Generally, the conditions in the family, the school, and the job have an impact on the individual's self-image (as a leader or a follower) and his conception of the functioning of the political system.

3. In totalitarian states, the accepted goals and values of education are outlined in detail by the central government. Textbooks, teaching guides, school curricula, and related school activities are rigidly controlled. However, the extent to which the official ideology is espoused by school children is undetermined. The few studies reviewed here suggest that young people are mostly interested in personal problems or those relating to their family and peer group rather than in topics and values introduced in the formal curriculum of the school. In some national systems, e.g., Japan and Germany, educators have made a conscious effort to revise ideas and notions of historic causality and of the ultimate purpose of national existence. Several educators and national leaders operate under the unproved assumption that many social dislocations and problems of youth can be solved in the social studies classroom. (In some cases it is perhaps politically expedient to operate under such a myth.) More evidence is needed to test the proposition that the school, in general, and courses in social education, in particular, are indeed instrumental in transforming attitudes and modes of behavior. More empirical studies should be conducted dealing with value and behavioral outcomes of students.

4. A great deal has been written on social studies, but most of it is included in general surveys of schools. Consequently, the task of the reviewer becomes formidable. Furthermore, the studies incorporate only one or two cultural areas, with special emphasis on the Soviet Union. In view of the scarcity of information, field studies should be conducted in Africa, the Near East, Latin America, and selected countries in Western Europe.

Adequate methodological schemes should be constructed so that future studies can include cross-national indices of the results of education.

5. Although the curricular pattern called "social studies" is mostly applicable to the United States, history and social science as school subjects generally serve the same educational ends in all schools under study. These goals may be grouped under three main categories: knowledge and understanding of civilizations past and present; values associated with good citizenship as defined by each society; development of certain skills, such as historical interpretation, documentation, and generalization.

6. The teacher of the social studies who has a commitment to reliable knowledge and a sympathetic understanding of people in other continents increasingly devotes more time and energy to (a) inquiry and discovery, (b) examination of values and attitudes, and (c) scientific prediction.

7. While historical information is important both as a source of hypotheses and as an instrument of verification, schools throughout the world have begun to emphasize the social sciences, especially anthropology, economics, political science, and sociology for the following major reasons:

a. They provide models, theories, and concepts about the function of social institutions that are analytical rather than purely descriptive, and thus they increase the learner's chances to understand and explain more accurately the world around him;

b. They examine the customs, practices, and beliefs of various types of people in all social classes instead of concentrating on the nobility, the clergy, or the monarch and his cabinet;

c. They include a segment of the world—i.e., the non-Western world— which has traditionally been excluded from historical investigation; in the absence of histories of various African states, the social scientist examines the structure and function of certain social institutions in the context of current mores, traditions, and aspirations of the populace. Indeed, it is claimed that this "societal" context allows the investigator to understand the country and its people better than mere reliance on the usual variety of history;

d. The social sciences being relatively new are more open-ended in their themes and tools of analysis than history, which has an old tradition and a method of analysis of long standing. In the classroom, it would be true to say that the social sciences offer considerable opportunity and indeed, by nature, encourage the students to engage in inquiry and discovery;

e. While at times studies in the social sciences tend to hair-splitting and deal with trivial themes, on the whole they yield reliable results with high predictive value.

8. Several studies indicate that history taught in various parts of the world is, in the last analysis, national history, written from a rather narrow point of view. Consequently, many historical events of significant import to mankind are either distorted or are left out of textbooks. This observation points to the need of establishing an international commission, preferably under the auspices of UNESCO, serving as a clearing house in the writing of textbooks in history and social science and disseminating information on current political and economic events in the world.

On the basis of this review, various ideas are grouped together and a number of questions are asked. The problems delineated here should help the researcher locate hypotheses relating to social studies theory and instruction in other lands:

1. *Social studies, nationalism, and cultural change.* (Research in this area should emphasize the newly independent states of Africa.) To what degree does social studies instruction foster or hinder the development of national consciousness? In this respect, what symbols and key figures are focal in the textbooks and official publications? From a philosophical viewpoint, is the fostering of nationalism desirable, especially among developing states, where a multiplicity of loyalties to local authority figures prevail? How are older institutions, such as that of the tribal chief, treated? To what extent are the teachers and their pupils tradition-oriented? Is there any validity in the hypothesis that nations with a relatively "poor" and "colorless" history (Puerto Rico), are more future-oriented (amenable to change) than nations with a rich and picturesque heritage (Greece, England)?

2. *Social studies and political socialization.* In what manner and under what conditions are political beliefs and attitudes—e.g., the image of the president or the monarch, the judge, the policeman—developed in children? What is the most crucial age in forming political values? (Does the hypothesis advanced by Easton and Hess that the preschool and elementary school age is important apply to cultures other than the United States?) Is it plausible to assume that early political maturity takes place only in economically advanced and stable pluralistic societies? What specific values and national objectives are emphasized in national systems representing varying levels of economic and social development—e.g., industrially advanced societies, such as France, societies in transition, such as Greece, or pre-industrial societies, such as Afghanistan? How successful is the school in changing political beliefs and attitudes of children?

3. *Social studies and mankind.* To what extent do national curricula and social studies programs reflect a concern for the human condition? Are universal problems (such as overpopulation, crime and delinquency, the Cold War, economic competition, illiteracy, unemployment, production, development, and allocation of scarce resources, mental health, ethnic minorities) discussed in the schools in an intellectually and morally responsible way? Do schools try to combat chauvinism and to foster a sympathetic appreciation and understanding of peoples who do not necessarily subscribe to the same ideologies and political doctrines? On the hierarchy of values what place does the concept of mankind or human brotherhood occupy? The work that has been done by UNESCO in this area provides a good beginning, but more studies should be conducted by each member nation and reported in international publications.

4. *Social studies and controversial issues.* Aside from world issues, what other issues are examined in the schools? Are national or local controversial issues discussed in the classroom of the respective nations—e.g., the Kashmir issue in India and Pakistan; the Berlin issue in East and West Germany; the Cyprus issue in Greece and Turkey; the race issue in the United States and the Union of South Africa; capitalism and Western-type democratic systems in the Soviet Union; the Trieste issue in Italy and Yugoslavia? Are there official positions concerning the treatment of controversial problems in the schools? What are the specific differences in policy and classroom strategy between totalitarian and democratic states? To what extent is the idea of a critical and judicious consideration of social cleavages and political issues accepted in the various educational systems of the world?

5. *Social studies and social mobility.* Does the school and its offerings in social studies provide the young the impetus and the skills to occupy positions of leadership in society? Or does it inhibit social mobility by perpetuating myths and superstitions concerning the sanctity of the existing social institutions? To what extent are egalitarian ideas discussed in the classroom? What are the school policies on recruitment, selection, differentiation, and promotion of students? How does the social-economic and ethnic background of students relate to their aspirations for social status?

6. *Social studies and scientific inquiry.* What are the dominant approaches in teaching social science and history? Are propositions treated openly? Does the teacher provide opportunities for the student to question various observations and related interpretations of social phenomena, or does he stifle creative and imaginative thinking by purporting to furnish all the "right" answers? Does the teacher operate in the spirit of scientific inquiry? (For example, does he indicate different sources of evidence, the

existence of conflicting data, biases of the source authorities, logical and empirical criteria for the acceptance or rejection of hypotheses?) Are the textbooks, source materials, visual aids, and instruments of measurement and evaluation consistent with the quest for public verification of knowledge? Assuming that the teacher seeks to find reliable knowledge about human events, past or present, does he draw data from all the social sciences or does he rely upon one only?

In the true spirit of inquiry, this chapter presents more questions than it answers. It is hoped, however, that it will provide the impetus for a fresh start on much-needed research in social studies.

BIBLIOGRAPHY

Adams, Don. "Rebirth of Moral Education in Japan." *Comparative Education Review,* IV (June 1960), 61–64.

Almond, Gabriel A., and Sidney Verba. *The Civic Culture: Political Attitudes and Democracy in Five Nations.* Princeton: Princeton University Press, 1963.

Benton, William. "Education in Red China." *Saturday Review,* XLIV (July 15, 1961), 46–47.

Bereday, George Z. F., William W. Brickman, and Gerald H. Read, eds. *The Changing Soviet School: The Comparative Education Society Field Study in the U.S.S.R.* Boston: Houghton Mifflin Company, 1960.

——., and Jaan Pennar, eds. *The Politics of Soviet Education.* New York: Frederick A. Praeger, Publishers, 1960.

——., and Bonnie B. Stretch. "Political Education in the U.S.A. and the U.S.S.R." *Comparative Education Review,* VII (June 1963), 1–16.

Brameld, Theodore. *The Remaking of a Culture: Life and Education in Puerto Rico.* New York: Harper and Brothers Publishers, 1959.

Bunn, Ronald F. "Treatment of Hitler's Rise to Power in West German School Textbooks." *Comparative Education Review,* VI (June 1962), 34–43.

Cekič, Miodrag. "Local Control and National Loyalty—A Yugoslav View," in *The Year Book of Education: The Secondary School Curriculum*, pp. 381–388, George Z. F. Bereday and Joseph A. Lauwerys, eds. London: Evans Brothers Ltd., 1958.

Chen, Theodore Hsi-en. "Education and Indoctrination in Red China." *Current History*, XLI (September 1961), 157–163.

————. *Teacher Training in Communist China*. Washington, D.C.: Studies in Comparative Education, U.S. Department of Health, Education and Welfare, Office of Education, Division of International Education, December 1960.

Conant, Grace Richards. "German Textbooks and the Nazi Past." *Saturday Review*, XLVI (July 20, 1963), 52–53.

DeWitt, Nicholas. *Education and Professional Employment in the U.S.S.R.* Washington, D.C.: National Science Foundation, U.S. Govt. Print. Off., 1961.

Division of International Education, U.S. Office of Education. *Bibliography: 1959 Publications in Comparative and International Education*. Washington, D.C.: U.S. Department of Health, Education and Welfare, Office of Education (prepared by the Staff in International Educational Relations), 1960.

Easton, David, and Robert D. Hess. "The Child's Political World." *Midwest Journal of Political Science*, VI (August 1962), 229–246.

Floridi, Alessio U. "Antireligious Education of Soviet Youth," in *The Politics of Soviet Education*, pp. 89–99, George Z. F. Bereday and Jaan Pennar, eds. New York: Frederick A. Praeger, Publishers, 1960.

Friedeberg, Ludwig von. "West Germany." *Review of Educational Research*, XXXII (June 1962), 308–319.

Fromm, Erich. *The Sane Society*. New York: Holt, Rinehart and Winston, 1955.

Hofman, Erich. "The Changing School in East Germany." *Comparative Education Review*, VI (June 1962), 48–57.

Hu, Chang-tu, ed. *Chinese Education under Communism*. New York: Bureau of Publications, Teachers College, Columbia University 1962.

Juviler, Peter H. "Communist Morality and Soviet Youth." *Problems of Communism*, X, No. 3 (May-June 1961), 16–24.

Katz, Joseph. "Common Ground between Communist and Western Education," in *Communist Education,* pp. 284–304, Edmund J. King, ed. Indianapolis: The Bobbs-Merrill Company, Inc., 1963.

King, Edmund J. *World Perspectives in Education.* Indianapolis: The Bobbs-Merrill Company, Inc., 1962.

―――――, ed. *Communist Education.* Indianapolis: The Bobbs-Merrill Company, Inc., 1963.

Kitchen, Helen, ed. *The Educated African: A Country-by-Country Survey of Educational Development in Africa.* New York: Frederick A. Praeger, Publishers (compiled by Ruth Sloan Associates), 1962.

Krug, Mark M. "The Teaching of History at the Center of the Cold War— History Textbooks in East and West Germany." *School Review,* LXIX (1961), 461–487.

―――――. "Young Israelis and Jews Abroad—A Study of Selected History Textbooks in Israel." *Comparative Education Review,* VII (October 1963a), 142–148.

―――――, in collaboration with Fuad Haddad. "History Teaching in Nasser's Egypt—A Study of Selected History Textbooks in the United Arab Republic." Unpublished manuscript, mimeo., 1963b.

―――――. "The Distant Cousins: A Comparative Study of History Textbooks in England and in the United States." *School Review,* LXXI (1963c), 425–441.

―――――, and Ida Paper. "History: Soviet Style." *Social Education,* XXVIII (February 1964), 73–80.

Lambert, W. E., and O. Klineberg. "A Pilot Study of the Origin and Development of National Stereotypes." *International Social Science Journal,* XI (1959), 221–238.

Levit, Martin. "Content Analysis of a Soviet History Text for University-Level Courses," in *Teaching in the Social Sciences and the Humanities in the U.S.S.R.,* pp. 19–29. Washington, D.C.: Studies in Comparative Education, U.S. Department of Health, Education and Welfare, Office of Education, Division of International Education, December 1959.

Lifton, Robert Jay. "Youth and History: Individual Change in Postwar Japan." *Daedalus,* XCI (1962), 172–197.

Lottich, Kenneth V. "Extracurricular Indoctrination in East Germany." *Comparative Education Review,* VI (February 1963), 209–211.

Malkov, N. M. "Education in Atheism in History Lessons." *Soviet Education,* III, No. 11 (September 1961), 8–12.

Medlin, William K. "Analyses of Soviet History Textbooks Used in the Ten-Year School," in *Teaching in the Social Sciences and the Humanities in the U.S.S.R.,* pp. 1–18. Washington, D.C.: Studies in Comparative Education, U.S. Department of Health, Education and Welfare, Office of Education, Division of International Education, December 1959.

———. "Teaching of History in Soviet Schools: A Study in Methods," in *The Politics of Soviet Education,* pp. 100–116, George Z. F. Bereday and Jaan Pennar, eds. New York: Frederick A. Praeger, Publishers, 1960.

Mitsuhashi, Setsuko. "Conceptions and Images of the Physical World: A Comparison of Japanese and American Pupils." *Comparative Education Review,* VI (October 1962), 142–147.

Monosnon, E. I. "On Teaching the Course on the Principles of Political Knowledge." *Soviet Education,* III, No. 11 (October 1961), 22–29.

Nikishov, S. I. "Marxist-Leninist Theory Must Be Taught in Organic Connection with the Life of the People." *Soviet Education,* III, No. 1 (November 1960), 20–25.

Oshiba, Mamoru. "Moral Education in Japan." *School Review.* LXIX (1961), 227–244.

Potapenko, N. Ia. "Atheistic Education in Elementary Schools." *Soviet Education,* III, No. 2 (December 1960), 3–6.

Pundeff, Marin. "History in Soviet Education since 1958." *Harvard Educational Review,* XXXII (1962), 66–80.

Shafer, Susanne Mueller. "Persistence of Postwar American Proposals for the Study of Contemporary Affairs in the West German Volksschule." Unpublished Doctor's dissertation, University of Michigan, 1962. Abstracted in *Dissertation Abstracts,* XXIII (February 1963), 2760–2761.

Shimbori, Michiya. "A Historical and Social Note on Moral Education in Japan." *Comparative Education Review,* IV (October 1960), 97–101.

Shteppa, Konstantin F. *Russian Historians and the Soviet State.* New Brunswick, N.J.: Rutgers University Press, 1962.

Stahl, Walter, ed. *Education for Democracy in West Germany.* New York: Frederick A. Praeger, Publishers, 1961.

Tavel, David Z. "Social Studies in Latin America." *Social Education,* XXVII (February 1963), 83–84.

"Teaching of the Social Sciences in the Higher Educational Establishments of the U.S.S.R." *International Social Science Journal,* XI (1959), 151–217.

Times Educational Supplement (London), January 22, 1960, No. 2331, p. 101.

Times Educational Supplement (London), February 19, 1960, No. 2335, p. 337.

Times Educational Supplement (London), February 16, 1962, No. 2439, p. 302.

UNESCO. *Education for International Understanding: Examples and Suggestions for Classroom Use.* Copenhagen: UNESCO, 1959.

UNESCO. *Reports and Papers in the Social Sciences,* No. 4, 1955. (Report of an inquiry presented to UNESCO by the International Federation of Secondary Teachers.)

Weir, Thomas R., and William J. Russell. "Status of Geography in the Social Studies Curricula of Canadian Schools." *Journal of Geography,* LVIII (September 1959), 280–285.

"What We Saw in the Schools of the U.S.A." *Soviet Education,* I (August 1959), 84–88.

APPENDIX

PRACTICAL CONSIDERATIONS FOR RESEARCH IN THE CLASSROOM*

Byron G. Massialas and
Frederick R. Smith

Periodic reviews generally reveal that the volume of research conducted in elementary and secondary schools by school personnel is steadily increasing. Although one could not safely claim that we have reached our research peak, one could probably advance the proposition that classroom teachers are beginning to exhibit some interest in pursuing inquiries in their respective fields of specialization. In the social studies, for example, examination of some of the specialized journals will justify the latter statement.[1] Additional evidence can be found in bibliographies and reviews of research.[2]

Research must have a qualitative as well as a quantitative dimension, however, and here much remains to be done. Quality may be anticipated when a study is planned and carried out under conditions which are educationally and ex-

---

* Adapted from an article in the *Phi Delta Kappan* (March, 1962), with the permission of the Editor.
[1] For example, see the volumes of *Social Education* and *Social Studies* for the last five years.
[2] Clarence D. Samford, *Social Studies Bibliography: Curriculum and Methodology,* Southern Illinois University Press, Carbondale, Illinois, 1959. Also see Richard E. Gross and William V. Badger, "Social Studies," in the *Encyclopedia of Educational Research,* pp. 1296–1319, edited by Chester W. Harris, Third Edition, The Macmillan Co., New York, 1960.

perimentally sound. The matter of quality is primarily a question of research design. It logically follows, then, that the reporting of the findings and conclusions of a study is really incomplete unless accompanied by an explicit and elaborate discussion of the method and frame of reference which governed the study. Many times in journal reports we see findings and claims concerning a variety of pupil outcomes attributed to certain variables (content or teacher). These frequently fail to indicate the strategy of attack and technique of investigation utilized in arriving at such findings. It is practically impossible to assess the end product of research where there is no statement about the methodological approach used.

The classroom teacher is in a key position to study the effect of new materials, methodology, and similar innovations upon the learning process. Yet no matter how research-minded he may be, he is apt to miss an opportunity for worthwhile basic investigation if he is not aware of the research potential of the situation. Even when research opportunities are recognized, the classroom teacher or even an entire department may fail to take into account some of the basic considerations crucial to quality research.

Let us assume, for example, that we are faculty members of a social studies department eager to embark on a research project. Here are some of the questions which we could ask ourselves. There is little doubt that the consideration of these questions will have significant influence upon the strength of our investigation.

1. *What is our research philosophy? For what purpose do we intend to conduct research?*

A number of alternative responses, not necessarily mutually exclusive, can be anticipated. A justification of research for purposes of problem solving might be to meet a specific and immediate problem confronting us. For example, in view of the fact that students are currently showing concern with civil rights, space exploration, and our policy in Viet Nam, how can we provide a new educational experience which would allow them to discuss these and related problems in a thoughtful manner? Could this problem be better met by creating a "current events club," or would it be more profitable to discuss such issues in regular classes?

On the other hand, a department might want to conduct research because of a long-range problem, i.e., since 90 percent of our graduates continue their education in college, what kind of social studies curriculum should we be offering? Should we include anthropology and social psychology or should we concentrate on history? What would be the best way of selecting content from a vast body of socio-economic data? Should we try to introduce a seminar at the senior level for the purpose of familiarizing our mature students with social science research tools and techniques?

The attitude of the school administration and the community itself may set limitations or offer encouragement to classroom investigation and experimentation. Thus we might legitimately ask ourselves what the prevailing attitude is toward studies such as we contemplate. What is more important is a determination that we as a department will take a position as curriculum leaders in our subject field while simultaneously working toward the creation of an atmosphere which will be conducive to research and possible curricular innovation.

Professional growth can be offered as an additional incentive for research activity. Through participation in research the teacher may become interested in readings about his subject and new approaches to teaching and learning; he could find himself involved in curriculum meetings, lectures, conventions, and summer workshops. Furthermore, research can provide a climate whereby communication and exchange of ideas and teamwork are made possible not only for members within one faculty but also among several faculties. A spirit of scholarly competition and drive to excel might be the justification and the outcome of such inquiry.

Finally and most significantly, one could justify research on its own merit. That is, our research could contribute to the building of a systematic body of social studies theory. Here, for example, a faculty could discuss and investigate basic philosophies appropriate to social studies instruction and research, conceptualization concerning logical operations employed in the act of teaching, or elements which could be operationally identifiable in the decision-making process in the classroom. The purpose of this approach is to accurately classify and systematize social studies knowledge. The ultimate ends are explanatory. Usually in pure research there are no immediate pay-off considerations, although many times there are measurable and tangible outcomes. We must remember that since Ptolemy it has taken many generations of scientists to build up, slowly and painstakingly, a satisfactory theory of our solar system; finally, one individual, Copernicus, published his thesis of a heliocentric universe in 1543.[3]

2. *What are some fruitful areas of investigation in the social studies? Considering our limitations and resources, what can we do productively?*

Here a number of considerations demand further discussion and analysis. For example, a team of teachers might desire to study the daily activities in the social studies classroom. Paradoxically enough, although many investigators have conducted research in the social studies, very few have dealt with actual happenings at the purely descriptive level. It seems only logical to assume that unless we can conclusively respond to the "what is" question we cannot intelligently proceed with questions of "why" and "how."

Teachers will also have to assess their strengths and weaknesses concerning the research process. Major weak spots are, generally, the following: (1) lack of background and formal preparation in the statistical and measurement procedures in education; (2) certain limitations in time and/or ability to pursue studies that go beyond the confines of the classroom, i.e., follow-up studies; (3) heavy teaching loads and extracurricular responsibilities. On the other hand, the classroom teacher also has a number of advantages appropriate to the conduct of quality research: (1) He has direct contact with the pupil and a knowledge of his problems, his intellectual potential, his socio-emotional development, and the like. (2) He is able to record happenings in the classroom and to put them in proper perspective as

---

[3] For an elaborate statement concerning the value of basic research, see Nicholas A. Fattu, "The Teacher and Educational Research, *High School Journal,* 44:194–203, March 1961.

they affect the teaching-learning process. (3) He can, with certain limits, manipulate the educational environment and observe the corresponding reactions of the pupils.

In addition, the faculty will have to consider some seemingly unimportant yet indispensable factors, such as availability of physical facilities and equipment, space for trained observers, and the like. This is not to imply that quality experimentation demands excessively expensive equipment or facilities. It is only realistic, however, to evaluate these factors in terms of their appropriateness to the over-all design of the study.

3. *What is the domain of inquiry? How do we delimit our problem?*

Acknowledging the fact that there is interrelatedness in nature, we realize that we need to reduce the problem to one which is manageable and operationally definable. For certain objectives, perhaps, global views are necessary and important. But for our purposes as classroom teachers we need to be selective; thus we attempt systematically to delimit our sphere of investigation.

A five-year research project conducted at the University of Illinois under the auspices of the United States Office of Education identified three domains of inquiry in the classroom: the linguistic, the expressive, and the performative. The first referred to the verbal intercourse that takes place in the classroom. The second referred to the behavior of children as expressed through certain signs, facial or others. The last referred to behavior centered on demonstration or performance of certain tasks associated with laboratory work. Although all these domains were identified, Smith chose to investigate only the linguistic in terms of logical operations involved in the act of teaching.[4]

---

[4] B. Othanel Smith, *A Study of the Logic of Teaching: The Logical Structure of Teaching and the Development of Critical Thinking.* A Report of the First Phase of a Five-Year Research Project, Bureau of Educational Research, College of Education, University of Illinois, 1962. Also see, by the same author, "How Can You Help the Student Teacher Become a Real Teacher?" *Teacher's College Journal,* 32:15–21, October 1960.

Bloom [5] and his associates, in an effort to classify and systematize educational objectives, identified three main domains: the cognitive, the affective, and the manipulative. The first included those objectives normally associated with knowledge, intellectual abilities, and skills. The second referred to objectives associated with interests, values, attitudes, preferences, adjustment, etc. The last included aspects of motor skill development. After he had operationally distinguished among the foregoing domains, he proceeded to investigate the first.

4. *What philosophical and psychological rationale are we employing? What constructs do we want to use?*

What assumptions appear to be warranted in planning our research? What postulates and propositions are we taking for granted? Are we going to accept Smith's [6] proposition that the act of teaching is related to but distinct from the act of learning? Does teaching involve a set of operations which could be logically and empirically discernible? Is it possible to categorize linguistic discourse in the social studies classroom? Can we assume, as Bruner [7] has stated, that there is an inherent "structure" underlying each discipline and subject matter area? Are we going to accept one particular theory of learning as valid and reliable and thus try to evaluate student behavior in such a light? Will we accept a connectionist theory of learning or a field theory as being most appropriate for achieving the desired outcomes in our subject area?

5. *What is our unit of measurement? What strategies and techniques could we utilize?*

Typical of the questions we might ask are the following: Would an existing standardized test provide an adequate measuring instrument? Do we need to construct our own evaluative instruments? If we

---

[5] Benjamin S. Bloom, editor, *Taxonomy of Educational Objectives,* Longmans, Green and Co., New York, 1956.
[6] Smith, *op. cit.*
[7] Jerome S. Bruner, *The Process of Education,* Harvard University Press, Cambridge, 1960.

are to measure or assess verbal exchange, what kind of measurement device can we apply?

Can we rely on teacher or student daily logs or anecdotal records as part of our evaluative design? [8] Would we need some additional objective evidence for purposes of validating our instruments? Can we use tapes and video-tapes to maintain a permanent record of our investigation in the classroom? Will it be desirable to hire trained observers to visit our classrooms and record activities using, perhaps, a time-sampling technique? Can we justify one approach or technique over another within the total project and its underlying rationale?

6. *In what aspects of this research would we need help from a specialist?*

A faculty ready to initiate a research project will have to determine what kind of professional, expert help it will need. For example, if we are utilizing standardized tests, or even tests constructed by individual researchers for specific purposes, we would need assistance in tabulating the scores and in determining whether the instruments are valid and reliable. We may need advice on the selection of statistical techniques which will enable us to determine whether outcomes are statistically significant, or whether our purported correlations are indeed positive. We may need to consider the possibility of consulting with a specialist in the content area to attest to the reliability of certain propositions and key concepts that we are using in our teaching.

7. *How do we evaluate and confirm our procedures and findings?*

Here we are mainly concerned with the validity of our product. We might be thinking in terms of replication and follow-up studies which will provide the necessary justification of our propositions. In this connection we might want to refine our procedures and investiga-

---

[8] For an analysis of promising new techniques in conducting research in the social studies see Byron G. Massialas, *Research Prospects in the Social Studies,* in the *Bulletin* of the School of Education, Indiana University, Vol. 38, No. 1, January 1962.

tive techniques as we proceed with our study. Ryans'[9] seven year project in teacher competence is an example of untiring devotion to obtain a logical and empirical confirmation of findings through an exhaustive attempt at the refinement of research tools and a continuous search for reconstruction of generalizations.

SUMMARY

At the fingertips of the classroom teacher lie innumerable opportunities for research which may be the source of additional insight into many of the problems of understanding the teaching-learning process. While we must operate within the limits set by the nature of our teaching assignment, level of training in research techniques, and necessary content background, the teacher should and can become skilled in conducting quality research. Among the principal points of justification for such endeavors, professional growth, problem solving, and systematic theory building are especially worthy of consideration. But whatever purpose the research is to serve, a statement of the underlying philosophy and rationale is indispensable. A systematic, thoughtful, and vigorous approach to the investigation is necessary if we are to expect a clear design and a valid strategy of attack. Only when tight and organized frames of reference are consciously employed will the field of social studies education move toward quality research.

[9] David G. Ryans, *Characteristics of Teachers,* Council on Education, Washington, D.C., 1960.

INDEX

INDEX

A

Academic freedom
  Classroom latitude, 121–122, 127
  Personal restrictions, 126, 132–133
  Pressure-group effects, 123, 124, 128–134

Adams, Fay, 22–24

Administrators, school
  Controversial issues
    Evasions, school role, 136
    Indifference to issues, 127–128
    Nonrecognition of pressures, 124, 146
    Policy formation, 125, 146
    Support of teachers, 126
  Curricular-planning role, 25, 56
  Television-usage control, 180

Affective factors in teaching, 102–103, 104–105

Africa
  Education, 203–204
  Stereotypes of, 195

Age-level limitations, *see* Maturation effects

Alexander, Albert, 160

Alexander, William H., 135

Alilunas, Leo J., 24

Allen, William H., 182

Almond, Gabriel A., 196–197

American Anthropological Association, 47

American Council of Learned Societies, 3

American Economics Association, textbook-study committee, 128, 162–163

American history
  Content organization, 48–49, 54, 93
  Course offerings, 23–27 *passim*
  Revision considerations, 42
  See also Civics and government; History studies

American Institute for Research, 170

American Legion, 13, 131

American Political Science Association, 143

American studies, 48–50, 55
  See also Civics and government

Anthropology, 37, 47, 55